HAROLD II

English Monarchs

A series of biographies of the kings and queens of England by acknowledged experts in the field.

Published

David Bates, *William the Conqueror*
'As expertly woven as the Bayeux Tapestry' *BBC History Magazine*

Keith Dockray, *Henry V*
'Well-crafted and thought-provoking' *History*

Michael Hicks, *Edward V: The Prince in the Tower*
'The first time in ages that a publisher has sent me a book that I actually want to read!
Congratulations' *David Starkey*

Michael Hicks, *Richard III*
'A most important book by the greatest living expert on Richard... makes for compulsive reading'
BBC History Magazine

Ryan Lavelle, *Aethelred II*

M.K. Lawson, *Cnut: England's Viking King*
'An exhaustive review of the original sources... excellent'
English Historical Review

Emma Mason, *William II: Rufus, the Red King*
'A thoroughly new re-appraisal of a much maligned king. The dramatic story of his life is told
with great pace and insight'
John Gillingham

W.M. Ormrod, *Edward III*
'Compelling and eloquently written... Nothing of comparable importance has been written on
the reign for the past thirty years' *History Today*

Peter Rex, *Harold II: The Doomed Saxon King*

Richard Rex, *Elizabeth I: Fortune's Bastard?*
'Polished' *History Today*

Ralph V. Turner, *King John: England's Evil King?*
'A portrait of John that should change a number of the more popularly held views of the king...
most valuable' *American Historical Review*

Forthcoming

Douglas Biggs, *Henry IV*
A.J. Pollard, *Henry VI*

Further titles are in preparation

HAROLD II

THE DOOMED SAXON KING

PETER REX

TEMPUS

For my son Richard, and my friends John and Jeanne Taylor, for
their unstinting support, assistance and encouragement.

First published 2005

Tempus Publishing Limited
The Mill, Brimscombe Port,
Stroud, Gloucestershire, GL5 2QG
www.tempus-publishing.com

British Library Cataloguing in Publication Data.
A catalogue record for this book is available from the British Library.

ISBN 0 7524 3529 9

Typesetting and origination by Tempus Publishing Limited
Printed in Great Britain

Contents

When beggars die, there are no Comets seen;
The heavens themselves blaze forth the death of Princes.

Introduction

Harold Godwinson was the last member of an Anglo-Danish dynasty established by Swein Forkbeard and his son, Cnut the Great. Even Edward the Confessor is, perhaps, better viewed as a member of this dynasty. He was of part-Danish descent, through his mother, the half-Danish daughter of Richard I, Duke of Normandy. Harold, also, was half Danish on his mother's side.

Research for this book has involved consultation of the original sources, as translated by scholars such as Frank Barlow, Elizabeth van Houts, Marjorie Chibnall and many others, including some from the nineteenth century. I am greatly indebted to those scholars, as also to all those whose works I have read, which are listed in the bibliography.

I am also grateful to the editors and contributors to the volumes of the journal *Anglo-Norman Studies*, which publishes the proceedings of the annual Battle Conferences, and to the contributors to the *English Historical Review* and other journals.

For one source, the *Chronicle of Florence of Worcester*, I have used Joseph Stevenson's translation of 1853. The editors of the modern edition call him John of Worcester.

My thanks go also to Dr Mark Nicholls, Librarian of St John's College, Cambridge, for his permission to consult the books and periodicals in the library.

I am grateful to my publisher, Jonathan Reeve, for his patience in waiting for this volume, and to my wife Christina for meticulously editing the text and correcting my errors of syntax and punctuation. She is my fiercest critic.

The views expressed, and any errors, are entirely my own responsibility.

Peter Rex
Ely, 2005

I

The Anglo-
Scandinavian Prologue

Harold Godwinson, son of that Godwine, Earl of Wessex, who had risen to power in the service of Cnut the Great, was born sometime in the first quarter of the eleventh century, into a kingdom which is best described as Anglo-Scandinavian, both in government and culture. Harold himself was half Danish, as his mother, Godwine's wife Gytha, was sister to the Jarls Ulf and Eilaf and sister-in-law to Estrith, who was the daughter of Swein Forkbeard, King of Denmark, and the sister of Cnut.

At the beginning of the eleventh century, the Scandinavian element was in control in half of England and acted as a counterpoise to the Anglo-Saxon, that is English, element elsewhere. The fresh stimulus brought by Swein and Cnut tilted the balance in favour of the Danes. England was now ruled by a Scandinavian dynasty in an England which was Anglo-Scandinavian rather than Anglo-Saxon. Cnut was succeeded by his sons, the half-brothers Harold Harefoot (son of Cnut's first wife, Aelfgifu of Northampton) and Harthacnut, son of his second wife, Emma of Normandy, widow

of Aethelrede II 'Unraede'. After their short reigns, they were succeeded by Hathacnut's half-brother, Emma's elder son, Edward (the
Confessor), under whom England still continued to be controlled by
the Anglo-Scandinavian aristocracy (put in place by Cnut), especially
the three great earls, Godwine of Wessex, Siward of Northumbria
and Leofric of Mercia. Edward himself was succeeded by the Anglo-
Dane Harold. As Freeman pointed out, the Danish followers of Cnut
and his sons were not looked upon in any part of England as foreigners, and in many areas they were seen as fellow countrymen. These
Danes had learned to identify themselves with the land in which
they had settled, and living in England under Cnut they lived under
English law. Differences of racial origin ceased to be important when
intermarriage between English and Danes became commonplace.[1]

So the Danish conquest, and the final transformation of England
into an Anglo-Scandinavian state, came only after some of the
greatest of England's families had been destroyed, over a period of
some thirty years. A chilling contrast to the rapidity with which the
Normans took over from an Anglo-Danish aristocracy which had
not had time to consolidate its power. It is with the life and career
of one of those nobles, Harold Godwinson, that the major part of
this book is concerned.

Many of the lands of the former aristocracy fell into the hands
of the king or his new secular officials, the earls, in the decades on
each side of the year 1000, and the survivors of the great kindreds
disappeared from the ranks of the Witan. This meant that Cnut's
new men differed fundamentally from their predecessors. At first he
used his own kindred, cousins, brothers-in-law and ritual kin, such
as godparents, but gave up doing so when there were rebellions in
Denmark and Sweden which compromised their loyalty. Then he
turned to others. The origins of one, the most prominent and eventually the most powerful of these, Godwine of Wessex, remain obscure;
a second, Leofric of Mercia, was of more distinguished ancestry; his
father, Leofwine, had risen to the rank of ealdorman of the Hwicce
in the West Midlands, under Aethelrede. His brother Northman
was murdered by Cnut in 1017, and Leofric was promoted to
replace him. The third, Siward Digera, the Dane, had married the

granddaughter of Earl Uhtred of Bamburgh, which made him acceptable to the Northumbrians, but otherwise nothing is known of his origins. But none of these men owed anything to King Edward. They were in power long before he ascended the throne and none was able to trace descent back to former West Saxon or Mercian kings, unlike the nobility they had displaced. But by the time Cnut died, the great office-holding aristocracy had been transformed into an Anglo-Scandinavian one. Only Godwine was to be connected to King Edward, and then only by marriage, and as that marriage was sterile and provided no heir, the bond remained a weak one.[2]

Yet it was a time of increasing peace and prosperity, as is evidenced by the reformed coinage, which also demonstrates the remarkable efficiency of the English administration. There were victories over both the Scots and the Welsh, as well as a few scattered Viking raids. The king could be seen as head of a successful royal administration with a firm grip on the kingdom, the sign of a competent, manipulative and active king whose rule produced prosperity and an improving native Church, and also extended the machinery of government (it is in Edward's reign that one royal clerk began to emerge as a proto-chancellor). Despite this, some argue for fundamental structural weaknesses and see this reign as the first act in the drama of the Norman Conquest. On this view, the Conquest was not some bolt from the blue, arising from the ambition of William the Bastard, but the climax of a long-running crisis.

The idea that Edward was a manipulative and active king looks like a hangover from the Victorian conviction that he deliberately, as a matter of policy, brought in a coterie of Norman favourites and worked throughout his reign to ensure as far as he could the eventual succession of Duke William. That view no longer holds. Few actual Normans can be shown to have been established in England under King Edward. Most of his foreign companions were French or Breton rather than Norman, associates for the most part of his nephew Ralf of Mantes, who was given an earldom in Herefordshire. Most of the king's episcopal appointments went to Lotharingians, or men trained there (in what is now Lorraine), and perhaps were part of an attempt at ecclesiastical reform. The 'Norman favourites' boil down to a handful of domestic clerks of the household with little political clout and three Norman bishops: Robert of Jumièges, Archbishop of Canterbury, Ulf of Dorchester and William of London. The first two were expelled after the return to power of Earl Godwine in 1052. Bishop William seems to have been politically neutral and was allowed to return and retain his see.

Although Edward was certainly manipulative, there is little evidence of competence or activity which cannot equally be attributed to his Witan, controlled after 1053 by Earl Harold, and particularly to his relationship with his leading earls. Together and separately, these men engineered the passing of the crown from Harold Harefoot to Harthacnut and from Harthacnut to Edward. They were present at court, willing and able to manage Edward's affairs from the moment he returned from exile, to ensure the continuation of the Anglo-Scandinavian colour of the régime. Although the chronicles attribute many political initiatives to the king, it should be remembered that the conventions of monarchy dictate that all good things come from the sovereign and that the bad emanate from his advisers. Many of the initiatives did indeed come from King Edward's earls, especially Earl Godwine before his death in 1053.[3]

Edward cannot have been unaffected by his background. Although exiled in youth and brought up thereafter in Normandy, where he made many French, rather than Norman, friends and assimilated French culture, he was in fact part-Danish by descent. Edward's mother, Emma of Normandy, was a descendant of Vikings on her father's side, great-granddaughter of that Rollo or Hrolfr who founded Normandy. More immediately, her mother Gunnor, Edward's maternal grandmother, was Danish. She must have been a formative influence on her daughter Emma, as an example of a widow's power and the value of shaping family history for political purposes. Emma was thoroughly Danish, which perhaps partly explains her readiness to marry Cnut.[4]

Since she was Danish-born in this manner, and probably culturally Danish, Emma not only passed Danish blood to her sons, Edward and Alfred; her Danishness must also have influenced their upbringing, which must be taken into consideration alongside the alleged

'Frenchness' of Edward's formative years in Normandy. Edward's part-Danish background certainly stood him in good stead in 1042, when the question of his succession to Harthacnut arose, so that he was not only acceptable to the English as son of Aethelrede and descendant of the ancient royal line, but equally acceptable to the Danes, through being of Danish descent on his mother's side. Perhaps this also explains Harthacnut's willingness not only to initiate Edward's recall to England but to associate Edward with himself in the kingship, in effect designating him as successor.[5]

That Anglo-Scandinavian state was strong enough to resist and repel attacks from overseas and on its borders from the Welsh and the Scots. They provided a background to the career of Earl Harold Godwinson and, indeed, were the occasion of his greatest military achievements. The threat of invasion from Scandinavia was always present in the minds of the Anglo-Scandinavian élite and formed the dominant feature of Edward the Confessor's foreign policy, especially with regard to Normandy. In pursuit of his own policy, Edward had the fleet disbanded and the heregeld (the tax devoted to the upkeep of the hired fleet) abolished, a striking indication that Edward felt secure in his kingdom. This action forms a watershed in Edward's reign. Before the disbandment of the fleet he and his Witan followed an interventionist policy abroad, but after 1050, or more properly after the crisis of 1051–52, there were no more foreign adventures and most of the action was concerned with the security of England's borders with Wales and Scotland.[6]

It has been suggested that Edward's own policy was a search for a Norman alliance as a means of obtaining protection against Danish raids. If there was such a policy, it seems to have been singularly fruitless. But at the beginning of Edward's reign the threat from Scandinavia was real enough. There seems to have been a secret project for invasion by Magnus of Norway, possibly financed by the Dowager Queen Emma, who had sent him huge sums of money. But the effect of this policy was to lead not only to the Norman Conquest but also to the invasion of England by Harald Sigurdsson, called Hardrada, and his defeat by King Harold at the battle of Stamford Bridge.[7]

The *Heimskringla* of Snorri Sturluson says, in the Saga of Magnus, that Magnus formally challenged Edward's succession. In 1043, he gathered an enormous fleet but, menaced by Swein Estrithson, was delayed. The threat ended when he unexpectedly collapsed and died. The English fleet was mobilised at Sandwich. Magnus' heir was his uncle, Harald Sigurdsson. The Norwegian claim derived from a treaty between Magnus and Harthacnut. According to some very late evidence, the two had agreed that if either died childless before the other, the survivor would inherit his kingdom. Both Harald Hardrada and Swein Estrithson seem to have considered that they had a claim to the English throne. Swein, according to Adam of Bremen, believed he had been promised the succession by Edward himself.[8]

But Edward, as the surviving son of Aethelrede and Emma, became king, as the descendant of both Alfred and Rollo and so equally acceptable to both Englishmen and Danes. He was also already in England, and had been adopted by Harthacnut as his heir. He was the only claimant actually available at the moment Harthacnut died and had the support of the Witan, led, it would seem, by Earl Godwine. Some historians, notably Eric John, while acknowledging the omnipresent Scandinavian threat, believe that Edward could count on 'Norman goodwill' to help him resist it. They stress that Edward was half Norman and brought up there, and use this to claim a permanent intent on his part to secure the succession to the English throne for Duke William. There is singularly little evidence for any goodwill, other than late Norman propaganda produced after the Conquest, and this ignores William's youth in 1043 and the fact that he had no control over the Norman channel coast until 1047 at the earliest. He was only an effective prospective ally after the battle of Val-és-Dunes. The suggestion, for which there is no real independent supporting evidence, is that Edward was prepared to offer the prospect of the succession in order to win Norman support.[9]

More to the point is the fact that in 1043 Edward faced 'a formidable group of Anglo-Danish warriors and statesmen', led by Earl Godwine, who had accepted him as king by 'popular' choice and right of birth rather than out of affection for his dynasty. For the rest of his reign, Edward had to deal with men representing the traditions of the Anglo-Danish monarchy through a system of government which had a Danish structure. The twelfth-century tradition, recorded in the legal text called *Quadripartitus*, was that King Edward had been recalled to England to become king at the instigation of Bishop Aelfwine of Winchester and Earl Godwine, with the agreement of 'a council of barons' (that is, 'thegns'), possibly at Horsted in Surrey. It has been argued that this place, 'Hurstshevet' in the text, was the Hurst or Hurst Beach, a sandbank in the Solent reaching out towards the Isle of Wight where Edward actually landed in England. There they accepted him as king, after he had sworn to preserve the laws of Cnut and his sons.

Cnut's Code became the foundation of future English law, embodying the content of much earlier law. If this is what happened, it explains why Edward never issued a code of laws of his own and why the northern rebels of 1065 demanded the reinstatement of the laws of Cnut after Tostig's meddling. This was granted to them by Earl Harold at Northampton. When Edward was accepted as king, he was seen as being of partly Danish descent, and was presented as such by his mother Emma in picturing him as full brother to Harthacnut. This story about Edward's accession also points to the Scandinavian method of selecting a king, who, while he had to be of royal blood, had to be accepted by all free men at an assembly. The *Anglo-Saxon Chronicle* has it that he was sworn in as king, *to cinge gesworen*, which looks like a kind of associative consecration in which the reigning king had his successor designated as such during his lifetime. It is possible that Edward had intended to associate Harold with the kingship in this way, as there are indications that the king and Harold were seen as joint rulers of England.[10]

Norway and Denmark ceased to be much of a threat after the death of Magnus. He was succeeded by Harald Sigurdsson, who began a prolonged effort to conquer Denmark, only to be frustrated over a period of sixteen years by the determined resistance of Swein Estrithson. The preoccupation of these two with each other casts light on the disbandment of the fleet by King Edward and his abandonment of the heregeld. It also explains the failure of Earl Godwine to persuade the Witan and the king to send the fleet to the aid of Swein in 1048. Harald Sigurdsson in 1064 was desperately in need of money, and that, perhaps, explains the alacrity with which he adopted the exiled Earl Tostig's suggestion of an invasion of England.[11]

The assassination of Uhtred of Bamburgh, at Cnut's instigation, in 1016 resulted in a breach between that king and the Northumbrians, allowing Malcolm, King of Scots to invade Tweeddale. Cnut then marched into Scotland and compelled Malcolm to acknowledge his superiority, but, preoccupied with the war against Olaf of Norway, he lacked the resources necessary to sustain an army in the north and entrusted Northumbria to another of his new men, Siward Digara.[12]

Malcolm, to Earl Siward's relief, died in 1034. His successor, his grandson Duncan, attacked the lands of Bamburgh and besieged Durham. It was a disaster. The Scottish army was destroyed and Duncan's reputation was ruined. Macbeth, Mormaer of Moray, rebelled and killed him at Pitgavery, near Elgin, sometime around 1040, and made himself king. Duncan's brother and sons fled to England, and that enabled King Edward to destabilise the Scottish kingdom. Siward was therefore commissioned in 1054 by King Edward and the Witan, now influenced by Earl Harold and his sister Queen Edith, to invade Scotland and put Malcolm on the throne. Macbeth put up a fight, making use of Norman knights who had been expelled from England in 1052, but Siward, with reinforcements from England, defeated the Scots in the battle immortalised as 'Dunsinane'. Macbeth escaped to Moray, but his power had been broken and he was eventually killed in 1057. When Siward died in 1055, his son Waltheof was still too young to become Earl of Northumbria, so the king and Witan, at Earl Harold's instigation, chose Harold's younger brother Tostig.[13]

Siward's settlement of the Scottish question did not last long. By 1057/58, Malcolm had killed both Macbeth and his successor Lulach and was free to turn his attention to enforcing his claims to Cumbria. With Siward dead, he was no longer bound by any ties of gratitude, so carried out raids in 1057 and 1059. Tostig, however (and this is somewhat puzzling), never attempted an invasion of

Scotland, although he was a vigorous and warlike man. It cannot have been because the northerners accepted Scottish claims, yet there are no recorded moves by Tostig. The *Vita Edwardi Regis* suggests that it was a preferential policy on his part and that, although harassed by the Scots, he preferred to wear them down 'as much by cunning schemes as by martial courage and military campaigns' so that 'they and their king preferred to serve him and King Edward than to continue fighting and, moreover, to confirm the peace by giving hostages'.

As Tostig had been made Earl of Northumbria on his brother Harold's advice, perhaps the policy he pursued in Scotland was devised by his brother. Earl Tostig, assisted by the archbishop of York and the bishop of Durham, persuaded Malcolm to attend King Edward's court, in a rare instance held at York, and a general peace was proclaimed. Tostig and Malcolm became sworn brothers to cement the alliance. All seemed well, until Archbishop Cynsige's death in 1060 deprived Tostig of a vital ally. The archbishop had provided a valuable insight into the ramifications of northern politics, and it is after his death that Tostig seems to have become less popular and to have made errors of judgement.[14]

Thus it was an error for Tostig to depart on pilgrimage to Rome in 1061, because Malcolm took the opportunity to raid England. No retaliation by Tostig is recorded. Instead, there were renewed negotiations, possibly facilitated by Gospatrick, son of Maldred, who was Malcolm's cousin and had links with the earl. Possibly Tostig felt too insecure to risk an invasion because he knew by 1062 that his rule in Northumbria was unpopular, yet he had felt secure enough to go to Rome in 1061, and he was ready enough to join Harold on campaign against King Gruffydd in 1063. However, his Anglo-Danish administration had affected adversely the interests of the Bernician aristocracy, and the Scots had taken control of the upper Tyne valley. Tostig's subsequent conduct gave rise to accusations of tyranny, the result of his efforts to govern an increasingly restive nobility. Tostig's failure to retain control over his earldom was to precipitate events which severely reduced his brother Harold's chances of successfully resisting the Norman challenge.[15]

A significantly more serious threat, from the perspective of an English court holding its formal sessions, the Witanagemots, at Winchester, Gloucester, London or Oxford, was the rise of Gruffydd ap Llewelyn. Ever since the mid-tenth century, the English had put pressure on Wales, attempting to browbeat its princes into attending the court of the English king to pay him tribute in gold, silver and even oxen. Gruffydd ap Llewelyn had changed all that. His victory in 1055 over Rhydderch of South Wales, the climax of a nineteen-year campaign, made him even more of a threat to English peace. He had dominated Wales from 1039 until 1063. He controlled Gwent and Archenfield and extended the boundaries of Wales. He was described as 'head and shield and defender of the Britons', who had 'hounded the pagans and the Saxons in many battles'. English countermeasures had proved inadequate and concessions had been made, while English settlements from the Dee to the Severn were devastated. Fear of the Welsh might indeed explain why King Edward created an earldom in Herefordshire for his nephew, Ralf of Mantes, and allowed, even encouraged, various Frenchmen – some of them Normans – to settle and build castles on the Herefordshire border with Wales.

Over the next few years, there were repeated conflicts arising from Welsh ambitions, notable especially for the alliance of Earl Leofric's son Aelfgar, Earl of East Anglia and, on his father's death, of Mercia, with Gruffydd. The two jointly attacked the western borders of England twice, with the assistance of Norse fleets. On each occasion, Aelfgar was exiled, on the rather vaguely defined charge of treason, and won his restoration to office by attacking Hereford. Earl Aelfgar's 'treason' seems to have consisted largely of having made common cause with Gruffydd and of objecting to the elevation of Tostig to the earldom of Northumbria in 1055. At some point, probably in 1057, the earl cemented his alliance with Gruffydd, who married his daughter Ealdgyth, and it might have been that, and other contacts with the Welsh king, that led to Aelfgar's second exile. But it should be noted that Aelfgar's succession to the earldom of Mercia strengthened his alliance with Gruffydd, by providing the two with a common frontier stretching from Hawarden to Ludlow.[16]

Thereafter, a series of incidents took place on the Welsh border until Gruffydd's death at the hands of his own men in 1063. The death of Earl Ralf of Hereford in 1057, leaving an infant son, allowed Earl Harold to absorb most of Ralf's earldom into Wessex. The Welsh border had to be held by a strong man, able to deal with the Welsh threat. Ralf's territories could not be given to Earl Aelfgar, who was not trusted after his first exiling, and the other brothers of Harold were probably still too inexperienced or too young. Aelfgar himself turned towards Gruffydd, perhaps, as some think, fearing encirclement by Godwinson power. But the alliance with Gruffydd protected his western frontier. Aelfgar was now the only earl in England who was not a Godwinson. His sons, Burgheard, Edwin and Morcar, were also too young. So the Welsh conflict and the death of Earl Ralf, which made Harold a 'marcher lord', mark a step forward for Earl Harold, who was given command of an army to seek reprisals against the Welsh for their attacks and the death of the bishop of Hereford, Harold's former chaplain Leofgar.

Earl Harold, assisted by Earl Leofric and by Bishop Ealdred of Worcester (now given pastoral care of Hereford), came to an agreement with Gruffydd, by which the Welshman became under-king to King Edward in Wales. The peace was an uneasy one, to which King Edward and Earl Harold were, perhaps, driven. The Norse attacks had been more serious than English sources admit, and they may even have attacked Northumbria. Oxfordshire seems at this stage to have been added to Mercia, perhaps because Harold still hoped to keep Aelfgar (then earl of East Anglia) 'on side'. Peace did not last and conflict came again in 1062, with a renewal of Welsh raids. Possibly Gruffydd had heard of the death of Earl Aelfgar, sometime after the death of the earl's eldest son, Burgheard, in 1061, and considered the treaty now void. This provoked king and earl to decide, at a Christmas court in 1062, to settle the Welsh problem for good. Harold, in a joint operation with his brother Tostig, mounted a campaign in 1063, which drove Gruffydd out of his 'palace' at Rhuddlan into Snowdonia and so harried the Welsh that they killed Gruffydd themselves and sent his head to Harold, who presented it to King Edward. Harold divided North Wales between Gruffydd's half-brothers, Bleddynn and Rhiwallon, as vassals of King Edward, and Wales fell to pieces. This was a striking contrast to earlier English failures and was remembered well into the twelfth century. Even to Englishmen, the years 1063–64 appeared a bright time, celebrated in verse by the author of the *Vita Edwardi Regis*.[17]

The more detailed history of much of King Edward's reign is, in fact, the history of the rise to power and ascendancy of Harold Godwinson, and it is his achievements that will now be described.

2

The Rise of the House of Godwine

No account of the life and career of Harold Godwinson can neglect the remarkable rise to power and influence of his father, Godwine, Earl of Wessex. It was from the example set before him by his father, in particular his career and misfortunes, that Harold gained so much that was to prove of value to him in his own career. He must have learned a great deal from watching the way in which his father handled the uncertain-tempered king, Edward the Confessor. Harold learned not only what was successful and what to do, but also what to avoid. Unlike his father, Harold never lost the king's confidence, even after his disastrous sojourn in Normandy.

The rise of Godwine was not due to his having been a member of the Old English aristocracy, despite the efforts of some writers to show that his father was of noble ancestry. He owed his elevation to the singular trust placed in him by Cnut the Great. He was undoubtedly one of Cnut's 'new men', promoted to replace not only the former servants of Aethelredee II Unraede but, when they proved unreliable, even Cnut's own Danish relatives and supporters.

There is still something of a mystery about Godwine's origins, and strange tales circulated in later years which sought to explain his rise. The available evidence, scanty and sometimes a little vague, supports the conclusion of most authorities that he was the son of 'Cild Wulfnoth, the South Saxon'. The twelfth-century chronicle known as *Florence of Worcester* alleges that Wulfnoth was related to King Aethelrede's treacherous councillor Eadric Streona (the Grasper), through his brother Aethelmaer (who the chronicler thought was Wulfnoth's father), but this is improbable. No other source supports it, and the sudden transition from names prefixed by 'Aethel-', meaning 'noble', to names like 'Wulfnoth' and 'Godwine' is against it. Furthermore, the *Vita Edwardi Regis*, written at the behest of Queen Edith, Godwine's daughter, studiously ignores the subject of Godwine's parentage. If he had been of noble descent, the queen's writer would surely have boasted of it. *Florence of Worcester* was probably determined to enhance Godwine's reputation by granting him noble ancestry. The *Hyde Chronicle*, in contrast, insists that Godwine was of low birth, while connecting him to Sussex.[1]

That Godwine's father was called Wulfnoth is proved by the will of Aethelstan, the son of Aethelredee, which makes a bequest to 'Godwine the son of Wulfnoth', and the Canterbury version (F) of the *Anglo-Saxon Chronicle* for 1008, which states that Cild Wulfnoth was Earl Godwine's father. In describing the manner in which Aethelmaer's brother Brihtric brought charges of treachery against Wulfnoth that year, possibly out of spite, neither the Canterbury nor the Abingdon version of the *Chronicle* suggests that Brihtric was Wulfnoth's brother, though *Florence of Worcester* claims that he was. As a result of those charges of treachery, Wulfnoth was driven into exile and spent time ravaging the English coast (c.f. the account in the *Anglo-Saxon Chronicle*).[2]

Later writers knew nothing of Godwine's ancestry and invented tales to explain how he won Cnut's favour and how he came to marry Gytha, sister-in-law of Cnut. Godwine is said to have been the son of a *ceorl* (a farmer, in effect), and to have either befriended King Aethelredee, who had become lost while hunting and rewarded the farmboy by making him an earl, or to have given shelter after the battle of Sherstone to the Jarl Ulf, Cnut's brother-in-law, who then gave him his sister Gytha in marriage and advised Cnut to make Godwine an earl. This scene was set on the borders of Gloucestershire and Wiltshire, a long way from Sussex.[3]

As a result of his banishment, Wulfnoth lost all his lands and Godwine, deprived of his inheritance, would have had to start again from scratch. It is thought that Godwine attached himself to the household of Edmund Ironside and performed loyal service to him during the Danish wars. If so, that would explain why Aethelstan's will restored land at Compton, in Sussex, to Godwine. It is known that Harold held four hides of King Edward in Compton (part of West Firl). Alternatively, Esbiorn, the man of Earl Godwine, held ten hides in another Compton, near Chichester; either could be the 'Compton' referred to, and the second is the more probable location, as it is more closely connected to Earl Godwine. It was a dependency of Laughton, which was held by Earl Godwine and valued with its berewicks at £15. Four of these dependent estates were held by 'Countess Goda' (possibly a scribal error for Gida, that is Gytha).[4]

There is an impression that Godwine did come to power under the patronage of Jarl Ulf, if only because of the marriage to his sister and the access, through Ulf, to the patronage of Cnut himself. The *Vita Edwardi* (pp. 5-6) alleges that Cnut 'gave him his sister Gytha as wife'. The date of the marriage is unknown, but it occurred between 1019, after Godwine had attracted Cnut's attention, and 1023. So it was the Danish conquest which brought about Godwine's rise, as Cnut came to value his skills as a counsellor and found him useful in ruling his new kingdom. Such marriages as that of Godwine and Gytha provided a bridge between the English and their Danish conquerors, by confirming the legitimacy of the new régime.[5]

Exactly how Godwine effected the transition from service with Athelstan and Edmund to that of Cnut will never be known. That he served these princely members of the royal family (known as 'aethelings') is indicated by his association with Aethelstan, as his will shows, as well as with those Danish thegns such as Sigeferth, Morcar and Thurbrand who supported the Aetheling Aethelstan and his brother Edmund. The latter secured the support of the Five

Boroughs by marrying Sigeferth's widow, Ealdgyth. Two of these men, Sigeferth and Morcar, were related to Ealdorman Aelfhelm, and Thurbrand was the Hold of York. They transferred their support to Edmund when Aethelstan died, and it would seem that Godwine did likewise. Note also that Cnut married Aelfgifu, Aelfhelm's daughter, in Danish fashion or *more danico* (without benefit of clergy), which left it possible for him to contract a later Christian marriage with Emma of Normandy.[6]

In the confused fighting during Aethelredee's last days, Godwine had lost any lands he had in Sussex, and so he had no reason to support that king. Instead, he remained loyal to Edmund until his death in 1016. It may be that it was during the fighting between Cnut and Edmund between April and November, when Edmund fought Cnut to a standstill and forced him to divide the kingdom between them, that Godwine earned a military reputation. The *Vita Edwardi* (p.9) describes him as 'most active in war'. But there is no plain evidence of it. Cnut, however, admired loyalty in his own and other men's servants. The *Encomium Emmae* records that Cnut 'loved those whom he heard to have fought previously for Edmund faithfully and without deceit', and this could be a coded reference to Godwine, among others. Godwine certainly escaped Cnut's initial purge of a number of prominent supporters of Aethelredee. Survivors at this time were those who were able to swim with the tide, and Godwine proved adept at that, as his reputation for patience and diplomacy shows.[7]

One account has Godwine win Cnut's favour in action against an enemy identified as the Wends (who lived on the south Baltic coast), where he was in command of an English contingent in Cnut's army. Cnut, planning a dawn attack, notices that the English have apparently gone missing, so sets out in force to find them and, in so doing, meets them still under Godwine's command, returning victorious from a surprise night attack on the enemy, having completely destroyed them. From then on, Cnut places complete trust in the English, and Godwine in particular. The account is a late one, but testifies to the tradition that Godwine earned his spurs, as it were, fighting for Cnut. A twelfth-century source, Geoffrey Gaimar, claims that Godwine was present at the battle of the Holy River in 1026 and gained much treasure 'from the King of Sweden (Anund) whom he killed'. It is an uncorroborated statement, but serves as evidence of Godwine's military reputation in his youth.[8]

In support of this tale, the *Vita Edwardi* asserts that Godwine served Cnut in Denmark at about this same stage in his career, but other sources say he was with Cnut a little later, in the Swedish war of 1025, which would be too late to be useful as an explanation for his rise to power. That Godwine fought for Cnut in command of men is supported by the runestone of Bjorn Arnsteinson, who 'found his death in Godwine's host when Cnut sailed to England'.[9]

A charter of 1018 (in favour of Bishop Burhwold) is the earliest definite evidence of Cnut's favour; in it, Godwine is given the rank of earl. This suggests that Godwine had already come to the king's notice as a loyal supporter. After that, Godwine is found to have replaced Jarls Thorkell and Erik at the head of witness lists, at least in those charters which have survived, and he replaces Earl Sired in Kent.[10]

When Cnut's brothers-in-law, Ulf and Eilaf, rebelled in 1025 and went to Norway, Godwine remained loyal while Cnut went into battle at the Holy River (Stiklestad), and he could have provided men for the army, as Englishmen are known to have fought there. Although the later writers think Godwine was at that battle, it is more probable that he remained in England, effectively replacing the rebel Thorkell as regent. The *Vita Edwardi* supports this; introducing Godwine out of nowhere, it says that 'when Godwine returned home' (presumably from the earlier war, not that of 1025) 'having performed all things well, he was appointed by him [Cnut] earl and office-bearer [*dux et baiulus*] of almost all the kingdom' and further says 'in the reign of the King Cnut, Godwine flourished in the royal palace, having first place among the highest nobles of the kingdom'. So, after the removal of almost all the surviving English ealdormen, especially any who were known to have changed sides like Eadric Streona, and the rebellion or removal even of Cnut's leading Scandinavian followers, Godwine emerges among the most favoured nobles, truly 'one of the new nobles... attached to the King's side' (*Vita Edwardi* p.9).[11]

His position was unique: an Englishman holding one of the high-est offices in a kingdom ruled by a Danish king, closely related to him and his followers by marriage and so, in a sense, a member of the Danish royal circle. But his survival and promotion remain a mystery. There is one possible explanation, in addition to Cnut's regard for men of proved loyalty. In 1018, Cnut raised a tax over all England of £72,000 (as well as £11,000 paid by the townsfolk of London), which was used to pay off most of the 'raiding-army', which was sent back to Denmark; then, at Oxford, the Danes and the English 'agreed on Edgar's law'. Perhaps Godwine had been zealously co-operative in assisting in the raising of that immense sum of money. He was then taken with Cnut to Denmark in 1019, where he distinguished himself in battle. His marriage to Gytha occurred at about this time, possibly as his reward for his conduct in Denmark. His earldom covered central Wessex (which had no ealdorman following Aelfric's death at Ashingdon in 1016) and was extended to take in western Wessex, after the exile of its ealdorman, Aethelweard, in 1020. Godwine then increased his landholding in Hampshire and Wiltshire. He retained and developed his unique position, and remained at the top of a very greasy pole until his death in 1053.[12]

During the rest of his reign, Cnut executed Jarl Ulf (probably around 1026), invaded Norway in 1028 and expelled Olaf Haraldsson, with the aid of English wealth. No doubt Godwine played a full part in making that wealth available to the king. Then, after Cnut died, Godwine supported Cnut's legitimate son Harthacnut, son of Emma, against the efforts of Harold I, Harefoot, to turn his regency into kingship. For a time, Harold held all England north of the Thames, reflecting his ties to the Midlands through his mother, Aelfgifu of Northampton, and Harthacnut's supporters, led by Queen Emma and Godwine, held Wessex. The threat of attack by Magnus of Norway prevented Harthacnut's immediate return from Denmark, so Harold was able to turn his regency into *de facto* kingship. Godwine played safe and effected a deal with Harold, while Emma went into exile with her son (1037). The sons of Emma by Aethelrede, Edward and Alfred, had been tempted into returning to England in 1036. Edward made a determined but cautious attempt at a landing, aiming to visit his mother, but was repelled at Southampton and returned to Normandy. Alfred attempted to go to London, but was intercepted and deceived by Godwine, who separated him from his escort and handed him over to Harold's men. Both his actions and his motives are the subject of much debate, but the reality is that his reputation was severely tarnished by his involvement. Alfred was brutally mistreated and taken to Ely. Somewhere along the way, he was so crudely blinded that his brain was pierced, and he died. The monks of Ely buried him 'at the west end, very near at hand to the steeple, in the south-side chapel'. By handing Alfred over, Godwine had secured for himself the favour of King Harold Harefoot.[13]

Harthacnut, freed of the Norwegian threat to Denmark, prepared an invasion to claim his kingdom, but no invasion proved necessary. Harold died in 1040 and Harthacnut, with a fleet of sixty ships, claimed his throne. He was welcomed by all and crowned. He took his revenge by levying heavy taxes, and had Godwine and Bishop Lyfing charged with responsibility for Alfred's death, affecting to be enraged by the murder of his half-brother. He also had a number of high-ranking nobles, of whom Godwine was one, disinter Harold's body and throw it first into a sewer and then into the Thames.[14]

Godwine defended himself against the charges by swearing an oath 'in company with nearly all the chief men and thegns in England' that it had not been by either his 'counsel or desire that the king's brother had been deprived of his eyes, but that he had only obeyed the commands of King Harold his master'. He was therefore clearing himself by compurgation, as English law provided: that is, by his own oath supported by the oaths of others. He then, in effect, paid compensation to Harthacnut by presenting him with 'an exquisitely wrought vessel with a gilded prow, well-fitted with all warlike stores and manned with 80 chosen soldiers splendidly armed'. Each man had a golden bracelet on each arm, weighing sixteen ounces, and wore a triple coat of mail and a helmet partly gilt. Each had a sword with a giltded hilt, a Danish battleaxe adorned with gold and silver, a shield with gilded nails and boss, and an *ategar*, or English javelin. This must be one of the earliest records in English history of the excuse that the accused was 'only obeying orders'.[15]

Godwine shortly afterwards joined Leofric and Siward, with all of the king's housecarls, in the harrying of Worcestershire, following the rebellion of the inhabitants against the tax raised by Harthacnut and his housecarls, two of whom, Feader and Thurstan, had been killed by the rebels – so he was back to obeying orders.[16]

It was after this that Harthacnut, possibly to avoid strife over the succession, recalled Edward from Normandy and associated him with himself in the government of the country, a common Scandinavian practice. The *Encomium Emmae* states that Edward became almost *regni socius* – that is, a partner in the kingdom – and that they ruled together *concorditer regnantibus* ('reigning in harmony'), until Harthacnut suddenly died while attending the wedding of Tofig the Proud. Edward was immediately seen and accepted as the obvious successor: he was on the spot, unlike other possible claimants such as Swein of Denmark or Magnus of Norway; he was acceptable to both Danes and Englishmen as Harthacnut's half-brother; and he was descended, through Emma, from Rollo of Normandy. Although it is unlikely that Godwine had favoured his return, the prime mover was the childless Harthacnut, so he was quick to throw his weight behind Edward's accession. The *Vita Edwardi* and *Florence of Worcester* both insist that it was Godwine who led the calls for Edward to become king. William of Malmesbury even claimed that Godwine had said that he would help Edward secure the throne in return for honours for his sons and the marriage of his daughter to Edward. That, of course, is a deduction based on the fact that Godwine's sons were honoured and Edward did marry Edith. There is an element of exaggeration in all this, but Godwine was the leading earl and no doubt played a prominent role in the smooth transfer of power.[17]

Edward had no natural circle of adherents, as he had not been back in England long enough to have acquired the land and influence which attracted commended men. He was able only to gather round him a coterie of Frenchmen, most of relatively low status politically. The only exceptions were to be the three bishops, including Archbishop Robert of Jumièges, and that not until 1050. That Godwine took no chances is demonstrated by his gift to Edward of a ship and its crew, comparable to the one he had given to Harthacnut. This can be seen not only as a move to pay compensation to Edward, as he had to Harthacnut, for his part in Alfred's death, but also as a demonstration of his power and wealth. This time, the ship had 120 crew members. It is described as having a golden-winged dragon on the prow and a gold lion on the stern, and purple sails depicting Edward's lineage and the seabattles of earlier kings.[18]

By early 1045, Godwine was so entrenched in power that he was able to have his daughter Edith married to the king. He had also, in conjunction with Leofric and Siward, carried out the king's orders with regard to Queen Emma. As earlier, under Harold I, she was residing at Winchester, whence she could have been controlling access to the royal treasury, as well as her own lands and wealth. Edward ordered the earls to deprive her of

> all the treasures which she owned, which were untold... in gold and silver... because earlier she had kept it from him too firmly... and... she did less for him than he wanted before he became king.

This cleared the way for Edith to marry the king and replace Emma.

Certainly Godwine was wealthy, especially in terms of estates. His holdings were overwhelming in Wessex and exceeded those of the king himself. The king had more land in some fourteen shires, of which six were the earldom of Mercia, and in Suffolk they were more or less equal, but in twenty-one shires Godwine had the greater number of estates. His total holdings amounted to 829, against the king's at 605. In ploughlands, the figures were 6,307 to 5,127 or, in value, £5,159 to £3,605. Some argue that this great wealth and power in Godwine's hands meant that the monarchy was in trouble. But that is to ignore other sources of monarchical wealth. The king could rely on the profits of justice, two-thirds in all shires, as opposed to an earl's 'third penny' only in the shires of his earldom. The king retained the yield of the geld, usually raised at two shillings on the hide (and not to be confused with the heregeld, raised to pay the fleet, abolished in 1050), and in case of need could demand 'gafol', as Aethelredee had done, to pay tribute to the Danes. He also had many other customary dues.

Arguments about Godwine's influence do seem to depend on the presumption that Edward resented Godwine's power and on the assumption that he intended all along to make William of Normandy his heir. Some see the king as effectively in Earl Godwine's pocket, and talk of chronic dynastic instability. Yet the king got his own way over the appointment of Robert Champart to Canterbury, and he was able to create an earldom not only for the Scandinavian Beorn but also for his own nephew, Ralf of Mantes, without demur from Godwine. It was Archbishop Robert who prevented the king from granting the bishopric of London to his goldsmith Spearhavoc, not Godwine. Nor could Godwine get what he wanted in the case of his kinsman, Swein of Denmark. Though the earl argued that a fleet should be sent to the Danish king's aid, no fleet was sent. Then, in 1050–51, Edward disbanded the fleet altogether, an act seen as ending the 'stranglehold' some believe was exercised over the royal household by the housecarls. The degree of control exercised by Godwine certainly had its limits and should not be exaggerated. He was not 'mayor of the palace', even though later writers saw him as virtually 'under-king' (*subregulus*). His role was perhaps to oversee the conduct of the administration and relieve the king of the tedium of day-to-day government. The *Vita Edwardi* calls him *dux et baiulus* of almost the whole kingdom: that is, earl and office-holder. Did this perhaps mean that, as earl, he was in fact 'the King's good servant', and does *baiulus* mean 'seneschal'? It certainly implies that he had charge of the royal administration. The title should be compared to that of Count Baldwin V as regent to Philip I of France; he was *Regni procurator et bajulus*.[19]

From this time onwards, Godwine's career was closely bound up with the fortunes of his whole family, as theirs were bound up with his. Harold, actually his second son (Swein appears to have been the eldest), begins to play an increasingly important role, not least because of the need to repair the damage done by the uncontrollable actions of Swein. Godwine and Gytha had a large family, six sons and three daughters, and the majority of their children bear Scandinavian names, denoting Gytha's influence. The two older boys were named in a manner which complimented Cnut: Swein, probably after Cnut's father (Estrith also named her son Swein), and Harold, after his grandfather, Harold Bluetooth. Even Tostig was probably named for a well-known warrior, famed on Swedish runestones, who might have served Cnut. Gyrth, the fourth son's name, is also Danish, but there is no known connection with Cnut. The youngest daughter was named Gunnhild, like Cnut's own daughter. The other siblings, Leofwine, Wulfnoth, Edith and Aelfgiva, have English names. The youngest boy is obviously named for Godwine's own father, and his brother Leofwine possibly for Leofric's father.[20]

Although Swein was the first son to receive an earldom (in Herefordshire, Gloucestershire, Somersetshire, Oxfordshire and probably Berkshire in 1043), it was Harold who received the fourth of the major earldoms, that of East Anglia, including Cambridgeshire and Huntingdonshire in about 1045. He had already been witnessing royal charters as *minister* or *nobilis* in 1044 and 1045, and appears as 'earl' (*dux*) at the head of the witnesses to the will of Thurstan, son of Wine, dated to 1044. He is from then on styled *dux* in all surviving royal charters.[21]

No earl had held East Anglia since the removal of Thorkell in 1021, and it could be that the earldom was revived to cope with the renewed threat from Scandinavia. It is possible that Harold led the ships from East Anglia to join the fleet, which was moved to Sandwich as a precaution against an attack by King Magnus. He was certainly with the fleet in the following year, when he and Tostig each commanded one of the king's ships and Godwine led forty-two local ships in a bid to see off hostile ravagers.[22]

Harold was now about twenty-five years of age, suggesting a birth date around 1020, certainly old enough to play his part in English political and administrative life. Like his father, he would have been a skilled horseman (one source says he was 'the best rider of either the old or the new time'), a hunter and physically able, well equipped for a prominent role in public life.

As earl, he was the king's local representative in the shires over which he, the bishop and the sheriff (*scir-gerefa*) presided, and all

writs were addressed to him. He had wide powers to act on the
king's behalf, to witness land transfers and the wills of prominent
thegns and landowners, to pass legally binding judgements in courts
of shire and hundred, and to lead the men of his earldom in war by
land and sea.[23]

As earl, he received the 'third penny' of the profits of justice in
shire courts and received wide lands, in this case in Norfolk, Suffolk
and Essex. It is known that he received the lands of the Danes Ulfkell
Snilling and Thorkell the Tall, and of the ealdorman Byrthnoth in
Essex. The will of Gunnhild, widow of Harold Thorkellson (exiled in
1014), implies that Harold Godwinson acquired her lands, and he had
lands at Colne in Essex which previously belonged to Byrthnoth's
wife. These lands went with the earldom to enable the holder of that
office to carry out his duties and allow him to dispense patronage
to those who sought to become his 'men', by commendation or by
holding land under his 'soke'. As Domesday Book shows, many men
sought to become his dependents so that he would use his influence
on their behalf. Men are found making bequests to him in their wills,
probably either in gratitude for favours received or in expectation of
favours to come. Thurstan, son of Wine, left him half a mark of gold,
and the Lady Wulfgyth left him an estate at Fritton in Norfolk.[24]

He was now one of a select number of royal officials, alongside
(if perhaps hierarchically a little lower than) the three great earls of
Wessex, Mercia and Northumbria. Those men exercised great power
and, in a sense, represented the former ancient kingdoms which had
once ruled the provinces they now administered. Harold held power
where there had once been the kingdom of East Anglia.

Recently created earls had to work hard to establish their authority and to recruit the support of the regional nobility, a task in which
Harold was to prove more able than Swein. One way of doing this
was to marry into that aristocracy. Siward of Northumbria married
into the family of Uhtred of Bamburgh; Leofric married a local heiress, Godgifu ('Lady Godiva'); and Harold's brother Swein probably
married (*more danico*) the mother of his son Hakon from among the
Danish nobility of his earldom. Harold himself contracted another
'Danish marriage' with Edith Swanneshals (the 'swan-necked', so

termed for her beauty), undoubtedly the heiress of a prominent, but unidentifiable, East Anglian family. This was a shrewd political move which helped to bind the local aristocracy more closely to the new earl and probably brought him more lands as part of the lady's dowry. It was not a Christian marriage endorsed by the Church (which would have been regarded as binding), and so the opportunity was left open for Harold to make a church wedding when that proved politically necessary. It is probable that Edith was in fact the lady known from Domesday Book variously as Edith the Fair, the Beautiful and the Rich.[25]

As an earl, Harold divided his time between the administration of his earldom, missions for the king, both abroad and in other parts of the kingdom, and attendance at court. He would usually have been at court for the three great Christian festivals of Easter, Pentecost and Christmas, when the king held great state and met with his earls and other counsellors of the Witan, the council of the great and good. This was not a formal institution with a constitution and defined powers, like a modern parliament, but consultations between the king, who in the last resort ruled by consent, and his natural advisors, those who by rank or wealth felt entitled to give the king their advice. There, decisions of policy were taken involving peace and war and the punishment of major offenders, and laws would have been promulgated. In Edward's case, despite the references after the Conquest to the 'Laws of King Edward', no written codes such as those of Aethelredee or Cnut were issued. He seems to have legislated by word of mouth, giving judgements in particular cases rather than issuing codes of law.[26]

There is no evidence that Harold took any part in Edward's decision to remove from his service influential Danes, those who had been Cnut's people. That was inspired by fears that they might not prove loyal in the event of a renewed Scandinavian assault. Not all those who were removed are noticed in the chronicles, but Cnut's daughter Gunnhild and her sons were banished in 1044, and also Osgod Clapa in 1046. These were prominent people, and the chroniclers were impressed. Certainly the earls did not oppose these removals, and might even have welcomed the exiling of potential rivals. The grandsons of Thorkell the Tall might have competed with the sons of the earls, and Osgod Clapa was a servant of Cnut. So they were seen as a danger in the event of further attacks from Scandinavia.[27]

Harold seems to have gained from these expulsions; his family certainly did. Wroxall, property of Osgod Clapa, was given to Countess Gytha, Godwine's wife. As an earl, Harold would have supervised the confiscation of the estates and goods of those who were exiled.

Many historians argue that Edward, having removed some of Cnut's supporters, sought to promote men whom he trusted more – that is, the companions of his exile in Normandy – and some go so far as to see this as a policy of arranging Norman infiltration of England in preparation for a Norman succession. The problem here is that many of those brought in by Edward were not Normans at all. There were some, of course, but most of those who came to England (and a few must have returned with Edward in Harthacnut's time) are better described as Frenchmen. Several were the companions and followers of Edward's own, partly English, nephew, Ralf of Mantes, and others, like Robert fitzWimarc and Ralf 'the Staller', were Breton (and likely to be hostile to Normans).[28]

In any case, Ralf, the king's nephew (earl of an unnamed area in 1051), was eventually given Herefordshire in 1054 as a sort of 'marcher earldom', in an experiment in the use of continental (not exclusively Norman) methods to control the Welsh. So he built castles and attempted to use cavalry, with a singular lack of success, which earned him the nickname of 'the Timid' because he and his men fled when attacked by the Welsh.[29]

The removal of the Danes came very early in Edward's reign, and the introduction of foreigners followed gradually. Many of the newcomers were clerics in the king's household, and these were largely, though not exclusively, Norman. But several of Edward's appointments to bishoprics were in fact Lotharingians, and their appointment can be seen as an attempt to improve the quality of the episcopate. The number of Normans appointed was quite small, three out of seven bishops and no front-rank laymen at all.[30]

Edward's policy can only be interpreted as pro-Norman if it is first postulated, as many historians have done, that Edward had from the very beginning of his reign, or at least once it became plain to him that he would have no direct heir, always intended that his rather distant relative, William of Normandy, should be his successor. But that is to assume as fact something that needs to be proved. That he probably did offer the succession to William at some time does not prove a settled intention. There is no English evidence to support such a view, which is the interpretation put upon events by Norman writers seeking to justify the legality of the Conquest.

Perhaps the recruitment of foreign clergy should be seen more as an attempt to create a source of advice to counteract the influence of the House of Godwine. Once Earl Godwine was removed from the scene by death in 1053, the king's policy seems to have become very different. Overall, out of twenty-nine ecclesiastical appointments during the reign, only seven were foreign, and of those just three were Normans.

Harold had been preceded in the acquisition of an earldom by his eldest brother Swein, who was in every way different from Harold. Swein Godwinson was a wild and unmanageable youth and proved a severe embarassment to his father and brothers. He is reported to have denied that Godwine was his father and even to have insisted that Cnut was his real father. His mother found this gravely insulting, and even gathered together a number of responsible matron ladies of distinction who supported her declaration on oath that Godwine was Swein's father. What Godwine thought of all this is not recorded. He does seem to have had a preference for his eldest son, nonetheless, as is shown by his efforts to get him reinstated, repeatedly, after each of his excesses. Swein was enamoured of all things Danish and sincerely wished to be regarded as a Dane. He certainly behaved like one, or as he imagined them to be.[31]

In 1046, Swein made raids into Wales to deter attacks on his earldom, as was the normal practice of marcher earls, but erred in allying with Gruffydd ap Llewelyn against the South Welsh. Although playing Welsh princes off against each other was also common practice, Swein's action had the effect of attracting Gruffydd's attention to the plunder obtainable in Herefordshire.

In 1049, Swein committed his first offence – the abduction of Edith, Abbess of Leominster – and, as one source has it, 'kept her as long as he listed and let her fare home again'. She was probably of noble birth, as were most abbesses, and he might have even intended to marry her and so acquire an alliance with her family, which would have strengthened his position as earl, as Harold had done in East Anglia. But his action was seen as intolerable and he was exiled, rushing off to Bruges and then Denmark. Despite his alleged power over the king, Godwine was unable to prevent the exiling of his son, though he worked to undo it and was able to have it cut short.[32]

The immediate effect of Swein's exile was to enhance the position of Harold, as the earldom was immediately divided between Harold and his Danish cousin, Beorn. This might have been done to placate Godwine, but it permanently enriched Harold, and reveals some of the limitations on Godwine's power when there was a consensus of opinion against him. His support for Earl Swein probably reduced his influence with Edward, who would have been angered by Swein's crime. That limitation in influence is indicated by the fact that when Swein of Denmark sought King Edward's aid in his conflict with Magnus of Norway during 1047, and Godwine favoured sending a fleet of fifty ships to his aid, the consensus of Leofric and the other magnates against doing so prevailed. They preferred to let Swein deal with Magnus alone, so keeping him away from England, and to retain the fleet for the defence of the realm.[33]

Meanwhile, Harold, like other earls, would have taken measures for the defence of his East Anglian earldom when the fleet was put on a war footing in 1048 and moved to Sandwich to oppose German raiders, who had been harrying the Essex coast. He is not named as present with the fleet, but he could have been with it, as he certainly was in the following year, when he and Tostig each commanded a ship under Godwine's overall command. This was a preliminary move to deter further piratical attacks and to prepare for Edward's decision that year to assist the German Emperor Henry III in his conflict with Count Baldwin IV of Bruges, who was in rebellion against him. The threat from England and its effect on Flemish trade caused Baldwin to make peace with the Emperor.[34]

Swein Godwinson returned to England during these moves seeking Edward's peace and the return of his lands. Both Harold and Beorn were opposed to this, no doubt unwilling to surrender the estates. Harold, for the first time, is seen acting independently of his father, possibly even in opposition to his wishes. Swein's request was rejected and he was given four days in which to leave England. He used the time to make overtures to Beorn, who was with Godwine, Harold, Tostig and the rest of the fleet at Pevensey, where they were held up by the inclement weather. Swein persuaded Beorn to agree to support a last bid to win over the king, and the two rode to Bosham where Beorn was seized, taken aboard Swein's ship and murdered. Swein buried him in an unmarked grave at Dartmouth.[35]

This was seen as an unspeakable crime, the betrayal and murder of a kinsman, and was immediately condemned by the king and the whole English fleet, who declared Swein to be *nithing*, utterly disgraced, in effect not only an outlaw but an 'un-person', who could be killed by anyone who encountered him. Swein, deserted even by most of his own men, fled the country. Strangely, Godwine still persisted in his efforts to secure his return.

Significantly, it was Harold who recovered Beorn's body and gave it Christian burial at Winchester alongside Cnut, so distancing himself from Swein's crime. The House of Godwine's reputation had been further and irreparably damaged by Swein's action, but Harold emerged from the affair with an enhanced relationship with King Edward. The redistribution of Beorn's earldom cost Harold nothing, and he would not have lost lands if Swein was allowed back. The king's nephew, Ralf, probably received his earldom at about this time.[36]

After the intercession of Godwine, supported apparently by Bishop Ealdred of Worcester (who had begun a long association with the Godwinsons on his appointment in 1046), Swein was allowed to return in 1050, escorted back by Bishop Ealdred, returning from his visit to Rome where he had attended a synod and secured a dispensation, permitting him to move Bishop Leofric's former see to Exeter. This reconciliation for Swein marks the beginning of Ealdred's career as a diplomat.[37]

Swein had to promise that he would make a pilgrimage to Jerusalem in reparation for his sins, but there is no sign that he had changed fundamentally, as he began disputing with Earl Ralf over his control of Herefordshire. Ralf had been endowed with the lands which had been given to Beorn. But of Swein's going on pilgrimage there was as yet no sign, and it was to be overtaken by other events.

Some historians regard Edward's agreement to the return of Swein as evidence of Godwine's ascendancy over the king. They argue that Edward lacked control over Wessex, the ancient heartland of the monarchy, within which Godwine's landed estates exceeded those of the king, and that he was in effect stifled by Godwine's influence. They see the successes of the king in refusing to send the fleet to Denmark and the expulsions of Swein in 1047 and 1049 as only minor, and argue that he was beginning to resent Godwine's tutelage. Some even suggest that he was now conscious that Edith was not going to produce an heir, and was beginning to see her as a symbol of her father's dominance. They point to the absence of her name from witness lists after 1046 as evidence of disfavour, though there could be other reasons for it, even ill health. It is unsafe to argue from the vagaries of witness lists, so many charters are suspect or falsified, and it may be that many more have simply not survived. To argue that he contemplated divorce (that is, an annulment of the marriage) is to assume that he wanted to do so, despite the fact that in 1051, although he sent her to a convent, no moves to end the marriage were actually made.[38]

More convincing are those who point to Edward's moves to secure his popularity by disbanding the fleet in 1050 (a sign of reduced apprehension of foreign invasion after the death of Magnus), in control of which Godwine had been prominent, and the suspension or abolition of the heregeld which had paid for it. But the dispersal of the fleet could not have been carried out without Godwine's consent.[39]

The Leofric Missal, which comes from early in the reign, contains a blessing for a childless king, suggesting that Edward was expected to beget an heir. It reads: 'Give from his loins offspring to reign'. The archbishop had prayed at his coronation that he might produce an heir, and undoubtedly similar prayers would have accompanied the wedding ceremonies. There was an expectation that Edward and Edith would have an heir. But by 1051 things were beginning to look bleak, and minds turned to the question of the succession. Edith was still of childbearing age, and men in that era were thought to remain potent up to at least sixty. Only after the crisis of 1051–52 and Godwine's death in 1053 were any steps taken to ensure the succession. There is no evidence whatever in English sources that anyone's thoughts had turned towards William of Normandy.[40]

3

Arrivals and Departures

The narrative sources for this period record major events (though not always all of them), but rarely explain them. Of no series of events is this more true than of the quarrel between King Edward and his coterie of 'foreign' advisors on the one hand, and Earl Godwine and his family on the other, which led to the expulsion of the Godwinsons from England in 1051 and their triumphant return to their former power in 1052. According to the accounts in the *Anglo-Saxon Chronicle* and in *Florence of Worcester's Chronicle of Chronicles,*[1] the whole thing was caused by the behaviour of Count Eustace of Boulogne and his men at Dover, during a visit to England to see the count's relative, King Edward, and by Earl Godwine's resentment at being ordered to ravage Dover and the surrounding parts of Kent, which lay in his own earldom, in punishment for the temerity of the citizens in resisting the high-handed behaviour of the French. No reason is given for the count's visit, nor indeed for the subsequent visit of Duke William of Normandy. There has, in consequence, been much speculation by historians about the purposes of these visits and whether they had any connection with each other.[2]

Light is cast on the politics of this quarrel and upon the under-
lying causes for it by the work known as the *Vita Edwardi Regis* or
'Life of King Edward who rests at Westminster'. The real title of this
work is unknown; the text itself has survived in a mutilated copy
(a large section is missing from the middle of the work), and the
actual author is unknown. It is certain that the work was commissioned by the king's wife, Queen Edith, towards the end of the
reign (probably after 1060) and completed after the cataclysm of the
Norman Conquest. It is probable that the author did not want his
name to be attached to the work, because the major part of the first
half is really a panegyric on the family of Earl Godwine and his sons
Harold and Tostig, and it would have done his subsequent career no
good to be associated with a work with such close connections with
the late King Harold. The author appears to have been a monk from
the monastery of St Bertin at St Omer, a town with close connections
to the Godwinsons, and opinion is divided still about which of two
possible writers from that monastery might have written it, Goscelin
or Folcard. The former has the stronger case for authorship, but there
seems to be no possibility of making a definite attribution.[3]

The *Vita*'s account provides at least some explanation for the events
of 1051, by revealing the enmity between Earl Godwine and Robert
Champart, Edward's choice as archbishop of Canterbury. First of all,
the church of Canterbury and its archbishop had lost control over
the 'third penny' 'of the shire of the archbishop' to Godwine in 1044,
when Archbishop Eadsige temporarily retired. Furthermore, the earl
was accused of 'stealing' land from the church of Canterbury. Some
of the lands held by Godwine, as entries in Domesday Book show
(they are listed as held by him in 1066, although he had been dead
since 1053), were to be the subject of Kentish land pleas under the
Conqueror, as the Church struggled to reclaim the lands. The *Vita*
seems to admit that some lands had been seized illicitly, but the exact
reason for Godwine taking possession of them is not known. The
Vita Edwardi does not deny the charge. Some could have been given
to him by the king, possibly to finance the cost of coastal defence
against Viking raiders, and others could have been the result of grants
of loan land. The location of some of Godwine's estates suggests

that the earl had profited from the assistance he gave to Archbishop Eadsige, in his declining years, in secular matters. Some of Godwine's commended men might well have had such land, granted away by the Church for the duration of one, two or three 'lives'. It was always difficult for churches which did this to reclaim the land when the lease ran out. Anyway, Archbishop Robert sought to recover some lands through the shire court, but had little success against Godwine's power.[4]

When Robert Champart, from the abbey of Jumièges in Normandy, who had previously been appointed bishop of London by Edward, was elevated to Canterbury at a Witanagemot held in March 1051, he immediately clashed with the earl, after returning from Rome with his pallium (the symbol of Rome's acceptance of his status as archbishop). His appointment would not have suited the earl, firstly because of his own ties to Flanders and the importance of access to that county (Robert's accession to Canterbury impeded that access), and also because it came at the expense of his own preferred candidate. When the see became vacant, the monks had elected one of their number, a kinsman of Earl Godwine, named Aelfric (Aethelric in the *Vita Edwardi*), but King Edward, despite Godwine's support for the monks' choice, preferred to promote his Norman supporter, on whose advice he had perhaps been coming to rely rather than on that of Earl Godwine. The new archbishop accused Godwine of 'invading' the lands of the Church and injuring the archbishop's own interests by reserving the lands for his own use. So there was now a permanent state of tension between the two men. The earl would have seen the archbishop as a threat to his own power.

The *Vita* paints a vivid picture of the archbishop poisoning the king's mind against Godwine. He is said to have suggested to the king that the earl might attack Edward as he had 'attacked his brother' (Alfred), so reviving afresh the events of 1036. This was allegedly proved by Godwine's having agreed to his son Tostig's marriage to Judith of Flanders, daughter of Baldwin IV. This was proof of his friendship with Baldwin, who was regarded by Edward as an enemy (the king had supported the Emperor Henry III against Baldwin in 1049). It has even been argued that there was a sort of Triple

Entente between England, Flanders and Normandy, and that it was
Godwine who was allied to Count Baldwin (who was ally to Duke
William) rather than King Edward. This would cast a new light
on Duke William's visit to England and, indeed, on the purpose
of Count Eustace's visit as well. As for Godwine, his command of
the south coast of England made him an attractive ally for princes
along the Channel coast of Europe. The earl might have preferred a
Scandinavian alliance but opportunism was a more important factor.
No chronicler connects Godwine's rebellion to any plans by Edward
favouring a Norman succession; the *Vita* does not include it in the
charges it makes against the archbishop, and even the Norman writers fail to mention the English crisis of 1051. It is modern historians
who make the connection in their efforts to find an explanation
for the crisis.[5]

One striking contrary interpretation of events is that given by the
Vita Edwardi, which entirely ignores the Dover affray as the cause of
the breach between Godwine and the king and attributes the whole
matter to the venom and spite of Archbishop Robert. It is the *Vita*
that raises the dispute over Robert's selection as archbishop, and says
that Aethelric was related to Earl Godwine. Immediately after his
appointment, the archbishop began to 'provoke and oppose' the earl
and to make himself the 'most powerful confidential advisor of the
king'. The *Vita* had prepared the way for this account by insisting that
Edward as 'master of the whole kingdom' had attracted to his side
several Frenchmen and 'enriching them with many honours... made
them his privy counsellors and administrators of the royal palace'. It
is of this passage that so much has been made to prove the case for a
pro-Norman cabal, but what it actually seems to be talking about is
the presence of French favourites who were not, with the exception
of Archbishop Robert and Bishop Ulf of Dorchester, men of any
great importance other than being members of the royal household
– chamberlains, chaplains, marshals and the like, not members of the
greater nobility.[6]

The archbishop is described as scheming against Earl Godwine and
exploiting Godwine's possession of Canterbury lands to 'direct the
hostile movements into a cause in which right was on the bishop's

side', making apparent use of a doubtful charter in the possession of Christchurch, said to have been granted by Cnut. The archbishop then dragged up the story of Alfred's murder causing a quarrel between Godwine and the king which resulted in the earl's immediate flight into exile, pursued by soldiers sent by the archbishop, 'driven on by his madness'. No doubt these allegations were used to add fuel to the fire started by Godwine's refusal to punish Dover. Frustrated in his efforts to have Godwine killed, the archbishop turned against Edith herself, so that no member of the family would remain in England to influence the king. He endeavoured to separate her from the king, 'contrary to the law of the Christian religion', but the king 'curbed the divorce proceedings' and sent her to Wilton (thus moving her from Wherwell, to which the archbishop had consigned her).[7]

Some historians do acknowledge that to connect the quarrel of 1051 with the king's desire to favour foreigners, both at court and elsewhere in England, is merely an assumption. It is based on the assertions of the *Vita*. It may also be suggested that too many other assumptions are made about English politics in the mid-eleventh century, for some of which there is little or no concrete evidence. Too many writers have made assumptions and then gone on to argue as though these theories are facts. As far as the 'foreign' (some would say 'Norman') influence is concerned, it is certainly all too easy to exaggerate it; the numbers of foreigners in positions of influence was really quite small, and the number of Normans even smaller. Land was the real basis of political power, and only the bishops and one layman (the king's nephew Ralf, Earl of Hereford) had enough of that to be major players. Most of the others were, as one historian has pointed out, 'strangers in a strange land'; they were not in England to build up an 'anti-Godwinist' party nor as a result of a deliberate policy. There is little evidence that the presence of foreigners was resented or that anyone objected to the king's friends, though it must have been the case that native and foreign influences were likely to clash eventually. Some have argued that Edward had successfully removed Cnut's men from office (though not, it must be said, his three great earls), and was seeking to promote men who had served him when in exile (although there is no positive evidence that he acquired his favourites when in Normandy), and that their real significance was as rivals to the House of Godwine for power and influence. Even so, it is admitted by some that there was no 'Norman policy'. One further point can be made. Most of the 'French' strangers were associates of Earl Ralf in Herefordshire, which would be a strange place to locate a 'fifth column' favourable to Norman ambitions, when a power base on the south coast would have been more useful. These men were mercenaries, as is shown by the safe conduct given them in 1052 to seek fresh employment in Scotland. They did not return to Normandy because they had not been sent from Normandy. If, as some have suggested, there had been an effort to put the 'burh' at Dover into 'French' hands, perhaps even those of Eustace of Boulogne, it would certainly have been in the king's interest to put some of his French vassals, such as Earl Ralf and his men, in Kent – yet he did not do so. In its account of Dover, Domesday Book does not mention any castle there, either before or after the Conquest. The fortification there was a burh set within the old Roman castra.[8]

As for the behaviour of Archbishop Robert, he was not the kind of man to identify himself with the cause of ecclesiastical reform. There is no sign that he was a reforming bishop of London. His refusal to permit Spearhavoc, the king's goldsmith, to succeed him in the see of London might have stemmed more from that man's possible but unproven association with Earl Godwine than from any critique of his suitability for episcopal office. It was merely convenient for the archbishop to be able to assert that 'the Pope had forbidden it him' (it is possible that a charge of simony had been made; Spearhavoc had been commissioned to make an 'imperial' crown for the king and could have 'bought' his bishopric). Edward did not remove Spearhavoc immediately; the archbishop's influence was still in its early stages. Interestingly enough, the king did not attend Robert's enthronement as archbishop. Robert Champart made no attempt to interfere otherwise with the king's right to exercise lay control over the Church, and it was the king himself who exercised that control, not the lay magnates of the kingdom. Control over the Church was one of the sources of King Edward's power.[9]

Nor is there any sign, before 1051, of a diminution in Godwine's power as reflected in the acquisition of land. During the 1040s, Godwine not only increased his land holdings, he also acquired earldoms for his elder sons, Swein and Harold, and as late as 1050 a charter of King Edward grants land to his 'faithful earl' Godwine. Then the ecclesiastical appointments followed, in which the king pleased himself (so much for any alleged dominance on Godwine's part) and opposed local connections, refused advice and routed all opposition. It can, of course, be observed that Godwine bore the brunt of this; he was, after all, still paying the price for the reinstatement of Swein on previous occasions and for his pardon for Beorn's murder. He might have paid even more for Swein's reinstatement as earl (though in this he was opposed even by his son Harold).[10]

So Robert Champart was in dispute with Earl Godwine, Swein Godwinson was at odds with Earl Ralf, and the king's mind had been inflamed against Godwine by the raking up of Alfred's death. Only a spark was needed to cause a conflagration, and Eustace of Boulogne duly supplied it. The fullest account is in the Peterborough version of the *Chronicle* (which for this period is based on a Kentish version, now lost, probably from St Augustine's Canterbury); the Abingdon version (C) omits it and the Worcester version (D), less well informed perhaps, puts the dispute at Dover at the beginning of Eustace's visit, whereas Peterborough says he was on his way home, and that is more likely to be correct. Most authorities believe the affair gave Edward the excuse, for which he was probably by now looking, to exile Godwine and attempt to destroy his power and that of his family. Some argue that the king might have planned the whole thing. This could have been simply an effort by King Edward to check the growing power of the earl. It does not, in itself, imply a decision about the succession. Eustace was his brother-in-law, needing his support against both Normandy and Flanders, as Boulogne lay sandwiched between the two powers. The alliance developing between Normandy and Flanders presented a threat to King Edward, a fact which argues against any real intention on his part to make William of Normandy his heir, and allows for another, more probable, explanation. One historian has even argued that a public offer of the succession to Duke William would have turned the major European powers, especially France and Flanders and probably Denmark, against both of them. But the threat was real enough to make an alliance with Boulogne an attractive proposition, though one Earl Godwine was sure to oppose, because of his links with Flanders.[11]

If the intention was to provide the king with an excuse for outlawing the earl (who was perhaps now seen, thanks to the whispering campaign of Archbishop Robert and his underlings, as an 'over-mighty subject'), by provoking him into defying his orders, then it worked perfectly. What, then, did Eustace do?

He is said to have arrived to visit King Edward, accompanied by a 'small fleet'. He had conversations with the king 'about what he wanted' and turned homeward. He and his men dined at Canterbury and advanced towards Dover. Outside the town, and in plain evidence of an intention to do harm, Eustace and his men donned their armour and went into Dover. There his men ('foolishly' according to the Worcester account) demanded accommodation 'where they themselves liked'. In the process, one of Eustace's men wounded a householder who was unwilling to co-operate, and the householder slew his assailant. Hearing this, the count mounted his horse, his men took horse also, and they came upon the householder and killed him. The man's neighbours reacted by killing seven of Eustace's men, and a general mêlée followed in which more than twenty of the Dover men were killed; they, for their part, killed nineteen of Eustace's men and wounded quite a few more. As the count is said to have 'escaped' with 'a few men', he had got the worst of it, and he returned to King Edward loudly complaining and giving a 'one-sided' account of what had happened. Edward accepted his story and granted him safe conduct out of England.[12]

It has been suggested, quite logically, that the affray took place during an attempt by Eustace to billet his men in the houses that lay within the burh of Dover, rather than in the lower town. This was not the last Dover was to see of Count Eustace. In 1067, after the Conquest, he again came to Dover, at the request of the men of Kent, who thought he would be a more acceptable lord than

Odo of Bayeux. They persuaded him to seize and hold Dover, and he was joined by a sizeable English force. Eustace, rashly, refused to wait for these reinforcements and attempted to seize the castle held by Odo's garrison, only to be ignominiously repelled. Before Odo, who had been otherwise engaged beyond the Thames, had returned, Eustace fled back across the Channel to his own County of Boulogne. The English rebels naturally dispersed. This story suggests that Eustace had retained an interest in Dover and its defences, and that in 1051 it had been the intention of King Edward that his son-in-law Eustace should control the burh and port, thus putting one of his own supporters where he could repel any attack from Flanders. It also explains Earl Godwine's reaction, since Dover was within his earldom and he would not have accepted a rival power base there. Also at this time, 'the Frenchmen in the castle' in Herefordshire, where Swein Godwinson was still claiming to be earl, had 'inflicted every injury and insult they could upon the king's men thereabouts'. That looks like a concerted effort to provoke Earl Swein, as well as his father. It is also probably a reference to other men, Normans and men of Boulogne, who, according to *Florence of Worcester*, were occupying a 'castle' at Dover. Perhaps the remnant of Eustace's force had taken refuge in the burh. There is no evidence that any of this was an attempt to garrison England with Frenchmen to ensure a Norman succession. The French in Herefordshire were there to protect the shire against the Welsh.[13]

Edward summoned Earl Godwine and 'ordered him to go into Kent with hostility to Dover, because Eustace had informed the King that it must be more the townsmen's fault than his; but it was not so'. Naturally it was 'abhorrent' to the earl to ravage estates and a town within his own earldom. The Latin version of the *Chronicle* (F) is even more graphic; it says Godwine was told to 'gather together an army and invade Kent, despoiling all of it, especially Dover; but Godwine, not wishing to destroy his province, concealed his anger'. It is perhaps significant that the *Abingdon Chronicle* (C) is either ignorant of or ignores the Dover affray, and appears to connect the return of Archbishop Robert with his pallium with the ensuing banishment of Godwine 'and all his sons'.[14]

Godwine and his sons, meanwhile, met together at Beverstone (or perhaps Langtree, which is just three miles away) in Gloucestershire, with many of their men, intending to travel together to a meeting of the Witan, at which they expected to secure 'the king's advice and his help' and that of the Witan, and so to avenge the 'insult to the king and the whole nation' perpetrated by Eustace. The *Worcester Chronicle* adds that they wanted Eustace and his men handed over to them, as well as the Frenchmen from Herefordshire, and had summoned 'a great and countless army all ready for war against the king' from all over their earldoms. This chronicler had accepted the version of events presented by 'the foreign men' who 'got to the king first' and persuaded him not to agree to meet Earl Godwine, accusing him of treason. Godwine's men had come from Kent and Sussex and the whole of the rest of Wessex; Swein's men would be those of the shires of Oxfordshire, Gloucestershire, Herefordshire, Somerset and Berkshire; and Harold's men would be from Essex, Norfolk, Suffolk, Huntingdonshire and Cambridgeshire – a formidable force.[15]

The king, in fear of this threat, sent for the Earls Leofric and Siward to come to his aid with their armed forces. They arrived with only their household troops (their 'genge'), but immediately summoned a great army, supported also by Earl Ralf and his men. Messages were sent to Earl Godwine from the king warning him of the measures being taken against him, and he in his turn put his forces in a state of readiness. Doubts were already rising in the minds of Godwine's supporters, who are said to have thought it 'abhorrent... that they must stand against their royal lord'. This again points to the limits that restricted the freedom of action of the earls. The men of the northern earls, however, were more resolute and prepared to attack Godwine's army if Edward desired them to do so.[16]

Others were having second thoughts and voices were raised, probably in both camps, questioning the wisdom of joining battle. Some pointed out that most of the finest fighting men in England were to be found in the two armies, and others stressed the danger of weakening the defence of the country by civil war, 'leaving the land open to our enemies' and causing 'great ruin amongst ourselves'. Cooler heads prevailed, and the Witan advised both sides to avoid more wrongdoing. Edward then apparently affirmed his friendship for both sides and, with clerical support no doubt, gave them 'the peace of God': that is, declared a truce.[17]

But that Edward was not yet satisfied that the danger was past is shown by the decision of the Witan to meet again in London on 24 September and by Edward's own decision to call out 'the raiding army' (used to oppose Viking intruders) from shires north and south of the Thames. He was, in effect, converting the men of both armies into royal soldiers and overriding the authority of the earls. That this is so is shown by Edward's demand that 'all those thegns that the earls formerly had' (their commended men) should be resigned into his own hands and become king's men. That this was done is confirmed in Domesday Book, which has entries naming men who were still, in 1066, regarded as the men both of the king and of a named earl. Significantly, the Worcester manuscript specifically states that Harold's thegns, in particular, were 'bound over to the King'.

That Godwine's position was becoming weaker is illustrated by the Witan's decision to renew the ban of outlawry on Swein Godwinson, and by the fact that Godwine and Earl Harold (again, Harold is particularly mentioned) were summoned to this meeting, under truce, and commanded to attend the London meeting. When Godwine demanded safe conduct and hostages to ensure his safety, his request was denied and he was told to attend with only twelve men – despite the Witan's original suggestion that hostages be exchanged. *Florence of Worcester* claims hostages were actually exchanged, but this does not seem to be the case. It might have been then that Archbishop Robert's revival of the accusation of involvement in Alfred's death was flung in the earl's face.[18]

Godwine and his sons went 'with a great multitude from Wessex' to Southwark (as they were to do again in 1052, which suggests that the earl had supporters there), in order to wait for the Council, but as time wore on, and probably as Edward's demand for the handover of commended men took effect, the earl's support began to dwindle. Men leaked away from his company, and he was unable to 'make a counter-plea against the king and the raiding army that was with him'. Overnight, Godwine decided not to wait for the Council to

meet, and went south towards Thorney Island, in Chichester harbour. The Council met and declared the earl and all his sons to be
outlawed, giving him five days in which to leave the country. The
earl, his wife Gytha and Earl Swein, together with the younger sons,
Tostig (with his wife Judith of Flanders) and Gyrth, went to Bosham.
In several ships, 'with as much gold, silver and other valuables' as they
could carry, they set sail for Flanders and the court of Count Baldwin.
Harold, and the last brother Leofwine, did not choose to accompany
their father. Instead they went to Bristol, where Swein had kept a ship
in readiness for his own use and now granted the use of it to Harold.
They were pursued by Bishop Ealdred, sent after them by Edward
with an armed force, to intercept them before they reached their
ship. However, it looks as though Ealdred was sympathetic towards
Harold because, as the Worcester chronicler put it, 'they could not
or they would not', and the two Godwinsons got clean away. In the
Irish Sea they met the autumn storms and suffered the loss of many
men, but managed to take themselves off to Ireland or, to be exact,
Dublin, where they were welcomed by Diarmaid macMael na m-Bo,
King of Leinster and, more recently, Dublin. He allowed them to
spend the winter there and to recruit ships and their crews for an
attempt to return to England.[19]

This apparently overwhelming defeat for the Godwinsons was
most unexpected. The Worcester chronicler was amazed. He asserted
that it 'seemed remarkable to everyone that was in England... that it
should turn out thus', because Godwine was 'formerly so very much
raised up, as if he ruled the king and all England; his sons were earls
and king's favourites ["darlings" in the text] and his daughter was
married and espoused to the king'. Interestingly also, the chroniclers
single out Earl Harold for particular attention, perhaps because when
these accounts were written it was known that he had succeeded his
father, Earl Godwine, as earl of Wessex. The account begins in 1049,
when attention is drawn to the objections of Harold and Beorn to
Swein's demand they hand back the lands he had formerly held and
which the king had given to them. His command of one of the two
ships sent to confront raiders (along with Tostig in command of the
other) is mentioned, and also the fact that Beorn (who may have

commanded the fleet) relieved him of the command; finally, it is pointed out that it was Harold who recovered the murdered Beorn's body and gave it honourable burial alongside his uncle Cnut. In 1051 it was Harold who, along with Swein, met Godwine at Beverstone before the confrontation with the king; it was Harold and Godwine who were summoned to Gloucester and commanded to attend the London Witan; and it was he and Swein who gathered their men from all over their earldoms. It was Harold's thegns, in particular, that Edward required to surrender themselves to him – perhaps they were seen as being particularly loyal to their earl – and, of course, it was Harold who commanded the separate expedition to recruit men in Ireland. It was only Harold and Leofwine whom Edward attempted to prevent leaving England.[20]

Harold is presented as his father's right-hand man in 1052, leading the return from Ireland, making a rendezvous with Godwine in the Channel ('they came together – his son Harold and he'), assisting him in recruiting men along the south coast, and it is 'they' who led their forces to Southwark and encircled the king's ships. Godwine and Harold landed on the north shore with their men and faced the king's council, in order to win reconciliation with the king and the restoration of their fortunes. And thus, when Godwine died, Harold simply succeeded to the earldom.[21]

Before considering the events leading to the restoration to power of Earl Godwine and his House, there are three aspects of the king's rule in Godwine's absence to consider: first is the conduct of government and the extent to which this was put into the hands of 'foreigners'; second is the matter of the treatment accorded to Queen Edith and the possible reasons for it; and third is the visit to England – one might almost call it a 'state visit' – of William *cognomento Bastardo* Duke of Normandy.

Few actual details of changes in the administration are recorded, and only the appointment of Ralf and Odda to command of the king's fleet is mentioned. But the emphasis, during the negotiations over Godwine's restoration in 1052, on the banishment of men responsible for unjust laws and false judgements and the 'promotion of illegality' points to a situation in southern England, at least, where 'foreign' servants of the king had been appointed to administer a legal system with which they were not fully familiar. Ralf of Mantes, the king's nephew, was only half French, from the County of Vexin. It is certain that he had been given the title of 'earl' by 1050 and probable that he was administering part of Swein's earldom, comprising Hereford, Gloucester, Oxford and Berkshire. Two Englishmen were promoted: Odda of Deerhurst was granted part of Godwine's earldom (Cornwall, Devon, Dorset and Somerset) and Leofric's son Aelfgar replaced Harold in East Anglia. It is possible that he had the assistance of Ralf the Staller, who certainly controlled Norfolk and Suffolk before the Conquest. The latter became a member of the court at some time; he is called *aulicus* in a charter of 1062 (from *aula*, a court). He was a Breton, not a Norman. The same applies to Robert fitzWimarc, who may have been sheriff of Essex (his son certainly was, although under King William). Other palace officials seem mainly to have been English, except for the chaplains, who were largely Lotharingian (several became bishops during the reign).[22]

But the complaints about bad government referred mainly to the conduct of the 'Frenchmen in the Castles' in Herefordshire and, by extension, would have included any who held land or office elsewhere. What is remarkable after 1042 is the complete absence of the greater men whom Edward is supposed to have brought from Normandy, and about whom Edith complained in the *Vita Edwardi Regis*. They are missing from the witness lists of charters. Robert of Jumièges himself dates only from 1046, when he became bishop of London; Earl Ralf appears only in 1050. In truth, Edward's court was a cosmopolitan mixture of Anglo-Scandinavian Englishmen, Danes (like Beorn), Bretons, Frenchmen and Lotharingians, and a few, mainly clerical, Normans. There is no real sign of a pro-Norman king's party in opposition to the House of Godwine. Of Normans in positions of real influence, there are only Archbishop Robert and his sidekick Ulf of Dorchester. Even the Norman bishop of London, William, was a well-meaning cypher and not appointed until after Godwine's expulsion. This fundamentally weakens the case for saying that Edward wanted William of Normandy to be his heir.[23]

The second major happening was, as mentioned previously, the removal from the king's side and from his bedchamber of the Lady Edith, daughter of Godwine and Edward's consecrated queen. She was not outlawed like the rest of her family; instead she was packed off unceremoniously to the abbey of Wherwell in Hampshire, in the charge of the abbess, Edward's sister – she was sent without honour and with only one maid. The *Vita Edwardi Regis*, which sought to lay the blame for the separation on Archbishop Robert rather than the king, claims that Edith was sent to Wilton, the convent in which she had been educated, and that this was done for her own safety; she was 'to await the subsidence of the storms over the kingdom... and... with royal honours and an imperial retinue... she awaited the day of salvation'. It does look as though the king had second thoughts and moved her to Wilton, permitting more honourable treatment. Perhaps he did this when he became aware of the strength of feeling against 'the foreigners' and of Godwine's preparations for his return. Most historians accept that Archbishop Robert was urging the king to divorce her; the Peterborough account says he 'abandoned' her (also translated as 'put away' or 'forsook') and took from her all she owned 'in land and in gold and silver' (just as he had treated his mother Emma, because she had not done as much for him as he would have wished). *Florence of Worcester* says he 'repudiated' her 'on account of his wrath against her father Godwine'. Edith herself testifies, in the *Vita Edwardi Regis*, that the king wished to separate from her 'contrary to the law of the Christian religion', which suggests that she rejected all arguments that might justify a divorce. She cannot actually have been divorced, as the king took her back immediately when Godwine returned, without further ado.[24]

The repudiation had to have been the work of Archbishop Robert, as he would have been involved in any proceedings for what would have been the annulment of the marriage – that is, a declaration by the Church that the marriage was canonically defective, therefore null and void. The distinction is an important one, since 'divorce' implies the breaking up of a legally valid marriage and was not recognised by the Church. Later writers purport to know the grounds for the separation. Queen Edith is reported to have denied on her deathbed – a most solemn occasion – the accusation of adultery, and that can be ruled out. Writers seeking to enhance King Edward's case for canonisation allege that the marriage was unconsummated because Edward remained celibate even after marrying Edith; the suggestion that he had lived 'like a monk' was essential to the proof of his sanctity (along with miracles worked after his death). Of course, if the grounds for a 'divorce' were of non-consummation, then allegations of adultery on Edith's part would have been irrelevant and unnecessary. What is known is rather different. No contemporary source suggests that the marriage was anything but normal. Edward could not have been forced into marriage if strongly opposed to that state, and if merely indifferent, or accustomed to a celibate lifestyle, it may be asked why he bothered to marry at all. But there would have been sufficient pressure to overcome that, not necessarily from Earl Godwine, but from the expectations of the clergy and laity around him who would have expected him to father an heir. The prayers used at his coronation included one asking God to grant him children, and those used at his wedding would also have asked God to cause them to bear offspring, and that they would be joined together in conjugal love. The *Vita Edwardi* insists that these prayers were listened to and that it was a happy united relationship; he writes as though it was a normal Christian marriage.[25]

It is true that there were no children and that there were rumours after Edward's death about non-consummation, but this was also said of Henry II of Germany, whose marriage was also childless. The inner truth of the matter cannot be ascertained, but there are many alternative explanations other than jumping to the conclusion (which celibate monks were only too ready to do, in order to promote the cause of his canonisation) that it was due to deliberate abstention from sexual relations. Edward might have been sterile or of low fertility, or Edith herself might have been barren: measles, for example, could account for that. There is even the possibility that Edith did conceive but that the child was stillborn. The case for deliberate abstention lacks any foundation in known fact. The king's doctor, Abbot Baldwin of Bury St Edmunds, records no rumours of that kind, nor do bishops like Wulfstan and Ealdred provide any tales of an edifying nature, while Bishop Leofric inserted into his pontifical (service book) a prayer for a childless king.[26]

Osbert of Clare, in his *Vita Beati Edwardi*, admits that it was thought right and proper that Edward should marry, and that Edith, as an earl's daughter, was thought to be most suitable. Although 'divorce' had been urged by Robert of Jumièges, the king did not go through with it and, as Edith's *Vita Edwardi* claims, he took her back with joy. One purpose of the *Vita* was to celebrate Edith's marriage to the king, and no blame for the separation is attributed to him. Monastic writers describe all laymen who remained faithful to their wives — like Earl Tostig Godwinson, for example — as chaste, and use the word *coelebs*. But *coelebs* means first of all that a person is unmarried and then, after marriage, it means chaste: that is, faithful to one's spouse. Monastic chastity or abstention from sexual relations is only the third possible meaning. Thus the *Vita* says of Edward: 'He preserved with holy chastity the dignity of his consecration and lived all his life dedicated to God in true innocence'. He was not thought guilty of any sexual sin. After the restoration of her family, Edith was 'brought back to the King's bedchamber' and remained 'his royal consort'.[27]

Since Edith's parents had married in 1022/23 and she claimed, after the death of Swein, to be the eldest child (and therefore possibly older than Harold), she cannot have been more than about twenty-seven years old in 1051, perhaps younger. She was therefore still of an age when a child might be possible, though women in the eleventh century rarely gave birth after the age of thirty. It would seem, therefore, that hopes of an heir were not abandoned until after the death of Godwine in 1053. It rather looks as though Edith acknowledged that no child would be born and resigned herself to a companionate marriage thereafter, as witness the tale that she and Edward behaved more as father and daughter than man and wife towards the end of the reign. Edward resigned himself to having no heir, and efforts were initiated in the mid-1050s to find Edward the Exile and bring him back to England; another indication that there was no settled intention to make anyone else Edward's heir.[28]

The third event in this period which needs consideration is the claim in the *Worcester Chronicle* (D), under 1052 for 1051, that:

> Then soon came duke ['earl' in the text] William from beyond the sea
> with a great retinue of Frenchmen, and the king received him and as
> many of his companions as it pleased him, and let him go again.

Much ink has been expended in discussing this passage and its significance. It is alleged by most authorities that it was on this occasion
that Edward promised to make, or actually made, Duke William his
heir (or that William came to accept an offer already made). Two
points can immediately be made. The passage itself does not say so,
and the Norman writers, so keen to assert William's claim, do not
themselves confirm it. None assert that William and King Edward
ever met after Edward became king, only that they knew each other
as boys and were friends. That in itself is unlikely; William was a boy
of thirteen or so in 1042 when Edward became king of England at
almost forty years of age, over twenty years older.[29]

Some authorities doubt the truth of the visit itself, arguing that
William could not have afforded to leave Normandy at that moment,
engaged as he was in a war around the border fortresses between
Normandy and Maine. In autumn 1051, Geoffrey Martel was threatening an invasion and William's uncles, Archbishop Mauger and
William of Arques, were in revolt. Doubts have also arisen about
the genuineness of the entry itself; it has been suggested that it was
interpolated into the text at a later date and is not contemporaneous
with the rest of the annal for that year. Nonetheless, the majority accept the reality of the visit, which was clearly a brief one.
What must be established is its purpose. That it was of diplomatic
importance is made clear by the fact that the language used is very
formal. Eric John has argued that 'the tensions and possibilities of a
Norman alliance meant the crisis of 1051 and William's visit had a
diplomatic purpose'. The word used in the *Chronicle* which is translated as 'received' is *underfeng*. As Eric John sarcastically remarks, the
modern word makes it look as though 'the King is supposed to have
"received" William and some of his men like a lot of debutantes
at a royal ball.' But *underfeng* is used in legal and political contexts,
suggesting that this annal is concerned with diplomacy. The root of

underfeng was *unfon*, and has the sense of submission, used when a man became another man's vassal. King Edward the Elder ruled that no lord was to *underfeh* another man's vassal without his leave. The kingdom of Oswald of Northumbria was so large that four peoples were said to have received him as lord (*hine underfengen to hlaford*). The annalist is clearly claiming that Edward received William and some of his men as, in some sense, his vassals. It might also be the case that some of those new vassals remained in England. But there is no sign of any other obvious result.[30]

There is corroboration of the idea that William became Edward's vassal. The Norman writers have William call Edward 'my lord and kinsman' in his statement of claim to the English throne. No stress is put on this vassalic relationship because it does not affect the claim, but it is noteworthy that a lord's vassal is not his heir. William would not have called Edward his 'lord' if he had not done homage and fealty.[31]

What had Edward gained? He now had William owing him, as a king and lord, service and loyalty. No Viking fleet would now be received in Normandy, from which it could attack the coast of England, left unprotected by the removal of Godwine and his sons. There were, in fact, no more such attacks until the fateful year 1065. Nor would William, an ally of Baldwin of Flanders, now be able to allow Godwine to use Norman ports. Edward might even have hoped for military aid against Godwine, should he attempt a comeback, and certainly for aid against Flanders if it caused problems. Conversely, Edward could guarantee that Baldwin would not be able to allow attacks by sea on Normandy. This straightforward interpretation of William's visit fits the facts without the need to invoke hypothetical promises about the English succession. In the event, no actual military aid was ever provided; William had his own problems and Godwine did indeed recover his earldom. The Normans do not mention the visit because nothing came of it and it had no bearing on the succession question. But William had seen England and formed an idea of its wealth, and his ambition could well have been stimulated. As the visit was not, on this interpretation, made by William in response to a promise of the succession, it follows that such a promise had not yet been made. It is equally unlikely that any such promise was made after the Godwinson restoration of 1052.

So, how, exactly, did Earl Godwine and his family win back their paramount position? It was at first a two-pronged attack. Godwine used his great wealth to recruit a fleet in Flanders and also to seek reconciliation with Edward through diplomatic pressure. He petitioned, unsuccessfully, for mercy, supported by Count Baldwin and Henry I of France, and returned to reconnoitre the situation, particularly investigating the effectiveness of Earls Ralf and Odda (of Deerhurst) as commanders of the royal fleet. These were not 'Norman' magnates. They proved unequal to the task, unable to catch Godwine or to cope with severe Channel weather. They took the fleet to London, possibly to repair storm damage, and then delayed so long that the naval campaign was abandoned altogether. The will to prevent Godwine's return just does not seem to have existed. One clue lies in the fact that, after his return, men turned against those foreign supporters of the king who had assumed positions of authority and handled it badly. Those who were in Herefordshire, in particular, were unable to prevent Gruffydd of Wales from taking advantage of Godwine's absence to raid around Leominster.[32]

Godwine summoned up reinforcements from Bruges and proceeded along the south coast as far as the Isle of Wight, seizing there any ships useful to his campaign. He did much damage at Portland, possibly because that island was a royal estate, and lay in wait for the arrival of Harold, which suggests some sort of pre-arranged rendezvous. All along the south coast, Godwine had 'enticed' men to join him – from Kent, from Sussex, and even from Surrey, further inland – and especially the boatmen ('butsecarles' or fighting sailors) of Hastings. While Godwine was thus engaged, Harold came out of Ireland into the Severn (only *Florence of Worcester* bothers to mention Leofwine) to Porlock on the Somerset/Devon border, and there ravaged the area. He was confronted by local levies from both shires – in neither of which he was well known – and put them to flight, killing thirty thegns and a good number of other men. His purpose seems to have been to secure stores and provisions. He seized cattle and property and also men. Some think he intended to make slaves of them but, as he had no intention of returning to Ireland, this seems unlikely. Possibly he was replacing men lost in the fight. After that, he sailed round Land's End to the Isle of Wight and joined his father. The two continued their policy of making landings along the coast to add to their supplies and to recruit more men, particularly butsecarles from Romney, Hythe, Folkestone, Dover and Sandwich, precisely the places later to become the Cinque Ports.[33]

From there, they sailed by way of Sheppey and Milton Regis to London, mooring at Southwark. This was on 14 September, the Feast of the Exaltation of the Holy Cross, and, as his endowment of the canonry of Waltham Holy Cross shows, that date struck a significant chord in Harold's heart. Taking advantage of the tide, they moved on, apparently unopposed, beyond the bridge to the south bank, and there rendezvoused with their land army (mostly from East Anglia and Essex, in all probability) which had come down to the shore. The king had drawn up his own land army along the northern side of the river but, again, the men on both sides were unwilling to fight men of their own race – and the only fighting men of any value on either side were Englishmen. Nor did they want to lay the country open to invasion by destroying each other. Instead 'wisemen' (meaning members of the Witan) were appointed to mediate between the two sides, and Bishop Stigand (singled out by the Canterbury manuscript F as the king's advisor and chaplain: *cynges raedgifu* and his *handprest*) played a prominent part, probably leading the negotiating team. Hostages were fixed from both sides, peace was agreed, and the armies were ordered to put aside their arms.[34]

Godwine and Harold landed and met the king in council; they were given back everything that they had previously held. Godwine received his earldom 'as fully and completely as he ever owned it'; his wife and daughter and his sons received back everything to which they were entitled and complete friendship was declared between them, the king promising 'good law for all the people'. All the French who had 'promoted illegality and passed unjust judgements and counselled bad counsel' were outlawed, with the exception of those the king liked to have about him (who had clearly not been responsible for the quarrel with Earl Godwine) and who

were faithful to him and his people. That would mean those who had
come with him from Normandy back in 1041, rather than any more
recent incomers. *Florence of Worcester* names some of them; Robert the
Deacon, his son-in-law Richard fitzScrob, Alfred, the king's marshal,
and Ansfrid, called Cocksfoot. There were certainly others whose
names are unknown. Later, Bishop William, the Norman bishop of
London, was allowed back, as he was a good-natured man who
had done no wrong. Others who had been faithful to the king also
remained, such as Ralf, who retained his earldom of Hereford, and
Odda of Deerhurst. Queen Edith, who had been sent to a nunnery
during her father's exile, 'abandoned' by the king and deprived of
lands and wealth, was now received back 'with honour', and the king
'gave the Lady all that she earlier owned'. She was, as the *Vita Edwardi*
insists, received back at his side and in his bed.[35]

It now becomes apparent just who the 'French' were who were
now outlawed. At the head of the list comes Archbishop Robert
– 'the cause of the wrath there was between [Earl Godwine] and
the king' (Canterbury F) and 'the most responsible for that discord'
between them (Worcester D). Also mentioned are Bishops Ulf and
William, and some of the French who had castles in Herefordshire,
such as Osbern Pentecost and his associate Hugh, and those, if any,
at Dover. It is reported that many of these did not wait about to
dispute their outlawry, but fled as soon as it became apparent that
the Godwinsons would be restored to power. They did not wait
for formal sentence to be pronounced against them. The archbishop and the other clerics fled east, to the Naze in Essex, and
set off for the continent in a not-quite-seaworthy vessel (the word
used is variously translated as 'unsteady', 'crazy', 'broken down' and
'unseaworthy'). In leaving London they had to force their way
out of the East Gate, killing and wounding several 'young men'
in the process, and they 'barely managed to escape'. The opposition to their escape has led some to suggest that Robert had
kidnapped Godwine's youngest son, Wulfnoth, and Earl Swein's son
Hacon, and that he took them to Normandy, leaving them in Duke
William's hands – though there is no evidence for this other than
the fact that they did become hostages in William's hands at some

time, and this was the most likely time for that to have happened. It is also at about this time that, according to William of Jumièges, Archbishop Robert had been 'sent' by King Edward to announce that he had made the duke the heir to the kingdom which God had entrusted to him, although some historians argue that Robert had actually done this earlier, when on his journey to Rome for his pallium. Certainly Archbishop Robert passed through Normandy in 1052, on his way to Rome to complain about his treatment and to get Stigand condemned as uncanonically appointed. That the archbishop told William that Edward wanted him to be his successor fits the available evidence and explains the duke's constant assertion that he was Edward's choice. It does not prove that Edward had made any such promise. The king might also have dropped hints to William during the negotiations for a treaty, without committing himself too firmly. William never claimed to have been granted the succession in person, only that he had been promised it through emissaries. Edward, raging at the prospect of Godwine's return, might have allowed Archbishop Robert to conclude that he would prefer the remote possibility of a Norman succession to any candidate proposed by Earl Godwine. Meanwhile, the Herefordshire men obtained leave from Leofric to cross through Mercia and fled to Scotland, where they took service with King Macbeth. Some others probably headed for the same destination, going north from London to 'Robert's castle' at Clavering in Essex, belonging to Robert fitzWimarc.[36]

The ultimate beneficiary of the restoration was Harold Godwinson, rather than his father. Shortly after the triumphant return ('soon after he landed'), and probably as a result of the great exertions he had made during the various excursions at sea, the earl became seriously ill; presumably he collapsed. This time he is said to have recovered, and the chronicler sourly remarks that 'he made all too little reparation for God's property which he had from many holy places', seeing the earl's illness as the consequence of God's wrath. Bishop Stigand was then chosen to replace Robert as archbishop, because Robert was deemed by the English Church to have deserted his see, an offence under canon law. King Edward had acted as he had always done, and chosen a successor. Leofric, nephew of the earl of Mercia, replaced Earnwig (who retired) as abbot of Peterborough, and this was probably a 'sweetener' for the Mercian. The new abbot brought great endowments to the monastery and it became known, for its wealth, as the 'Golden Borough'; it 'grew greatly in land and gold and silver'.[37]

Stigand's position proved to be anomalous. He never even attempted to go to Rome for a pallium of his own, making use instead of Robert's pallium, left behind in the rush to escape. No less than five reforming Popes were to deny recognition to Stigand. Archbishop Robert, possibly with Norman support, soon informed the papacy of the situation; Stigand was rejected as having 'intruded' himself into Robert's see and was probably condemned as a pluralist as well. For the rest of the reign, most southern bishops went overseas for their consecration, though the Norman bishop Remigius (of Dorchester/Lincoln) did accept consecration from Stigand; King William allowed him at first to continue to administer his see, until he was deprived of it by the Pope's legates.[38]

At Easter 1053, while dining with the king, Earl Godwine had a stroke; as the *Abingdon Chronicle* says 'he suddenly sank down against the footstool, deprived of speech and of all his strength; he was carried into the king's chamber and it was thought that it would pass over, but it was not so; but he remained thus unspeaking and helpless, through until Thursday, and then gave up his life'. Fanciful and unsubstantiated stories became attached to this event. Godwine and the king were alleged to have again begun arguing about Godwine's part in the death of Edward's brother, Alfred, and, as William of Malmesbury relates without endorsing the tale, Godwine was said to have dramatically seized a large morsel of bread and cried out that he was innocent of the charge and that if he was not, then might the bread choke him. He attempted to swallow the morsel and promptly choked to death. Like so many dramatic medieval vignettes, it is simply wishful thinking by those who saw Godwine's sudden death as God's punishment for his many sins. It is, in fact, a well-known medieval folk tale about the punishment of malefactors by divine intervention.

The king immediately promoted Harold to fill his father's place as earl of Wessex, and he 'succeeded to the earldom and to all that his father owned'. Harold's former earldom of East Anglia passed to his son Aelfgar, in another move to mollify Earl Leofric. The stage was now set for the rise of Harold to a position of almost unparalled power and influence. He was well on the way to becoming the richest and most powerful man in England, after the king. [39]

4

The Earl in his Earldom

From 1044 onwards, Harold Godwinson was an earl and, until 1053, earl of East Anglia. That earldom had been vacant since the departure of Thorkell in Cnut's reign. It extended from the Thames to the Wash, with the inland addition of Cambridgeshire and Huntingdonshire.[1] It included many of the estates held under Cnut or earlier by such prominent figures as Ulfkell Snelling, Thorkell the Tall and Ealdorman Byrhtnoth, in Norfolk, Suffolk and Essex.[2] Harold now had a local power base and could dispense patronage to and use his influence on behalf of other men. Bequests were made to him, intended to secure his support for the provisions of wills; he received half a mark of gold from Thurstan, son of Wine, and land at Fritton, Norfolk, from the Lady Wulfgyth.[3] He probably also benefited when men were exiled and lands were forfeited to the king. As earl, Harold would have supervised the seizure of such lands and been rewarded for doing so. For example, when his brother Swein was outlawed as 'nithing' in 1049, Harold gained a share of Swein's former earldom and refused to surrender it to Swein when he was briefly allowed to return in 1050.[4]

Land was the source of all power in agricultural societies, providing for all men's needs – food, clothing and wealth generated from any surplus. It was therefore also a source of political power. Earls were appointed by the king and had to be confirmed in office,[5] as is demonstrated by Edward's last act as king, the confirmation of Morcar as earl in Northumbria in 1065 (although there was a natural tendency for son to succeed father). This power of appointment was vital to the king's own power, and his right, as king, to the fealty of all adult males meant that he could call on them to obey him rather than the earl – as Edward did in 1051, in his capacity of lord of all thegns, calling upon Harold's men to hand themselves over to him as king.[6]

As earl, Harold commanded the 'shire militia' (of all the shires within the earldom) in war, presided over the shire court and heard lawsuits,[7] and was compensated for his work by receiving the 'third penny': that is, one third of the profits of justice. The other two thirds went to the king, as also the same proportion of the customs (*consuetudines*) of boroughs. Earls were addressed by name in royal writs and a number of estates were apparently also reserved for an earl's maintenance. But of other more specific powers little is known. The actual main function of an earl was political, as adviser to the king and member of the Witanagemot, rather than purely administrative, though Earl Godwine is credited with relieving the king of much of the administrative detail of government. Earls regularly attended court for the three major Christian festivals, Christmas, Easter and Pentecost, or to witness charters issued by King Edward.[8]

An earl was the king's representative in the district, or more properly province, under his control. These provincial units were larger in the eleventh century than had been the case in the tenth, when they were known as 'ealdordoms' or 'ealdormanries'. Aethelrede seems to have begun a process of amalgamating ealdormanries into larger units, so reducing the number of ealdormen. It has also been suggested that the growth in importance of the sheriff ('shire reeve' or *scir gerefa*) was due to the need for a local administrator to relieve earls of routine duties and permit their constant attendance upon the king. Kings also made use of the large number of king's thegns, who formed an aristocracy supporting him and his earls, and they were a source of contact between the king and the local middle-ranking thegns in the shires – the monarch's eyes and ears.[9]

Every earl was the lord of a large number of thegns and freemen, as well as having sokemen under his lordship. The greater an earl's resources in land and portable wealth, the greater his status and reputation, and so he attracted an ever-increasing number of men who 'commended' themselves to his lordship by 'bowing' to him, in an act of homage. *Commendatio* in Old English is *mannraedenn*, which means homage – the condition of being the 'man' of another man. Harold had forty-five men (and one woman) commended to him in East Anglia, and many unnamed others, with land worth £230. Some sought Harold's service when their own lord was outlawed, such as the men of Eadric of Laxfield. But an earl's lands were scattered and there was no tendency for the accumulation of large blocks of adjacent estates, such as were formed in the Norman period as a result of the Conquest. However, there was a solid block of shires in the north-west Midlands, where the earls of Mercia had no rivals, so the House of Leofric was never a completely negligible factor in the politics of Edward's reign.[10]

One of the main obligations of an earl was to provide for the defence of the kingdom, and Harold's appointment to East Anglia was intended to provide a figure capable of organising the defence of that area against the incursions of Danish raiding armies. Several of his East Anglian estates were located where defensive measures needed to be taken, along shores and inlets. Waltham, where Harold built his House of Canons of Waltham Holy Cross in the Lea valley, was the link to a group of estates.[11] Harold's holdings can be compared to Earl Godwine's holdings such as Singleton and Folkestone, which might have been comital land and were certainly intended to assist an earl in defending the area against Danish raids. There were two main reasons for granting such estates to the earls: income and defence. That is, either to provide large amounts of cash or because of their strategic location, or both. Cnut the Great and his successors had granted their earls ecclesiatical, royal or ealdormanic estates, not by confiscation but by the piecemeal patching together of lands as they became available where the services of the earls, and the Godwinsons in particular, were needed.[12] Harold was not only able to govern his East Anglian earldom but could raise forces in 1049 for the fleet when it was called out and, in 1051–52, support his father Godwine against the king. But the earl spent a great deal of his income on all of his duties as earl – administrative expenses, the cost of the administration of justice, attendance at court and of going on royal embassies abroad, as well as the cost of defensive measures. There were also his own daily household expenses and those of his family. He paid stipends to his housecarls, who formed his armed retinue, the 'genge', for their attendance on him or performance of garrison duties. He paid the expenses of his reeves, priests and household servants.[13] In Harold's case, as also that of his brother Earl Tostig, there was the cost of his pilgrimage to Rome, the education of his daughter Gunhild at Wilton Abbey, the purchase of large numbers of holy relics, the cost of his leisure pursuits, hunting and hawking, and even the purchase of books, which were enormously expensive.

Some of these lands were very profitable, but others were located in areas devastated by the Viking Wars (or in Herefordshire by the Welsh). Cnut had rearranged the estates of his earls to suit the needs of defence. Plotting the holdings of the Godwinsons (especially Harold's in East Anglia) reveals this. Many were located near Roman roads; Harold owned two estates in Wiltshire. The first was Aldbourne on the junction of Ermine Street with the ancient road from Wanborough to Cunetio, and that was connected by Ermine Street to the second, at Aldermaston. This cannot have been a coincidence. Ancient roads are used in charters to act as boundaries between estates, and served manors which held markets. Nor was it a coincidence or fortuitous that Earl Godwine and his sons met in 1051, at the commencement of the crisis, at Beverstone near the Fosseway and its intersection with Ermine Street and the Icknield way. It linked Swein's lands to Harold's in East Anglia.

Domesday Book shows that Essex was strategically important in 1044, when Harold became earl, and he is shown holding lands draining into the rivers Colne and Blackwater. There he had fourteen manors worth some £1,300 (or over 300,000 silver pennies)

including the value of twelve nights' farm: that is, one day's provision
for the royal household. Another estate, Lexden, included the Lexden
ramparts, a two-mile dyke near the Old London Road. Other estates,
previously the property of Ealdorman Byrhtnoth's wife Aelflaed
(daughter of Ealdorman Aelfgar of Essex), near Colchester, were
on the Great Road (the Roman road from Colchester to London)
and linked to his Blackwater estates. At Maldon, nearby, Edward the
Elder had built a double-ring defensive work in 912. Benfleet, another
of Harold's estates, was the site of the earthwork built by Haesten
the Dane in 894. All of this assisted Harold in the organisation of
the defence of East Anglia. The same sort of links were to be found
in Harold's greater earldom of Wessex. Exactly how, and sometimes
when, all these lands were acquired will be considered, along with
the extent of Harold's landholding and of his wealth. Something can
also be said about the number and kinds of men who chose Harold
as their lord.

Even as earl of East Anglia, before he was elevated to earl of
Wessex, Harold enjoyed the lifestyle of an earl and benefited from
the wealth of his vast estates. The exact nature of the administration
of these estates is unknown, although individual manors would have
been managed by reeves in the usual way[14] (the names of some of
them are in Domesday Book) and he might have imitated the king
by appointing his own shire reeves, although it is not known that
he actually did so. Those thegns and earls with a great deal of land
did not necessarily farm it themselves but rented it to tenants who
supported their own families and were therefore dependent upon
the lord.[15] Landlords could secure resources and military services
in return for their protection and support. The manors of an earl
were probably organised like the royal demesne, the 'home farms' of
the monarchy, into either provisioning or revenue-producing units.
Entries in Domesday Book note the number of nights' farm that
could be obtained from a manor. They were the cost of overnight
provisions[16] for the king or lord and his whole household when visiting the manor. The overall value of a manor was reckoned to be the
sum of money that went out from it to the overlord or landowner.
This probably involved the relationship called 'soke', (a form of

overlordship). If so, then these values represent soke dues and in origin were most likely shares in the royal farm due from the estate and paid at least partly in coin.[17] The overlords were those described in Domesday Book as having sake and soke in particular counties. As well as earls, these overlords included the king's thegns, who are seen as greater landowners with full rights over their land, the aforesaid sake and soke, and the men dwelling on them. They had no lord but the king, and even if commended to an earl, such as Harold, their loyalty was still to the king first. They were required to attend his army and bring their men with them.[18]

Harold's household would have been the centre of control, and it can confidently be said that, like the king himself, he constantly travelled around consuming those provisions which were not sold for cash, and collecting revenue. It is likely that a great earl's household would have mirrored that of the king, with stewards and butlers, household clergy, marshals in charge of the horses, chamberlains to look after the lord's apartments in the halls at which he stopped, and so on. It is not known whether Harold had any favourite residences, but he would certainly have visited the larger and more luxuriously appointed estates. His visits to shire courts were for the transaction of royal business, and such courts would have been grouped into provincial centres, as he governed many shires, to make his attendance practical.

English earls, like thegns, had protected residences,[19] which were not castles as the Normans understood them, but enclosures surrounded by a stockade or a ditch and rampart, so constituting a burh with a gatehouse and belltower. Such a 'ring-work' enclosed a hall, often also a church, a kitchen and probably other buildings, and the whole complex was entered by way of the gate-tower. Whether this should be called a castle is a question of definition and usage, and its difference from the Norman type is a matter for consideration by archaeologists. Thegns' seats were a kind of fortified residence which can be taken to include Norman castles which lacked a keep or donjon, such as Richmond, Chepstow and Ludlow.[20] When Orderic Vitalis denied that there were castles in England before the Conquest, he seems to have meant that they did not have the motte and bailey castle, not that they had no fortified residences of any kind. Several sites have been uncovered which show large aisled halls and alongside them separate chambers (*cameras*) for the use of the lord's family. A dignified 'setl', or seat, required both private and public accommodation on an enclosed site, often of an acre or more, and a church.[21] Such churches could be quite large. Earl Leofric and Godgifu (Godiva) built one at Stow, Lincolnshire with transepts eighty-five feet long and the arches of the central crossway thirty-three feet tall, on the scale of an Anglo-Saxon cathedral. The size of Harold's church at Waltham is uncertain but was certainly impressive.

There is little or nothing now above ground to show where these lordly residences were, because the Normans suppressed the thegns' burhs,[22] so allowing Orderic to assert that 'there were few of the works [*munitiones*] which the Gauls call "castella" in England'. But 'castles' were the private fortified residences of princes and other lords, as distinct from Anglo-Saxon fortified cities and boroughs. The Normans scattered a multitude of 'estate castles' over the landscape, state-of-the-art fortresses (as distinct from the mainly royal castles built in or on the edge of towns), which were not modified versions of thegnly burhs but replaced them. That gave rise to the idea that castles were entirely new, yet most castles were rural, not urban, and were not built on entirely new sites. It is common to claim Anglo-Saxon predecessors for many rural churches (not always correctly), but this is rarely claimed for castles, which demonstrates the effectiveness of the Norman takeover.

Although moated mounds are not converted thegns' burhs, the frequency with which churches adjoin castles has been ignored, and mottes are emphasised, to the neglect of ring-works.[23] The lord, his church and the parishioners formed a unique whole, into which the castle which had replaced the burh had been absorbed. The building of castles after the Conquest was intended to erase and eclipse Anglo-Saxon buildings. For example, at Bramber, excavated in 1966–67, the apparently enigmatic motte with no ditch was revealed as the remnants of a tall 'keep-gatehouse' (a burh-gate?) with a masonry enclosure and a church.[24] This castle-church juxtaposition is more common than is often realised.[25] At Sulgrave, Northamptonshire, the pre-Conquest gateway had been the entrance to a free-standing tower, which was blocked when it was incorporated into the Norman ring-work.[26]

The new aristocracy, the new élite, to which Harold Godwinson belonged, had different priorities from those of the previous élite which it replaced, and a different mode of life. They were, in fact, nouveau riche, and Godwine in particular was 'an Anglo-Danish parvenu'. These new aristocrats put the large-scale foundation of monasteries a long way down the list. There are far fewer new foundations between 1020 and 1066 than earlier (or than there were to be later).[27] There are only three: Abbotsbury (Orc), Coventry (Leofric) and Waltham (Harold).

The new élite replaced the tightly knit ealdormanic aristocracy united to previous kings through ties of kinship, marriage, lordship and close association. The kings had been aware of the benefits of ruling with the aid of their cousins, uncles and in-laws. It could be argued that perhaps the Godwinsons (and Harold in particular, by allying himself with Edwin and Morcar) were unconsciously trying to recreate the previous situation, through Edith's marriage to Edward which united the Godwinsons to the royal kin. The old aristocracy was virtually extinguished during the later years of Aethelredee's reign and the opening years of Cnut, as the ties binding the aristocracy to the monarchy loosened and were then severed. The ealdormen were stripped of wealth and influence (and much wealth was lost through the huge payments historians call danegeld), and then, as the ealdormen grew old, retired or died (and some were killed), others replaced them. Many of these new men were Anglo-Danish, or at least Anglo-Scandinavian, in origin, adherents of the Viking king risen, like Godwine, from the dust. These were the men whom William of Normandy was to fight, even including England's king, Harold, but they had not had the time – barely fifty years – in which to consolidate their power, so they fell quickly.

Many of the lands of the former ealdormen and their associates, as surviving wills show, fell to the king or to his new secular officials in the decades each side of the millennium, and the survivors of once great kindreds disappeared from the ranks of the Witan. Only

Earl Leofric of Mercia was the son of an ealdorman, Leofwine, and he had only come to power under Aethelredee, as ealdorman of the Hwicce.[28] So by the time Cnut died, the great office-holding aristocracy had been transformed, and under Harold it was to be transformed again. None of the new great families of Godwine, Leofric and Siward owed their position to King Edward, but neither could they trace descent back to former West Saxon kings. This perhaps explains their devotion to conspicuous display and expenditure. They have been called an 'aristocracy without cohesion', yet they presided over a period of peace and prosperity, until the very end of Edward's reign, as witness the impressively reformed coinage, the remarkably efficient administrative system, and a forward-looking interventionist policy in international affairs. The major figures, especially Harold, all played a decisive role in the government for half a century, defended the kingdom and protected it from the assaults of the Welsh and the Scots — and they did all this while accumulating wealth in land and treasure.

These great lords derived wealth not only from land but from a variety of customary dues, judicial fines, and labour services such as sesters of honey, blooms of iron cartage and the 'third penny' of justice. The Godwinsons predominated, holding sixty-six per cent of the total of land held by comital families. The Leofricsons held thirty-one per cent and the Siwardsons only three per cent.[29] It has been calculated that the Leofricsons had an income of over £700 (168,000 silver pennies) and that this rose to £2,700 in 1065 (480,000 silver pennies). But the Godwinsons had £7,500 and, if Tostig is included, £8,400 (1,800,000 and 2,016,000 silver pennies). Those holdings equalled the combined total of the seventy wealthiest thegns in England. No post-Conquest Norman baron ever even came close.

Harold and his brothers therefore attracted a large following, including many of those wealthy thegns, and did so in part because their prodigious holdings allowed them to alienate property to thegns and housecarls hungry for land. They could offer their aid in court, help dependants stave off the attacks of their neighbours, and pressure local churches into leasing them land. The greater the family's resources and the more offices they held, the more effective and sought after was their lordship. In return for their protection and support, the Godwinsons were in turn provided with service, cash and land. Lordship was very profitable.

This new political class produced its own political style, which required an ostentatious display of wealth. Their clothing, for example, both impressed and scandalised the Normans with its use of cloth of gold and gold embroidery. The clothes were thickly encrusted with precious metal thread, so that it was said to look like the chainmail used for hauberks. King Edgar is said to have worn a purple cloak and gold corselet, but such finery was now also found on the new earls. Such garments were available to those who received them as diplomatic gifts, or whose womenfolk were free to do fancy needlework as Edith did for King Edward. She found him relatively plainly dressed, rustic and uncultured, coming as she did from a wealthy Anglo-Scandinavian background, and insisted on choosing or fashioning suitably decorated robes for him. These, too, were in complicated floral designs in gold and precious stones. Edith insisted on his using a staff encrusted with gems and gold and a saddle and horse-trappings hung with golden beasts and birds, on having fine Spanish carpets on the floors, and gold embroidered hangings on the throne.[30] England became awash with de luxe fabrics, as Aelfric's *Colloquy* reports: 'purple cloth and silks, precious jewels and gold, unusual clothes [employing] ivory and bronze'.[31] The Northumbrian thegn Gospatrick was 'wearing garments suited to his noble rank' when he was seized by bandits during the pilgrimage to Rome. They thought he had to be the Earl Tostig.[32]

Great rectangular brooches were fashionable, and robes were trimmed with fur: marten skins for a king, sable, beaver and wolf for those who could afford them. There were chests full of tapestries, bedclothes, and wall-hangings, all for their lordly residences. It did not stop there. The splendour of their gifts to churches of copes and altarcloths is noteworthy. Waltham was given stunning vestments and hangings by Harold,[33] and a chasuble valued at twenty-five marks of gold and named 'The Lord Spake to Me'. Harold's gifts to his church are detailed in the *Waltham Chronicle*: thirty-one large gospel books in gold covers, and five other books in silver gilt, precious metal artwork, altar vessels (silver for ordinary services and gold for feast days), gold and silver reliquaries and candlesticks. Like Judith, his sister-in-law, Harold was a connoisseur of de luxe manuscripts and owned books on hunting. Included in Harold's taste for display is the cost of his personal standard or banner, called 'The Fighting Man', the figure of a warrior in armour worked in gold and jewels.[34] His household was also elaborate, and the Bayeux Tapestry shows feasting, grand palaces, fine horses and ships and his own finery in dress, as well as that of his followers, reflecting his status. He gave King Edward the gold figurehead from the ship of Gruffydd of Wales, and could easily afford to build a hunting lodge at Portskewet in Wales, for the king's use.[35]

Real evidence of Harold's religious impulses is to be found not in the criticism of his conduct by the Norman scribes of Domesday Book, who faithfully recorded all allegations of misappropriation of Church lands they could find, but in his foundation of Waltham Holy Cross. Lands which had previously been those of the staller Tofi the Proud came to Harold. Among those lands were the endowments of a small church at Waltham in Essex, devoted to the Holy Cross. Tofi had founded a small house of canons there. In the 1060s there were only two canons, dedicated to the service of the miracle-working image of Christ on the Cross. This was said to be a life-size crucifix discovered at Montacute in Somerset. It was of black marble, from Tournai, or perhaps polished blue lias, with a Black Book, possibly a missal or set of gospels. It has been suggested that it was Scandinavian in style and ornament. Inspired by this, Tofi had set up a small shrine, staffed by canons not monks. The movement for houses of secular canons had begun in the eighth century and Chrodegang of Metz had devised a rule for them, so it was a Lotharingian movement. Knowledge of this rule apparently reached England by about 1059 (possibly as a result of Ealdred and Harold's visits to the continent), some time after the Council of Rome of that year. Perhaps the idea of recruiting secular clerks commended itself to Harold as a source of trained clerks for his chapel, and even for a writing office. A great earl certainly had need of such staff. Harold might well have had a devotion to the Holy Cross arising from the fact that during the family's restoration to power in 1052 they arrived at Southwark on the Feast of the Exaltation of the Holy Cross, 14 September. Evidence at Waltham and elsewhere (Peterborough, Bury St Edmunds, Evesham, Durham) speaks of huge man-sized crucifixes, bearing the figure of the crucified Christ, as well as other crosses. Harold gave a collection of gold and silver crosses at Durham, as did Tostig and his wife, and as did the original benefactor of Waltham, Tofi the Proud. Leofric and Godgifu gave crosses to Coventry. Harold also gave Waltham a set of life-size statues of the Apostles and two full-sized lions, all covered or cast in gold. All this was wildly expensive and envied by the Normans. William Rufus robbed Waltham church of much that Harold and Tofi had given it, and gave it to Caen. The *Chronicle* values Harold's endowment at £6,000, almost 1.5 million silver pennies, or over two tons of silver.

The rule required that the canons live a life in common, dining together and sharing a dormitory, and living a life of faith, love and chastity. Harold appointed twelve canons in all, led by a 'Primicerius' or dean, later called Praepositus, and an archdeacon. These two were to be learned in the gospels and the fathers of the Church, and to instruct the community in divine law. The psalms were to be sung reverently, conduct was to be orderly and boys were to be educated there. The Church was well endowed with land, generating the 'farm' of forty weeks. The first man to be appointed to rule the community was Adelard, described as an educator and physician, who had been in the service of the German Emperor. He is alleged to have cured Harold of a paralysis after his campaign in Wales, but if that was done it must have been earlier, because Waltham was founded in 1060 and received its charter from King Edward in 1062. More probably, they might have met during Harold's continental visit of 1056–57.[36]

The Godwinsons had some 2 million silver pennies in annual income by 1065, and although their households fed hundreds of people and consumed the produce of estates as the earls travelled across the kingdom, they could not have consumed 2 million silver pennies' worth. So vast sums were spent on conspicuous consumption, great feasts and gifts to maintain friendships, alliances and support. The surplus was still available and had been building up for a generation: 2 million silver pennies amounts to almost three tons of silver. Of course, not all of this was available in collectable cash and a great deal had to be spent on their comital outgoings, but this estimate shows the scale of their operations, and explains why Gytha could credibly be said to have offered the victorious duke his weight in gold as ransom for Harold's body, and why Hugh the Chanter claimed that Archbishop Stigand left so much treasure that on his deposition it propped up the Conqueror's régime.[37] Even lower down the hierarchy, thegns with estates worth £40 a year had 28.5lb of silver a year. Even one tenth of that would have been a small fortune. A simple five-hide manor could render 1lb of silver, which could be used to buy stone for a church, or just fancy shoes. A silver penny was so valuable that it could not actually be spent at all by villeins or serfs. One such penny would supply the subsistence of a slave woman for three months. As Aelfric's *Colloquy* remarks: 'He who has pennies or silver can get anything he pleases'. But Wulfstan sourly remarked that a ceorl with a gold-plated sword but who lacked five hides of land was but a ceorl still. Yet having the cash would allow a man to 'thrive to thegnhood'.[38]

The Confessor's reign was relatively peaceful, with no oppressive gelds or warfare, and estate owners could spend or hoard their money. In the inner circle at court, men could finance a noble lifestyle and influence political life. Godwine's treasure financed his comeback in 1052. It can be seen that after Cnut's death three factors become the leitmotifs of the chronicles: treasure, ships and paid retainers. England was a wealthy country, as shown by Aethelredee's ability to raise vast sums to pay off the Danes. William of Jumièges asserts that the king was as rich as Croesus,[38] and dug up treasure from the earth before fleeing to Normandy. Queen Emma twice had her treasure hoard confiscated, in 1035 and 1043, but recovered it. Godwine, in 1051, loaded the vessel in which he escaped with 'as much gold and silver and precious things on board as it could carry'.[39]

Wealth was deployed without subtlety. Emma threw hers around after Cnut's death to bolster her position as queen dowager. Others bought political favours. Godwine bribed – there is no other word for it – both Harthacnut and Edward with the gift of a fully manned and equipped warship and, in Harthacnut's case, 160 gold arm-rings and eighty gold-hilted swords. Edward was given a 120-man ship with a gold lion on the stern, purple sails, and a golden winged dragon on the prow. Both ships were state-of-the-art warships.[40] Godwine himself kept ships at Bosham and Thorney, and Swein had one at Bristol.[41] Harold used it in 1051 and might well have taken treasure with him, with which he was able to recruit Norse-Irish freebooters from Dublin. Men of prominent position were expected to have their own ship, men like Harold's Danish cousin Beorn, Osgod Clapa and Earl Aelfgar, and Archbishop Robert of Jumièges was scorned for escaping in a broken-down scow (*unwraeste scip*). Other courtiers and exiles could hire ships and their crews.

Great men also travelled with bodies of retainers, including household troops, the housecarls. English aristocrats had always been expected to have a large mounted retinue,[42] and both Edric Streona and Leofric's brother Northman were killed in 1017 'with many of their soldiers'.[43] William of Malmesbury[44] comments on Harold and Godwine's refusal to meet King Edward in 1051 unarmed and unaccompanied, because 'if they brought few men in their train, this would be a stain on their honour'. The men in these retinues (their 'genge') were expected to defend their lord by force of arms.[45] When Leofric and Siward were summoned in 1051 to come to Edward's aid, they arrived with 'heora genge', their usual retainers, and promptly sent for a larger force when they discovered what was happening. As the Bayeux Tapestry shows, Harold travelled as a high-born magnate would with his retinue, held feasts in his manor house, attended to his religious duties at Bosham and, as *Dux Anglorum*, was chief counsellor to the king.[46]

5

Earl of Wessex: Character, Wealth and Achievement

There is sufficient information available, if handled with due caution, to permit an appreciation of Harold's character, although the portrait which emerges will be governed by the conventions observed by eleventh-century writers. It is not feasible to expect deep psychological insight from that period, but a broadly painted character study in conventional terms can be attempted. The main source for information is the *Vita Edwardi Regis*, commissioned by Harold's sister, Queen Edith, and written by an as yet unidentified monk of the abbey of St Bertin at St Omer. Other comments about Harold are available from later sources, including major historians such as William of Poitiers and William of Malmesbury (both hostile) and from the Waltham Abbey material, the *Waltham Chronicle* and the *Vita Haroldi* (with much legendary matter).[1]

The real overall purpose of the writing of the *Vita Edwardi* is still problematical. It was not intended as a biography or hagiography of King Edward, although the second half of the work is concerned with him, and the text is untitled as well as anonymous. Whatever the purpose, the events of 1065 to 1066 destroyed it, and forced a certain amount of rewriting, in an attempt to salvage the text. It was perhaps left anonymous because the author no longer wished his name to be associated with a text devoting so much attention to the defeated English king, Harold, and his family – not a popular subject in William the Bastard's newly conquered realm.[2]

In appearance, then, Harold was tall, graceful, handsome and incredibly strong, envied, according to observers, by French and Normans alike, and seen as courageous and honourable. Both the *Vita Edwardi Regis* and Orderic Vitalis agree on this, as does the more partisan *Waltham Chronicle*. He was capable of feats of both strength and endurance. During the notorious sojourn in Normandy, he easily distinguished himself among the knights of the Norman army on campaign in Brittany, and is depicted in the Bayeux Tapestry single-handedly rescuing two of them from a quicksand. To William of Jumièges, Harold was 'brave and audacious, very handsome in body and agreeable in manner and in expressing himself, and affable to everyone'.[3]

He was a fine sailor, commanding royal vessels in the Channel campaigns of 1046–47, shortly after his elevation to the earldom of East Anglia, and subsequently in command of his own force of ships, during the return to power in 1052. He also commanded the fleet in the Welsh campaign of 1063 and during the summer of 1066, when he probably met and put to flight a Norman fleet. The final assault on Gruffydd ap Llewelyn was a combined operation and was followed by an arduous pursuit of the Welsh king through the mountains of Snowdonia. He truly was, as the *Vita* boasted, 'well-practised in endless fatigues and doing without sleep'.[4] The year 1066 proved his strength of mind and body, as he not only conducted all the expected affairs of government but oversaw and directed the preparations for the expected Norman invasion. He no doubt travelled the length

and breadth of southern England and East Anglia, stirring up resistance and organising defences. Then, when Harald Hardrada, King of
Norway, accompanied by Harold's brother Tostig and a large raiding
army, invaded the north, defeating the Earls Edwin and Morcar at
Gate Fulford near York, Harold launched a counter-strike, requiring
a forced march by horse and foot of over 200 miles. At the end of
that, he outfought and overcame Hardrada, the most formidable
warrior in the northern world.

No sooner had he accomplished this than he had to return in the
same manner to London, gather a new army, and march over sixty
miles further to Senlac near Hastings, to confront the invader, Duke
William, in a long, bitter and bloody battle. In the end, at almost the
eleventh hour, he lost to a wilier and fresher foe, possessed of the
vital force of archery.

Of his personal appearance, of course, little can be established.
There is not even a drawing of him in any manuscript, as there is
for King Edward. (Edward is shown with Harthacnut, looking on
as Queen Emma is presented with a copy of the *Encomium Emmae
Reginae*).[5] Harold is portrayed, of course, in the Bayeux Tapestry, but
even allowing for the limitations of needlework as a medium, the
representation is iconic rather than realistic: he has long blond hair
and luxuriant moustaches, and is either well armed for battle, dressed
in the height of fashion as an Anglo-Danish magnate, or shown as a
crowned king in regal majesty. This is representational art and por-
trays him as he appeared to friend and foe alike, as a great nobleman,
a magnificent warrior, or a king enthroned.[6]

That representation is confirmed by his appearance on his coinage,
a surprisingly large amount of which has survived. He is presented
in profile, fierce and aquiline with a small crown, well-trimmed
moustache and neat beard, signifying the gravitas of a king (Edward
too is shown bearded). The image – almost an icon – is modelled
on Roman imperial exemplars, even to the depiction of prominent
neck muscles. It is Harold as he wished to be thought of, a strong
and virile warrior king capable of defending his people. To expect
more realism than this is vain; it was not the convention of the age,
nor did it become so for several centuries.[7]

As for his character, Anglo-Norman sources are largely hostile in describing him, as are some continental sources. They are all the more willing to admit his graceful bearing, his strength of body and his courage, in order to enhance Duke William's achievement in overcoming him. He is also attacked and vilified in the strongest terms. To Master Wace, author of the *Roman de Rou*, he was nothing less than treacherous. To Adam of Bremen, he was a *vir malificus*: the epitome, as it were, of evil. The *Chronicle of St Maixent* saw him as a false usurper and called him 'pseudo-King'. William of Poitiers, above all, lambasts him for his alleged perjury and disloyalty towards Duke William and calls him 'the basest of men... defiled by luxury... a cruel murderer... the enemy of justice and good'. All this is too far-fetched to be accepted and all hinges on the one charge of perjury. He is a murderer, say the Normans, because he was involved in the death of the Aetheling Alfred in 1036, which is absurd, or because he killed his brother Tostig at Stamford Bridge, though there is nothing to indicate that the two met in battle face to face. The allegation of fratricide is made also by Adam of Bremen. Other Norman sources accuse him of adultery, presumably because of his marriage *more danico* to Edith (Eadgyth) Swanneshals (whom they call his concubine) and later Christian marriage to Edwin and Morcar's sister, Ealdgyth.[8]

Harold was also much criticised by Anglo-Norman clergy, notably Bishop Giso of Wells, somewhat ungratefully, for expropriating, as they saw it, the lands of various churches and monasteries. They complain, in chronicles and especially in Domesday Book, of his seizing lands 'violently', 'by force' or 'unjustly'. By this, in those cases where some of the facts are known, they seem to mean that he used the civil law against them (he is credited with a thorough knowledge of English law) to settle property cases, either to enforce the terms of a will or to enforce the terms of a lease made for several lives. The actual amounts of land involved are mostly quite small, other than thirty hides taken from the church at Hereford (probably on royal authority to provide for defence against attacks by the Welsh), forty-three hides from Shaftesbury Abbey, and the fifty hides taken from the see of Wells and disputed by Bishop Giso. This was a case of dispute over the terms of the will of Giso's predecessor, Dudoc, involving Harold as president of the shire court and probably held pending the resolution of the dispute.[9]

Many of Harold's lands ended up in the hands of Norman lords, including the king himself, and were never returned to the Church, which suggests either that the Normans were no less prone to take over Church lands than their English predecessors had been, or that the churches had not been able to make good their claims. Other members of the English aristocracy, even Earl Leofric, usually regarded as rather pious, had been 'guilty' of seizing Church lands with one hand while simultaneously acting as benefactors to other churches. They were prone to picking and choosing which churches to endow, while passing judgement against those they did not favour. The intention of alleging that land had been seized illegally was largely to persuade the Norman officials that the estate in question should be returned to the Church. It did not always work, and churchmen had to accept a Norman holding the land from the Church. This casts some doubt on the justice of at least some of these cases.[10]

Harold's character is also delineated in the pages of the *Vita Edwardi*. Much is found in what has been described as a rhetorical piece on the character and attainments of both Harold and Tostig. The *Vita*, as a source, is regarded as biased, but then few sources which comment on the character and achievements of major historical figures can be said to be unbiased. But even a biased source must be based on some degree of truth if it is to be acceptable to the audience for which it was intended. The *Vita* was written for one very special and particular patron, Harold's sister, Queen Edith. The author had certainly been at court in the years immediately before the Conquest, and probably afterwards, and might well have encountered both Harold and Tostig. He had access to the opinions of other courtiers and to those of his patron, the queen. His views cannot be entirely discounted.[11]

The portrait which results is in accord with the conventions of the age, as all such vignettes must be, and makes full use of rhetoric, metaphor, simile and antithesis. Harold, then, is a second Judas Maccabeus, the hero and saviour of his people. He can be as fierce as a lion towards malefactors, yet affable towards men of good will. He is compared and contrasted with his brother Tostig (or perhaps it is Tostig who is being compared with Harold), not always to Harold's advantage. The author seems to know rather more about Tostig than he does about Harold. Harold's visit to Rome is only cursorily mentioned, while Tostig's pilgrimage and adventures are related at length. But as the writer piles up antitheses, adjectives and images, a consistent picture emerges which can be supported from other evidence.[12]

The brothers are said to have been carefully educated, probably brought up at least in part at court, and trained in the arts of government necessary to prepare them to be 'a strength and help to future rulers'. Harold is termed Earl Godwine's eldest son (as he was after Swein's death) and also the wisest, who 'wielded his father's powers and walked in his ways'. He was mild of temper, neither rash nor given to levity, and of ready understanding. He suffered contradiction without retaliating and was affable and courteous; the picture of a true diplomat, which is easily confirmed by his actions. He often shared his designs with his supporters, but was prone to defer action too long, to his own detriment. Tostig, on the other hand, was secretive and disinclined to share his plans with anyone. Whereas Harold's aim in life was happiness and he was prudent in action, Tostig's aim was success and he acted vigorously, which explains his chagrin when expelled from Northumbria in 1065. Both men were capable of dissembling and could disguise their true intentions when necessary.[13]

Harold's portrayal here is borne out by the *Waltham Chronicle*, the author of which claimed to have derived his information about Harold from the aged Turkill the Sacristan, whom he had known in old age and who had been a contemporary of Harold in the 1060s, regarding all Normans as perfidious. The *Chronicle*, too, saw Harold as a fine soldier, tall in stature and incredibly strong, 'more handsome than all the leading men in the land'. He was skilled in military arts, knowledgeable, astute, vigorous, prudent, with all knightly prowess and wisdom, and well conversant with the laws of the land. Yet he could be headstrong and prone to trust too much in his own courage. The two descriptions are not dissimilar and neither is entirely mere convention; both sets of qualities can be illustrated from his career.[14]

Lastly, from Harleian MS 3776 fol. 62n and 62v comes what is said to be his epitaph, as it was on his tomb at Waltham before it was destroyed; he was 'blessed father of our country... brave... renowned among men, a man of character and authority'. From his character, the focus now changes to his wealth.

That Harold was wealthy is beyond doubt. A more difficult matter is to establish just how rich he was. Estimates can be and have been made of the extent of his estates, as given in hides, carucates and sulungs. But there are two problems here. The first is that the rating in such measures is a measure of his tax liability. When geld was collected, usually at two shillings on the hide or carucate (a sulung was equal to two hides), the number of those measures determined the amount payable, a kind of rateable value. How rich he was can then be illustrated by comparing his assessment with that of other nobles, and with the income from his estates of the king himself, as though today a man's wealth was estimated by comparing the size of his income tax bill with that of one of his peers. Secondly, even that comparison takes no account of what historians refer to as 'beneficial hidation'. It is known that Harold had seen the hidage of at least some of his lands reduced; Domesday Book contains examples where the assessment is actually said to have been reduced – that there were so many hides on an estate, but Harold paid on fewer than that. Also, the number of occasions on which the hidage on his estates is in suspiciously low round numbers, given as five hides and assessed at twenty shillings, is greater than one might expect in reality. As Edward's chief minister, Harold was generously treated by his lord, with gifts of land.[15]

It is also a fact that Domesday Book is much less systematic and comprehensive than it appears to be. Some large towns, especially London and Winchester, were not included at all, nor was the extreme north of England up to the border with Scotland surveyed, so that there is a possibility that the earls of Northumbria had estates

up there, of which nothing is recorded. If that is the case, then the
wealth of the House of Siward may be seriously under-reported, and
accordingly that of Tostig and Morcar, who succeeded Earl Siward. It
is also the case that Domesday is sometimes rather vague about the
relationship between estates which were the centre of a soke, and
the several, often many, berewicks and sokes attached to them. This
makes it very difficult to establish the exact assessment of a group
of estates, especially in Norfolk and Suffolk.[16]

Allowing for all these difficulties, it is nonetheless possible to suggest that Harold had something approaching 2,000 hides and 500
carucates (and three sulungs in Kent), far more than any other person.
In assessing his power, it is worth noting that his men held a fair
amount also. Because hidage or rateable value was arbitrary, and
could be changed by royal action, it is accepted that the monetary
values assigned to estates by Domesday Book are a better guide; those
monetary values are a more realistic estimate of revenue yielded by
the estates. Although some see these sums as representing tax yield
(not just of geld but including all customary dues), a better definition
is to suggest that they represent the sum of money that might go out
of an estate to its lord.[17]

The Godwinson family estates are estimated to have produced some
£7,000 a year (1.75 million silver pennies), of which Harold had some
£5,000 (1,200,000 silver pennies). The Leofricsons, on the other hand,
had £2,400 (just over half a million silver pennies) and the Siwardsons
a mere £350 (84,000 silver pennies), although that figure might be an
underestimate; consider how much of the north was 'wasted' by the
Conqueror, so that no estimate of income was available even in 1086.
The royal demesne which supported Edward the Confessor is thought
to have produced roughly the same as Harold's estates, so that he really
was as rich as royalty on one level. However, Domesday Book does
not report how much the king received from London and Winchester,
nor how much he received in all other customary dues and from
the profits of justice throughout the country. The king's true annual
income is an unknown, but one estimate has put it at £8,000 (almost
2 million silver pennies), although others give a more conservative
estimate of around £6,000 (1.5 million).[18]

Harold had substantial amounts of land in fourteen shires, mainly in Wessex itself, which extended from Kent to Cornwall, right across southern England south of the Thames. He had smaller amounts in several other shires, and little or nothing in Mercia. There he may have gained a little from his marriage to the sister of Edwin and Morcar, Ealdgyth, widow of Gruffydd of Wales. To all this can be added land, money and valuable objects which came to him as gifts or bequests, the lands of his vassals, the men recorded as commended to him or under his soke, and lastly the lands he acquired 'illegally', 'violently' or 'by force' (that is, by the use of secular law) from various churches.

In the light of such wealth as Harold is shown to have possessed, it is no wonder that William of Jumièges could describe him as 'the greatest of all the counts of his kingdom in wealth, dignity and power'. Even William of Poitiers, who elsewhere consistently vilifies him, confesses that 'he abounded in riches whereby powerful kings and princes were brought into his alliance'. He was certainly richer than William of Normandy, whose duchy was only about the size of East Anglia. As an English earl, he was of at least equal hierarchical status to the duke, as the use of the term *Dux Anglorum* in the Bayeux Tapestry indicates.[19]

In order to understand Harold's impact on events and on the position as king of Edward the Confessor, this wealth must be accounted for and some effort made to assess on what it was spent, other than on ostentatious display. The sources of his wealth can be accounted for quite readily. A large proportion, not necessarily the greater part, was certainly inherited. Many of his estates would have been in the possession of Earl Godwine and have come to Harold on his father's death. The family held over 1,200 hides in Sussex, for example: about one third of the whole shire. That in itself partly accounts for the speed with which Harold was moved from the earldom of East Anglia to succeed his father as earl of Wessex. He was already too wealthy for anyone else to be even considered.

Much of what Harold held had come to him while he was earl of East Anglia. Some have argued that he held on to land in that earldom after he ceased to be the earl, and so reduced the amount of land available to his successor. But that was Aelfgar, who would not have been ready to accept a depleted earldom. The more likely explanation is that some of the lands Harold held in East Anglia had simply been given to him by King Edward. The absence of charters as proof is not a convincing argument against it, since charters for the last ten years of Edward's reign are scarce anyway, and religious houses, the main source of them, would not have retained much that connected them to Harold. One estate, Writtle in Essex, is recorded as 'of the fief of Harold' (*de feudo Haroldi*) but elsewhere is said to have belonged to the king, which points to a gift. Hitchin, Hertfordshire, producing £60 a year, with another £40 from the sokemen, belonged to Harold but had all the hallmarks of a royal estate: preferential assessment and rendering (not 'valued at') sixty pounds assayed and weighed. Hertfordshire had been part of Beorn's earldom, which Harold and he had acquired when Swein Godwinson was outlawed. There are other examples elsewhere which point to royal gifts to Harold. Thus the *Waltham Chronicle* says forfeited land was given to Harold by the king. As earl, he also gained land by bequests from those who wanted his guarantee that their will would be upheld, as in the case of the will of the Lady Wulfgyth, who left an estate called Fritton, Norfolk, to Harold and his father Godwine in about 1046. From men who were commended to him or sought his patronage, Harold received gifts of land, as when Ansgar the Staller gave him 'Leighs' in Essex, some two and a half hides valued at £4, which Harold in turn gave to his housecarl Skalpi (who after the Conquest 'died in outlawry at York', unreconciled to King William).[20]

Other lands held when Harold was earl in East Anglia, and later in Wessex as earl there, were what F. W. Maitland termed 'comital' estates (from *comes*, a count or earl): that is, lands officially set aside, some no doubt from royal ancient demesne, to support the earl in the exercise of his duties. Such estates can be recognised as attached to the office of earl, since they render to him the 'third penny' of the profits of justice in certain hundreds which are attached to the estate. Molland and Molton in Devon (fol. 101) and Puddletown, Dorset (fol. 75) are examples of this, as is Hereford itself (fol. 178), which Harold took over after the death of Earl Ralf the Timid. Finally, Harold's lands belonging to the earldom of Wessex in Somerset are actually headed *mansiones de comitatu* in Domesday Book.[21]

In consequence of his wealth, many men entered Harold's service as commended to him. Some became his thegns, just as some nobles became the thegns of the king, or became his housecarls, members of his retinue or 'genge', and, of course, held land from him or under him. The full tally of such men is unknown, not least because several of the 'circuits' of Domesday Book do not mention the names of under-tenants at all. Such men varied immensely in wealth and rank. Leofwine, of Bacton in Suffolk and of Essex, was one; he is termed *cild*, implying noble descent. He was like another of Harold's men, Aethelnoth Cild of Canterbury, the Kentishman. *Florence of Worcester* calls him a *satrap*, which suggests he came from the family of a former ealdorman. There was Eadric the Steersman, benefactor of St Benet's at Holme, and many king's thegns like Azor in Sussex, Eadmaer Attile of Berkhamstead, Edward Cild of Wing, Buckinghamshire and Eadnoth the Staller. These and many other men were beholden to Harold for land or for the use of his influence on their behalf, and provided him with a powerful following.[22]

Lastly there is the question of Harold's marriage to Edith (Eadgyth) Swanneshals. He probably married her at around the same time as he became earl of East Anglia. To contract a marriage with the daughter of a powerful local family was an easy and obvious way of securing local support. Harold would have had need of securing such backing, since he had been given an earldom which had been dormant since Cnut expelled the last known holder, Thorkell the Tall, in 1021. That Edith was a wealthy heiress was an added advantage, bringing Harold the support of her own landed estates and commended men.[23]

The important additional point here is that, like Cnut's marriage to Aelfgifu of Northampton, the marriage was *more danico*, a hand-fast marriage without the blessing of the Church. Again like Cnut, that would permit Harold some time later to contract a Christian marriage, to Ealdgyth, widow of King Gruffydd of Wales and sister of the earls Edwin and Morcar. To marry for political and economic advantage was a common tactic among eleventh-century nobles.

King Edmund Ironside had married another Ealdgyth, widow of the
powerful Sigeferth, in order to secure the support of the men of the
Five Boroughs, and Cnut contracted a second Christian marriage
to Emma of Normandy, King Aethelredee's widow and mother of
Edward the Confessor, to strengthen his hold on the English throne.
Edward the Confessor himself cheerfully married Edith, daughter of
Earl Godwine, and this too can be seen as a move to strengthen his
position as king of the line of Alfred the Great, after the period of
rule by Cnut and his two sons. Earl Godwine too had married Gytha,
sister-in-law of Cnut. That Harold's marriage to Edith Swanneshals
took place in the mid-1040s is confirmed by the fact that their
sons were old enough to lead raiding forces against William the
Conqueror in 1068.

From considering the sources of Earl Harold's wealth and power,
attention can now turn to the use to which that wealth and power
was put. At first the earl would have been busy enough, in 1053–54,
consolidating his hold on his earldom. As a leading member, if not
yet quite the leading member, of Edward's Witan, he agreed to
the king's rather whimsical decision in 1054 to put Malcolm, son
of Duncan, back on the throne of Scotland. Why he wished to
do so is a mystery. There is no evidence that Macbeth, who had
overthrown Duncan in battle at Dunsinane near Perth (he certainly
never murdered him), was any threat to the security of England, and
indeed Malcolm turned out to be a bigger nuisance than Macbeth
ever was, permitting the Scots to raid Northumbria and sometimes
leading the raids himself. Perhaps Edward, who had given Malcolm
Canmore ('Bighead') and his brother Donaldbane a refuge at the
English court, thought he would be grateful and that his gratitude
would translate into increased security for the Northumbrians.
Whatever the reason, Earl Siward of Northumbria was commissioned to overthrow Macbeth and put Malcolm in power. In the
short term, he was successful. Macbeth was duly defeated, but not
killed, and Malcolm secured the throne of Scotland, though it was
some years before Macbeth died in one of many skirmishes at
Lumphanan in Aberdeenshire in 1057, and Malcolm became the
unchallenged King of Scots.[24]

One unfortunate result of the battle against Macbeth was the death of Earl Siward's eldest son Osbeorn, leaving his other son, Waltheof, still a mere child. That meant that when Siward died the year after his victory, the Witan decided that Waltheof was too young to take over from his father, and Harold's brother Tostig was appointed instead. This may be the first occasion on which Harold used his newly acquired power to support the elevation of his brother, though evidence in the *Vita Edwardi*, which shows that Tostig was in some way her favourite, suggests that Queen Edith might have had a hand in it too. The result was to enhance greatly the power of the House of Godwine, as Harold and Tostig now controlled two of the three major earldoms, eclipsing the House of Siward altogether.

At the same Witan at which Tostig was appointed earl, Leofric's son Aelfgar was outlawed, and thus began a long-running conflict between Aelfgar, supported by King Gruffydd of Wales, and King Edward, supported by Harold and Tostig. The chroniclers were confused about this outlawry, two versions alleging that he was outlawed 'well-nigh without fault' or quite guiltlessly, with the Peterborough writer claiming that he 'admitted his guilt before all the men assembled there, although the words slipped out of his mouth against his will', which sounds as though he made some rash and ill-considered remarks to infuriate the king. To say anything which directly challenged the declared policy of a king could easily be transformed into a charge of treason. Aelfgar fled to Wales and enlisted the support of King Gruffydd, who was only too willing to go fishing in troubled English waters.[25]

Aelfgar fled further, to Ireland, and recruited a force of eighteen Viking ships, using it to ravage the west coast of England, and then allied himself with King Gruffydd to harry Herefordshire. They inflicted a severe defeat on Earl Ralf, not least because Ralf and his remaining Normans and Frenchmen tried to compel their English levies to fight on horseback, a tactic totally unfamiliar to them and unsuitable for the terrain. They lost 400 or 500 men, and the Welsh suffered no losses when the English on horseback fled, possibly in panic, as the Welsh 'spooked' the horses. Gerald of Wales says that the Welsh method of opening a battle was to 'shout, glower fiercely at the enemy, and fill the air with fearsome clamour, making a high-pitched screech with their long trumpets' and shower the enemy with javelins. Having repulsed Ralf's force, Aelfgar and Gruffydd attacked Hereford itself and burnt St Aethelberht's Minster (killing seven canons) and the town itself, first stripping the minster of its treasures, killing many of the inhabitants and taking others captive.[26]

And then look what happened: 'it was decided, after they had done most harm, to reinstate Earl Aelfgar and give him back his earldom'. Aelfgar had bullied King Edward into reinstating him, just as Earl Godwine had been able to do in 1052. Harold had intervened immediately after the sacking of Hereford, driving the Welsh back with a great body of men drawn from the fyrd (national army) of almost the whole of England. He drove Gruffydd back to a natural strongpoint, the Black Mountain, and then encamped in Golden Valley. Then, instead of pursuing the enemy, Harold offered terms to Aelfgar, that if he abandoned Gruffydd he would be granted pardon and peace. It may be that Harold and Earl Leofric together persuaded the king to accept this, because a little later they and Ealdred made a truce with Gruffydd, who swore oaths (he seems to have done so very easily, with no intention of keeping his word) that he would be 'a loyal and undeceiving under-king' to King Edward. This was agreed at Billingsley in Archenfield. It might also be that Gruffydd was recognised as lord of Archenfield, which lay between the Wye and the Monnow and, if Domesday Book is right, included all the land beyond the river Dee, on the Welsh side. But the real outcome was that Gruffydd had established close links with Aelfgar, the heir of Mercia. Harold then fortified Hereford against future attacks, constructing a ditch to surround the city and erecting fortified gates. Archaeologists have uncovered timber and stone walls and ramparts. Another consequence seems to have been that it caused the deaths of Tremerig, the assistant bishop of Hereford, and of his superior Bishop Athelstan (who had been given an assistant when he had gone blind thirteen years earlier). Harold cannot have been entirely happy at the outcome and, when Athelstan died, he persuaded the king to make his Mass-priest or chaplain, Leofgar, bishop in Athelstan's place.[27]

The reason is not far to seek. Leofgar was notoriously belligerent. He was said to have retained his warrior's moustaches (his *kenepas*) after he was ordained, although the custom was for clergy to be clean shaven. Unwisely, the new bishop decided to take immediate action to seek revenge for the damage to his minster. Calling up the Herefordshire levies under the sheriff, he 'abandoned his chrism and his cross and his spiritual weapons, took up his spear and sword and went thus on campaign' against Gruffydd, near Glasbury on Wye, 'and there he was killed'. His priests, the sheriff Aelfnoth and many other good men died with him, while the rest fled. Leofgar had rashly taken on the Welsh without waiting for further reinforcements, and paid the penalty. The one good thing that came from this was that Bishop Ealdred of Worcester was put in charge of the diocese until it was decided to appoint a new bishop, thus cementing his alliance with Earl Harold. But the campaign against the Welsh went from bad to worse. The reinforcements for poor Leofgar had arrived too late to do any good and Gruffydd easily evaded them. As Gerald of Wales explains about Welsh tactics: 'if the enemy resists manfully and they are repulsed, they are immediately thrown into confusion; with further resistance they turn their backs... seeking safety in flight... in retreat they will frequently turn back and, like Parthians, shoot their arrows from behind... although beaten today, tomorrow they march out again no whit dejected by their defeat or their losses... and harass the enemy by their ambushes and night-attacks'. No wonder that the Abingdon chronicler complained how difficult it was to describe the hardship and all the travelling and campaigning and the labour and loss of men and of horses sustained by the English army.[28]

The ensuing year saw more prominent deaths. Earl Odda of Deerhurst died and was buried at Pershore and his earldom was incorporated into Wessex; then the great Leofric of Mercia finally died, having been earl there since Cnut's time and Aelfgar, so recently reconciled to the king, succeeded to his father's earldom, surrendering his earldom of East Anglia just as Harold had done when he became earl of Wessex. East Anglia was perhaps being used as a kind of training ground for the heirs of the greater earldoms, and when Aelfgar gave it up Harold's brother Gyrth was given an earldom there, though at first perhaps only in Norfolk. Somewhat later, possibly after Aelfgar's second outlawry, Gyrth became earl in Suffolk along with Cambridgeshire and Huntingdonshire and, curiously, also Oxfordshire, which seems to have been regarded as a kind of marcher county between Wessex and Mercia. At the same time, the fourth Godwinson brother, Leofwine, had an unnamed earldom created for him consisting of Essex, Buckinghamshire, Middlesex, Bedfordshire, Hertfordshire north of the Thames estuary and Kent and Surrey south of it, so that he controlled access to London. Thus the Godwinson brothers had consolidated their hold on the earldoms and extended their authority.[29]

The Welsh did not long stay quiet, and it could be that Gruffydd and Aelfgar were still in league together. At some point in this period, Aelfgar's daughter Ealdgyth was married off to Gruffydd, the sure sign of a definite alliance. It is also noticeable that while Leofric lived, the Welsh attacks were always directed at Herefordshire, south of Leofric's earldom, evidence perhaps that Leofric was successful in deterring the Welsh from attacking him. After Aelfgar became earl, the same pattern continued, this time because Gruffydd did not harass his ally's earldom. In 1058, however, Aelfgar was again outlawed, but few details are available about either the cause or the course of events. Partly this is due to the failure of the monks responsible for the *Chronicle*. Only the Worcester version mentions the outlawry, giving no reason for it, and merely remarking that he 'came back again with violence, through the help of Gruffydd' and that a raiding army from Norway was involved. Otherwise, he found it 'tedious to tell how it all happened'.[30]

Florence of Worcester maintains that the Norwegians came to assist Aelfgar, although they were there only by chance, cruising in the Irish Sea. But the *Annales Cambriae* report that this was a much graver attack than one would think from the chronicler's air of boredom, and Irish sources, such as the *Annals of Tigernach*, support this. They relate that there was a quite large-scale invasion led by Magnus, the son of Harald Hardrada, with a fleet drawn from the Orkneys, the Hebrides and Dublin, and that the invasion was only frustrated 'by the will of God'. As a result, the Witan and the king caved in and reinstated Aelfgar once more. Harold again appears as the great exponent of compromise in order to avoid civil war, although some remark that it might have suited him better to have crushed Aelfgar. There is no indication that the cause was friction between Aelfgar and Harold. In fact, it was at about this time that Oxfordshire was for a time added to Mercia. It is possible that Aelfgar had become increasingly aware of the growing dominance of the Godwinsons and, relying on his alliance with Gruffydd to bale him out if need be, had passed some ill-advised remarks about the king's favourable attitude towards them. The Welsh problem had not figured at the forefront of the Witan's deliberations between 1054 and 1058, because the major worry was the question of King Edward's successor, since Edith had still not produced an heir. Some moves had been made to secure the return from Hungary of Edward the Aetheling, son of Edmund Ironside. Nothing more is heard of Aelfgar; even his death is not noticed by any chronicle, and he is last mentioned in 1062. He, like Harold, supported the choice of Wulfstan as bishop of Worcester. He also saw to the burial of his son Burgheard, who died late in 1061 at Rheims, during his return from a pilgrimage to Rome in the company of Earl Tostig. The church of St Remi was given land by Aelfgar, at Lapsley in Staffordshire, on the occasion of his son's burial. As he is not mentioned anywhere after that, largely because of gaps in the chronicles, especially for 1064, and was clearly succeeded by his elder son, Edwin, by 1064, it is assumed that he died in unknown circumstances, probably early in 1063. His death is seen by some as a determining factor in the events which followed, not least because he might have been unwilling to accept Harold as king.[31]

This assumption is perhaps supported by the fact that at Christmas 1062, and therefore possibly after Aelfgar's death had removed the likelihood of civil war, it was decided to settle the Welsh question once and for all. This time Harold took the initiative and concocted a careful strategy to deal with Gruffydd. In conjunction with his brother Tostig, a two-pronged attack was planned, the ostensible cause justifying it being Gruffydd's raids on the borders of Mercia, a further indication that Aelfgar wass dead, as Gruffydd might have regarded that as signalling the end of the peace. He is said to 'have carried wrongful war across the Severn and England's realm endured his hostile blow'. First Harold struck in mid-winter, penetrating Wales in a daring cavalry campaign, riding 'in all haste', hoping to catch Gruffydd in his chief residence at Rhuddlan on the Clwyd. The town and Gruffydd's 'palace' were captured and a great deal of treasure was taken, especially ships (which ended any further evidence of Welsh naval power). But Gruffydd himself escaped. This was the first of Harold's three great rides; the others came in 1066. In the spring of 1063, Harold and Tostig sought out Gryffydd. Harold took a fleet from Bristol right round into Cardigan Bay and launched an attack at the heart of Wales, while Tostig attacked from inland on the north. The Welsh were repeatedly defeated in several skirmishes, following their pattern of fighting as described by Gerald of Wales. He confirms that, although ferocious in their first headlong assault, if they were resisted they fled: 'Their sole idea of tactics is either to pursue their opponents' – as they had Earl Ralf, for example – 'or else to run away from them'. The *Vita* says that Gruffydd 'with Earl Harold directing the English army, was often defeated and in the end was killed'. It further says that Harold and Tostig 'terrified the foe, till then so bold, with close attacks in strength, with fire and sword'.[32]

Gerald of Wales says that the Welsh were lightly armed fighting men, who depended on their agility in combat rather than on brute strength, and that therefore they were unable to meet an enemy on equal terms. However, he adds, as Harold and the English had found out, they were difficult to defeat in a long war because they were inured to hunger and cold, were not tired by fighting and did not lose heart when things went wrong, but were always ready to fight again. Harold's strategy was simple: to pursue them into the fastness of Snowdonia and beat them at their own game. That is why the *Vita Edwardi* says of Harold that he was 'well practised in endless fatigues and doing without sleep'. Eventually, the Welsh themselves despaired and deserted Gruffydd. He kept up the fight until the bitter end, 'inured to lurk in distant dykes from which with safety to fly upon the foe, exploiting barren lands with woods and rocks, he galls the brother earls with drawn-out war'. Eventually, in August, some of his own followers, angered by his obstinacy, turned against him and killed him.[33]

Harold, therefore, had demonstrated the method by which the Welsh could be defeated and which was followed by the Normans in their successful colonisation of Wales. As Gerald explains, those who wished to conquer Wales could not hope to do so in one single battle because the Welsh refused to meet an enemy in the field. Nor could an invader hope to subdue them by beseiging them in fortified strongpoints, since they did not have recourse to them. They could only be defeated in the way Harold did: 'by patient and unremitting pressure applied over a long period'. An attacker had to 'invade their secret strongholds which lie deep in woods and buried in forests. They must be cut off from all opportunity of foraging and harassed... by frequent attacks... using... assault troops... lightly armed and not weighed down by a lot of equipment'; thus, explains Gerald, by constantly bringing up fresh troops and making no break in the assault, they can be overcome. Gerald confirmed this view in his account of Harold's assault on Gruffydd. He advanced, as has been related above, at the head of lightly clad infantry, and marched up and down and round about the whole of Wales so energetically that he 'left not one that pisseth against a wall', and defeated the Welsh so thoroughly that it was to his victory that 'the first three Kings of the Normans owe the fact that in their lifetime they have held Wales in peace and subjection'. Gerald also claims that as Harold's army passed through the country, stones were set up to mark his victories, bearing the inscription '*Hic fuit victor Heraldus*' ('Here Harold was victorious'). No such stones have ever been found and Gerald is probably exaggerating, although it is possible that these cairns have long since collapsed due to weather erosion, and that the inscriptions were merely scratched on the topmost stone and so did not endure for long.[34]

The final step was to replace Gruffydd ap Llewelyn in North Wales with the brothers Bleddyn and Rhiwallon, sons of Cynvyn and half-brothers of Gruffydd. They submitted to Harold and his master King Edward jointly, and it was then decided to elevate Caradoc ap

Gruffydd ap Rhydderch in South Wales. (His father had been slain by Gruffydd ap Llewelyn nine years previously.) The latter proved to be something of a nuisance in 1065, making a raid on Portskewet and destroying Harold's hunting lodge there, built for the recreation of King Edward. It was part of a trading dispute between Welsh and English merchants and had no lasting consequences. But Harold's victory subdued the Welsh for several generations and one result of it was to add the first substantial area of land to England for three centuries, as annexations were made beyond Offa's Dyke. The frontier in South Wales was moved from the Wye to the Usk; in mid-Wales, Ewias Harold and the defunct principality of Ercyng became part of England, extending the boundaries of Herefordshire, Shropshire and Radnor. Another small area was probably taken back along the border opposite Chester, in Flint, as Domesday Book reflects evidence that Gruffydd held the whole area between the Dee and the Clwyd, except for the estuary shore. The victory would have ensured Harold's popularity in all the shires along the Welsh border and left him the most powerful man in England after the king. No subject had ever been so powerful in relation to other nobles, or so great a figure in the country at large.[35]

6

Queens and Countesses

T he career of Harold Godwinson, his upbringing and education, and his rise to kingship were all influenced by
the presence in the Anglo–Scandinavian society that was
eleventh-century England before the Norman Conquest of a number
of powerful and influential women. They were powerful not only
because they were wealthy in lands and money but because of their
status, deriving from the fact that they were the wives of either
kings or earls.

Their presence not only among Harold's immediate family (his
mother, Gytha, was countess of Wessex, sister to two Danish jarls and
sister-in-law of a Danish king, Cnut the Great) but also in the extended
family that formed the court of King Edward the Confessor – where
his sister Edith was Edward's queen – was a formative influence on
his character. They also played a crucial role at several turning points
in his career. The support of two women in particular was vital, and
an understanding of their part in his career is essential to explaining
his rise to prominence at court and in the country at large.[1]

He was probably born around the year 1025, which would make
him about twenty years of age when he became earl of East Anglia,

twenty-seven when he succeeded his father as earl of Wessex, and
about forty when he became king in January 1066. It is not possible
to be precise about his date of birth because it is not recorded, and
there is uncertainty about the exact year in which his father, Earl
Godwine, married his mother, Gytha. There is further uncertainty
about the order of birth of Godwine's children. The five older boys
were certainly born in the order in which they are usually listed:
Swein, the eldest, followed by Harold, Tostig, Gyrth and Leofwine.[2]
The problem is that the position in this line of Edith, Godwine's
eldest daughter, cannot be ascertained. Some argue that she was born
after the first four boys, on the grounds that they all have Danish
names and hers is English, but female names were less critical than
male and this gets the argument no further. In any case, one solution
would be to suggest that she, like her mother, was originally Gytha,
and that her name was changed to the English 'Eadgyth' as befitted
an English queen and in honour of Saint Edith of Wilton.[3]

The *Vita Edwardi Regis*, written under her patronage, claims that
she was the eldest, but remains vague about whether this means eldest
child or eldest daughter. That she was older than Tostig is suggested
by evidence in the *Vita Edwardi* of a preference for Tostig, such as
might be the case concerning a younger brother. She was certainly
older than Gyrth and Leofwine. Swein Godwinson, dead by 1052,
is never mentioned. The author of the *Vita Edwardi* might well have
assumed that she was older than Harold and, knowing nothing of
Swein, concluded that she was the oldest child, but there is no possibility of certainty.

Godwine and Gytha were married sometime between 1018, when
Godwine was raised to the rank of earl by Cnut, and 1023, by which
time Godwine was fully established as Cnut's chief English supporter.
A date closer to 1018 than 1023 seems probable and allows for the
birth of the three elder children – that is, on this conjecture, Swein,
Edith and Harold – between 1019 and 1025. If this was the case, Edith
would have been in her twenties when she married King Edward in
1045. Closer than that it is not possible to get.

As children of Countess Gytha, who was wife of an earl and
a member of the highest kin of Cnut the Great, Harold and his

siblings were descendants through Thorkils Sprakaleg of Harold Bluetooth, King of Denmark, and therefore members of the Danish royal kin. (Thorkils was married to an unidentified daughter of King Harald.) That gave the children of Gytha aristocratic lineage, and they received the upbringing and education fitted to their station. Edith herself was something of a bluestocking, learned in several languages, literate and artistic, a credit to her mother Gytha. There is an epigram written by Godfrey of Cambrai, Prior of Winchester between 1082 and 1104, about Edith's death, which says that she knew astronomy and mathematics: 'You teach the stars, measuring, arithmetic'. He goes on to talk of her knowledge of music, grammar and rhetoric: 'the art of the lyre, the ways of learning and grammar, an understanding of rhetoric'. This is the stock curriculum of the quadrivium and trivium, the basis of medieval education. All this she would have learned at Wilton, where she received her education. The *Vita Edwardi* adds that she was literate and skilled with the needle and the brush.[4]

Godwine had served Cnut well and was firmly established by him as one of the new men, the earl of Wessex, and his family spent much of its time at the Anglo-Danish court presided over by Cnut's wife, Emma of Normandy, widow of King Aethelredee. (Some confusion has arisen in the past because after her marriage to Aethelredee, Emma took the English name of 'Aelfgifu', which seems to have almost been used as a royal title.) Emma herself was proud of her Danish ancestry, which came to her not only from her father Duke Richard, direct descendant of Rollo or Rolfr, the first duke of Normandy, identified by Dudo of St Quentin as Danish, but also from her mother Gunnor, a woman who was inordinately proud of her own Danish ancestry and who instilled that pride in her daughter Emma.[5]

The Godwinsons, therefore, were born into and raised in an Anglo-Scandinavian aristocratic environment, influenced by a queen who preferred to emphasise her own Danishness, despite having been the wife of an English king. So proud was Emma of that ancestry and her marriage to Cnut that in the work written at her direction, the *Encomium Emma Reginae*, she successfully gave the impression that Cnut was her only husband and that the Aetheling Edward,

Aethelredee's son, was, like Harthacnut, her son by Cnut – whereas in fact Cnut was his stepfather. King Aethelredee was effectively airbrushed out of her life.[6]

Queens like Emma and Edith played a vital role as the daughters, wives, mothers and widows of kings. They were responsible for the transmission of kingship from father to son as their sons became aethelings: that is, 'thronerightworthy'. It is, indeed, the politics of succession which are fundamental to the study of the status of aristocratic women in the Middle Ages. Their influence, their power and their status arose from and were determined by their traditional role within the royal family and court politics, so central to personal monarchies. They had a pre-eminent role as continuators and transmitters of the dynastic claim and as protectors of children during their minority. They were framers of family policy and preservers of its tradition, and were protected by an envelope of royal status and territorial endowment which could extend beyond the death of a husband into widowhood, especially if they were then also the next king's mother. Something similar can also, perhaps, be said to apply to a countess as the wife of an earl, the English equivalent of the continental titles of duke and count. A countess, too, transmitted the dynastic claims of her husband's family, was responsible for the care, education and protection of his offspring, and could continue to enjoy the status of an earl's wife after his death, retaining a controlling interest in much of the family's lands and wealth.[7]

Queens, and no doubt countesses, had their own personal household, while, in the case of queens, simultaneously ruling the royal household. Through their possession of estates and the income they generated, even through the possession and use of their own seals, they could exercise patronage, both direct and indirect.

As was the case with Edith, and no doubt Emma also, queens were cultivated and educated women, well versed in the courtly arts of music and poetry and in modes of courtly conduct; they acquired these attributes at their mother's knee. They were certainly neither powerless nor mere ciphers in the shadow of their lord, the king. Emma and Edith were in their time the richest women in England. Gytha, Edith's mother, seems to have been not far behind them, and

Edith Swanneshals, the long-standing wife *more danico* of Earl Harold, was rich in her own right.[8]

There is a sense in which the legitimacy of the old English royal House of Aethelrede was passed on to Cnut by marriage to his widow Emma, and, as the *Vita Edwardi Regis*, perhaps unwittingly, testifies, King Edward's action on his deathbed of entrusting both Edith and the kingdom to Earl Harold legitimised the earl's assumption of the crown.

Because the king's wife, by the eleventh century, was also queen (*cwen*), it was essential that she be of the correct status, in order to maintain the royal dignity and so that she might bring treasure, land and supporters in her train. King's wives were chosen from among the daughters of great nobles, in order to attract their support and to secure a useful alliance. Emma, daughter of a duke of Normandy, was chosen by, or perhaps for, Aethelrede in order to secure Norman support during the Danish Wars, and it is probable that she brought with her an entourage of Norman servants, clerics and courtiers, some no doubt of distinguished lineage themselves. It would seem that many of the Normans who settled in England before the Conquest came from this group, and some of them can be identified. They were in due course reinforced by the coterie of Normans, Bretons and miscellaneous Frenchmen who accompanied the Aetheling Edward on his return to England under Harthacnut. He certainly had some kind of entourage and was probably accompanied by the sort of household which accompanied his ill-fated brother Alfred in 1036. They would have been largely household officials and clerics, or members of a military escort provided by his Norman relatives, or men who had chosen to accompany him in order to seek their fortune in England. Few became really powerful at court or in the country; even fewer were actually Norman, and those who were were churchmen.[9]

That did not prevent Anglo-Norman writers like Henry of Huntingdon from claiming that the Norman Conquest originated from Emma's marriage to Aethelrede, asserting that 'from this union of a King of the English and a daughter of a Duke, the Normans... according to the law of nations [*ius gentium*]... claimed and acquired England'. This caused E.A. Freeman, in his *History of the Norman*

Conquest, to remark that it was the 'strangest theory of international law on record'. Orderic Vitalis, in his *Ecclesiastical History*, also said that it was through Emma's marriage that the Normans first entered England and won positions of influence. These claims are, of course, rather damaging to other Norman assertions that Duke William owed his claim to King Edward.[10]

While still fighting for control of England, Cnut the Great had married Aelfgifu 'of Northampton', daughter of an ealdorman of the north Midlands, from the same area of the Danelaw where Edmund Ironside had sought support by marrying the widow of Sigeferth of the Five Boroughs. The *more danico* nature of this marriage allowed Cnut's subsequent Christian marriage to Aethelrede's widow Emma. It was an example which was to be followed in due course by Harold Godwinson.[11]

From that marriage to Emma, Cnut secured English acceptance of his rule and the benefit of her expertise as a guide to the ramifications of English politics. It might even have been she who pointed out to Cnut the importance of securing the support of a man like Godwine Wulfnothson, with his family connections in Sussex. Certainly, Emma and Godwine co-operated after Cnut's death during the power struggle between Harold Harefoot, supported by Earl Leofric of Mercia and the shipmen of London, and Emma's son Harthacnut, who was detained in Denmark. By marrying Emma, Cnut had also ensured that her influence was turned to his advantage rather than to that of her English sons. In doing so, he prevented any hostile move from Normandy. As Edward's marriage to Edith likewise shows, a marriage to the daughter of an English noble was also an attempt to capture the support of her father in the delicate politics – a kind of chess game – between king and nobles. Edward is frequently pictured as having been compelled or intimidated into marrying Edith, or as having married her in gratitude for Earl Godwine's support for him in taking over the throne, after Harthacnut's sudden death. But the case for arguing that is weak.[12]

Edward had already been, in some sense, accepted by his half-brother Harthacnut (possibly already aware of his own ill health) as his obvious successor, and, as Emma's frontispiece to the *Encomium*

Emmae suggests, he was associated with Harthacnut in the kingship. The Abingdon version of the *Anglo-Saxon Chronicle* clearly states that in 1041 Edward was 'sworn in as king', and the *Encomium* itself says he was asked to come and hold the kingdom with Harthacnut. All sources say he was a popular choice, received by all the people as king. Godwine's role should not be exaggerated; only the *Vita Edwardi* and *Florence of Worcester* – which are not contemporary with these events, while the *Encomium* is – suggest a dominant role for Earl Godwine. Also, according to the *Vita Edwardi*, he had to ensure his position at Edward's court by means of the gift of a fully equipped and manned warship, just as he had been obliged to do in 1040 to secure his position under Harthacnut. In both cases, he was forced to make this gesture because of the accusations concerning his part in the death of the Aetheling Alfred, Edward's brother and Harthacnut's half-brother.[13]

It can equally well be argued that Edward married Edith of his own volition in order to bind Earl Godwine more closely to the régime, just as he had won over Godwine's sons, Swein and Harold, by creating earldoms for them. He was later to create some sort of subordinate earldom for Beorn, brother of Swein Estrithson, and for Ralf of Mantes, his nephew, son of his sister Goda. It should always be remembered that many of the actions of kings and earls in eleventh-century England can be interpreted in more than one way, because of the chroniclers' reluctance or inability to provide explanations for them.

The queens were required to be educated and cultivated women. Emma, as daughter of a duke of Normandy, had been well educated there, at the insistence of her mother Gunnor. She not only commissioned the writing of the *Encomium*, controlling in minute detail its interpretation of events – it was really a highly political tract – but saw to it that the frontispiece would display her as an enthroned queen accompanied by her two sons, both as kings: a visual demonstration of her claim to power during their brief dual kingship. She is the anointed queen whose power is confirmed and legitimised by the presence of both of her sons as kings. In the *Liber Vitae*, she is pictured with Cnut: he on the left and she, significantly, on the right of a cross. He stands beneath an image of St Peter and Emma is seen beneath an image of the Virgin Mary, Queen of Heaven. The picture is powerfully symbolic of Emma's status as king's wife, as queen – a consecrated office-holder like her husband, on a par with him as the Lord's Anointed. She was patron of the creators of both of these works. From the *Encomium*, historians learn what it meant to be wife and mother of a king, a powerful woman presenting herself as she wished to be seen. Emma pictures herself as a prominent actor in the events her panegyrist narrates, and wishes to be seen as a major player in events. Edith, Godwine's daughter, is more self-effacing. For her, it is her family that matters: her father and her brothers, especially Harold and Tostig. But the *Vita Edwardi Regis* is just as surely a political tract as the *Encomium*.[14]

Both works were written by Flemish monks. No evidence exists to identify Emma's panegyrist other than as a monk of St Omer, but suggestions have been made that Edith's writer was not just any monk of St Bertin at St Omer but either Goscelin or Folcard, whose other works are well known to students of hagiography. Both had the opportunity to have encountered and been recruited by Edith, and the balance of probability favours Goscelin. But there is no direct evidence to connect either with the *Vita*, which in its surviving state is untitled; it is not known what title the anonymous author gave it.[15]

The author of the *Encomium Emmae* was no doubt encountered and recruited to Emma's service during her exile in Flanders under Harold I, and written *circa* 1041 to extol her part in all the politics, exonerating her from all blame in the crisis following Cnut's death and from all responsibility for the Aetheling Alfred's death. She is pictured controlling the treasury at Winchester and, like Godwine, forming a party to work for the return of Harthacnut to assume the kingship. The work whitewashes her decision, again like Godwine, to end her support for Harthacnut. The *Encomium* is a piece of propaganda, intended to influence events after Cnut's death. In particular, it rehearses her title to be queen, as opposed to Aelfgifu of Northampton, daughter of Ealdorman Aelfhelm, regarded as a mere

concubine. It also asserts her claim against the earlier 'Aelfgifu', Earl
Thored's daughter and Aethelrede's unidentified wife, mother of so
many of his children. Both Emma and Edith tell their story through
men: husbands, fathers, brothers and sons. The *Encomium Emmae*
devotes much space to the deeds of Cnut and the *Vita Edwardi* is
all about the Godwinsons, especially Harold and Tostig, as well as
about King Edward.[16]

The *Vita* presents Edith as an educated and intelligent woman,
of royal stock through her unnamed mother, found to be the most
suitable bride for Edward when it was thought right that he should
marry an earl's daughter. There are resemblances between the *Vita*
and the *Encomium*, although Emma is never mentioned in the *Vita*.
That work was begun before 1066 and after Tostig's pilgimage to
Rome, which it describes in some detail. (Harold's pilgrimage there
is also mentioned, but no details are provided regarding it.) Whatever
the original purpose of the *Vita* might have been, that purpose was
frustrated by the events of 1065 and the subsequent Conquest. Edith
had been in some danger during that time, involved in Tostig's fall
and implicated in the murder of Gospatrick. After the Conquest,
the author hardly knew what to write or how to please his patron.
The work was probably never published in any sense, surviving in
an incomplete and damaged form, and whoever wrote it had no
wish for his name to be attached to a work in praise of the House
of Godwine.[17]

In building up a laudatory picture of that House, the author sin-
gles out Harold and Tostig (the brothers Gyrth and Leofwine might
have received more attention in the missing pages) as pillars of the
state, deliberately educated as fit counsellors of a future king, and
paints a picture of Edith as responsible for the care, protection and
upbringing of 'boys of royal stock'. Edward certainly provided a
home at court for Edward the Exile's children (Edgar, Margaret and
Christina) and their mother Agatha, as well as Harold, son of Earl
Ralf of Mantes and Edward's great-nephew. They were raised as if
they were his own children, mothered by Edith.[18]

But, as the *Vita* implies, these 'royal boys' might also have included
the younger Godwinsons, even Tostig, who was not made an earl

until 1055. They were arguably of Danish royal stock. If Edith was the
eldest daughter and almost the eldest child, then, as assistant to her
mother Gytha in Cnut's time, she might well have helped nurture
and raise the younger boys at court. It is also possible that Edward's
willingness to regard Edgar and his sisters and Harold, Ralf's son,
as his adopted children, after the deaths of their fathers, indicates a
frustrated wish to be a father himself (the *Vita* pictures him as he
became more elderly, perhaps prematurely, regarding Edith as more
of a daughter than a wife), while recognising that it was God's will
that he would have no heir of the body; this seems more probable than the lack of an heir being the result of deliberate celibacy.
Edward's policy between 1054 and 1066 regarding the succession, as
presented in English sources, is that of a king determined to find a
legitimate heir acceptable to God.[19]

The *Vita* celebrates Edith's marriage, presented as an entirely
normal one. She is restored to 'the King's bed' after the crisis of
1051–52. There is also a clue as to the hazards of childbearing in the
eleventh century. The *Vita* extols the Church as a spiritual Mother
with numerous progeny, who has not endured the pangs of a stillborn child nor suffered the pangs of birth and tedious pregnancies.
Does the writer perhaps imply here that Edith had indeed been
pregnant, only to give birth to a stillborn child? She might have done
so more than once. She is contrasted with Holy Mother Church,
who *can* have children without childbirth. Edith is then described
as mothering the noble children brought up at court, acting as a
surrogate mother.

However, Edith's failure to produce an heir, whatever the reason,
had an impact on the whole position of her family in 1051. Alongside
the superficial causes for the breach between Earl Godwine and the
king, such as Godwine's quarrel with Archbishop Robert of Jumièges
over Canterbury lands and his refusal to punish Dover for its conduct
towards Eustace of Boulogne, lies the vexed question of the succession. Edith had not produced an heir, and the archbishop's advice was
that Edward should put her away and seek an annulment.

Grounds for divorce included failure to consummate, the bar-
renness of the wife, or adultery. Edith's case is presented by the *Vita*

Edwardi Regis. It argues that the Danish conquest had caused the rise to power of Earl Godwine, as well as the exile of Edward, the divinely protected heir, designated as king, to whom allegiance had been sworn while still in his mother's womb. The vision of Bishop Brihtwold is adduced to show that the kingdom of the English belongs to God. He predicts a 'chaste' life for Edward and foretells that God will dispose of Edward's kingdom after his death.[20]

The inference is that the next king will owe his throne to the support of the House of Godwine, and the *Vita* presents three arguments for this: the greatness of Edith's family, the divine choice of her husband as king, and the question of the English succession in 1066. The work closes with the fate of the English left undecided and the Conquest seen as the result of English divisions. Edith's propagandist also reworks the deathbed scene, in a manner which recalls the regency of Baldwin of Flanders over Henry of France, and the account of Edward's last testament is left a little ambiguous: Harold is entrusted with the care of both Edith and the kingdom (although he is expected to behave in a merciful and kingly manner towards Edward's French servants and courtiers), while the author studiously avoids the language used by the chroniclers, in which Edward is said to have 'committed the Kingdom' to Harold (no mention of Edith), who is then consecrated king. *Florence of Worcester* states that Harold was nominated by Edward and elected by the chief nobles of all England.[21]

If there had been a regency council formed after Edward's death, Edith, as queen, could have expected to be the regent, perhaps on behalf of Edgar Aetheling, who was only about fourteen years old in 1066. The formation of such a regency might have been exactly what the *Vita* was originally intended to advocate. But the events of 1065 had wrecked whatever plan Edith had in mind. That this plan intended a prominent role for the House of Godwine seems certain, but what it actually was will never be known. It is unlikely to have involved a change of dynasty, unless the Aetheling was to have been persuaded to marry a daughter of one of the Godwinson sons, or perhaps their sister Gunnhild; in that way the House might eventually have attained the throne. Events dictated otherwise. As Frank

Barlow remarks, 'The Vita does seem to have intended to prepare for the family taking over the government in some way'.[22]

This, of course, argues against the idea that Edward had designated anyone as his sucessor. But what is certain is that steps were taken to initiate divorce proceedings as soon as Godwine and the rest of the family had been driven from the country. Edith was 'repudiated' and sent to a convent; in the first instance probably to Wherwell, at Archbishop Robert's instigation, only for the king to move her to Wilton (where she had been educated, and where Edward's unnamed stepsister was abbess) as soon as it became apparent that Godwine's outlawry was not going to stick and that he was on his way back. The king's changing his mind reconciles the conflicting evidence regarding his choice of convent for Edith.[23]

It has been suggested that the move to repudiate Edith was the real cause of the events of 1051, and that the outlawry of her family was engineered to facilitate her removal. It is an attractive solution, but relies on a conspiracy theory of events and over-simplifies a complicated situation. These events occurred in parallel, and it is equally likely that Archbishop Robert seized the opportunity presented by Godwine's fall to suggest that Edith be divorced. That would then have left Edward free to remarry and father an heir. Such an interpretation also rules out the idea that he had already designated William of Normandy as his heir, making it more probable that the duke's alleged visit at that time was a diplomatic manoeuvre to secure an alliance. What is left open is whether it was Edward who wanted an ally to help him keep Godwine in exile or whether it was William seeking an alliance with the wealthy English king in order to shore up his hold on Normandy. What it did was to ignite William's ambition, especially if Edward, in order to secure an alliance, hinted at his lack of an heir and allowed William to dream of his own designation.[24]

In any case, Godwine's triumph resulted in Edith's return to her former royal status. She was given back her lands and wealth and, according to the *Vita Edwardi*, restored to the king's bed. Then, shortly after Earl Godwine's death and the elevation of Harold to the earldom of Wessex, it was decided to seek out the whereabouts of

Edward the Exile, son of Edmund Ironside, with a view to bringing him back to England. As a king's son, he was aetheling, and thus the strongest claimant to the English throne in the absence of a direct heir for Edward. This also casts doubt on the idea that Edward had made William of Normandy his heir, but does not rule out the possibility that the Norman duke now had designs on the English throne. The idea of a divorce seems to have emanated from Robert of Jumièges' fertile brain rather than from any initiative on the part of King Edward, who took his wife back very readily. The marriage thereafter seems to have remained a harmonious one.[25]

The *Vita Edwardi* claimed that Edith's dismissal had left a void at the heart of English government, an exaggerated but not totally incredible claim. The anonymous author was seeking his patron's approval and advancing her cause, and so paints a picture of the royal couple as effectively one person, implying that Edith was the power behind the throne – a theory in which, after 1051, there is an element of truth. The author might have also been trying to counteract the growing tendency, down to 1063, to regard Earl Harold as holding that role, as acting as a kind of 'mayor of the palace'. Edith is described as strong and wise in counsel, and the court is said to have relied on her advice. It is a partisan portrayal and ignores the darker side of her character. Her patronage could be bought by gifts (her interest in estates had sometimes to be bought off), and she had such a passion for collecting relics that abbeys and churches feared her visits. Nor must it be forgotten that she was credibly accused of political assassination in 1065.[26]

Her decision to side with Earl Tostig helped to bring about his downfall by triggering the Northumbrian rebellion (as well as his own murders of prominent Northumbrians who were under safe conduct), and her support encouraged him to refuse to surrender his earldom voluntarily. He and Earl Harold then fell out when Harold, ever ready to seek a diplomatic solution, persuaded the king, after negotiating with the Northumbrians who were threatening civil war, to dismiss Tostig from office and accept the Northumbrian demands for the appointment of Morcar, Aelfgar's son, as earl and also for the renewal of the laws of Cnut. Tostig went into exile and fomented trouble, which led directly to the Norwegian invasion and the battles of Gate Fulford and Stamford Bridge.[27]

The dismissal and exiling of Earl Tostig turned Edith against her brother Harold and filled her, according to her own account, with a foreboding of disaster. She is said to have been overwhelmed with grief by the breach between the brothers, which had ruined all her hopes, weeping at Tostig's fall and plunging the court into mourning as 'all men deduced future disasters from the signs of the present'. This passage, written after the event, is proleptic and includes the effect of the death of King Edward in January 1066, which certainly cast a shadow over the whole court. Edith would have feared for her own future after Edward's death, and the ominous atmosphere described in the *Vita* reflects that. She has herself pictured at the end as the sorrowing and devoted daughter (rather than wife) of a saintly king, aged prematurely by the events of the autumn of 1065.[28]

William of Poitiers, for his own ends, pictures her as the sister of Earl Harold and wife of King Edward, opposing her brother's usurpation of the throne by her pleas and counsel. Poitiers is indulging, as usual, in special pleading, asserting that she preferred Duke William's rule because her husband had made him his heir. The *Vita Edwardi Regis* offers no support for this whatsoever. The Norman is using Harold's family connections to further blacken his reputation, claiming he was the murderer of his own brother (who actually died in battle), and rejected by his own sister who, as a widow, conveyed to Duke William the wishes of her deceased husband. Thus Edith becomes part of the Norman justification for the Conquest.[29]

The picture is carefully crafted. A widow's position as her husband's alter ego is used, and, although incapable of bearing arms, she is shown confronting Harold as a woman of 'virile discretion', who displays male attributes in preferring Duke William. Even to the end, she is King Edward's wife. The *Anglo-Saxon Chronicle* records her death in 1075 as that of 'the Lady, King Edward's wife' and in *Florence of Worcester* she is the former queen of the English and Harold's sister. It was usual for rich widows, even queens, to be remarried to a new husband, but this did not happen to Edith, perhaps because she was known to be unable to bear children.[30]

Florence puts her at the beginning of a sequence of events leading inevitably to Hastings. Edith engineers the death of Gospatrick, triggering the Northumbrian rebellion and dividing the nation's resistance to invasion. Her unholy alliance with Tostig brings a disastrous outcome. Henry of Huntingdon, on the other hand, sees her as part of a plot devised by Earl Godwine to control the simple and innocent Edward, a picture which influences some historians even today. In truth, Edward was neither simple nor innocent but rather, like Charles II, determined never to 'go on his travels again'.[31]

Edith was not the only powerful woman to have affected the career of Harold Godwinson. His character would have been in part moulded during his upbringing at the court of Cnut and Emma. The *Vita* asserts that Godwine and his wife Gytha had all their children carefully educated 'in those arts which would make them useful to future rulers' and, further, claims that Harold in particular so admired his father that 'he wielded his father's powers and walked in his ways'. The younger brothers would have spent a great part of their youth in the royal household controlled by Emma and, after 1042, by Edith. As for Harold, the *Waltham Chronicle* asserts that he had won the favour of his sister the queen, and of their father, and that he remained close to Edith until the fateful breach in autumn 1065.[32]

The *Vita* pictures Edith as showering Edward with a kind of motherly love, which was extended to 'those boys of royal stock' – not only those who lived at court after 1054 but also, perhaps, her own younger brothers, who, like her, were descended from King Harald Bluetooth through their mother Gytha. Godwine's wife was daughter to Thorkils Sprakaleg, brother-in-law of Swein Forkbeard and son of Harald Bluetooth. Her brothers were Jarl Ulf who married Cnut's sister Estrith (mother of Swein, Beorn, and Osbeorn) and Eilfr, Cnut's earl of Gloucester. Gytha had married Godwine by about 1020, confirming his membership of the close-knit circle around Cnut. Their older children were given Danish names, but subsequent children had English names, including Edith, although she was perhaps originally called Gytha after her mother.[33]

Very little is known about Godwine's wife otherwise, although there are stories of her scruples over accepting produce from the former estates of Berkeley Abbey after it was somewhat illicitly dissolved, and about her outrage at Swein Godwinson's insistence that he was Cnut's son rather than Godwine's. She is said, rather obscurely, by the *Vita Edwardi* to have sorrowed over the exile of Tostig, yet it was Harold's body that she sought to recover for burial after Hastings, offering his weight in gold, which Duke William refused to accept.[34]

She took with her into exile in 1068 an immense treasure, which ensured a welcome from Baldwin VI of Flanders, and, with her daughter Gunnhild, she did good works at Bruges. Her resistance to Duke William probably lay behind the revolt of Exeter (one of Godwine's residences was there) and led to her exile. A copy of Aelfric's works at St Bertin in St Omer might be a gift from Gytha to the abbey and, if so, is evidence of her eventual exile in St Omer. She had seen a nephew ascend the throne of Denmark and a daughter and son on the throne of England. Her other children and kinsmen ruled like princes in England and allied themselves with the princes of foreign lands. She had been the benefactress of several churches and made offerings at New Minster, Winchester, for the repose of her husband's soul, granting the monastery estates at Bleadon and Crowcombe; she also gave gifts to the Church of St Olaf at Exeter. It is even claimed that she founded a college (of canons, presumably) at Hartland in Devon. If so, that might have inspired Harold in his foundation of Waltham Holy Cross.[35]

7

The Wives of Harold Godwinson

T he last major female figures in Harold's life were his wives: his first wife, *more danico*, Edith (Eadgyth) Swanneshals, the 'swan-necked', and his political wife, according to rites of Christian marriage, Ealdgyth (Alditha), widow of Gruffydd ap Llewelyn and daughter of Earl Aelfgar, sister to Edwin and Morcar. Ealdgyth became Harold's official wife – in effect, his queen, although there is no evidence of a coronation – at a marriage early in 1066, in order to cement an alliance with, and ensure the support of, Edwin and Morcar. That the tactic worked is proved by their action against Harald Hardrada and Tostig. Rather than wait for reinforcement from southern England, the earls took the Mercian army, and such of Morcar's Northumbrians as he could recruit at short notice, including Earl Waltheof's household, to Fulford, where Morcar held an estate, and attempted to prevent Hardrada from capturing York. The attempt failed. The earls were heavily defeated, although in an action which must have depleted the forces of Hardrada and Tostig, and Edwin and Morcar barely escaped with their lives.[1]

Some argue for an earlier date for Harold's marriage to Ealdgyth, perhaps around the time Harold accepted the Northumbrian demand to have Morcar for their earl. It might even be the case that Harold took her to wife after the assassination of Gruffydd by his own people in 1063, but there is no evidence for it and it is not particularly likely. Two children are attributed to the marriage: Harold, named for his father, born in 1067, and Ulf or Wulf, who is noticed as a hostage held by King William in 1087 and possibly captured at Chester in 1071. (Chester had been Ealdgyth's refuge after the Conquest.) But it is suggested that this second child could have been Edith Swanneshals' last child, since his name is Danish. Ealdgyth had twice been used as a political pawn, first married off by her father to Gruffydd to cement that alliance, and then by her brothers to King Harold as an earnest of good faith.[2] King Harold also benefited from his marriage to Ealdgyth by gaining land in Mercia, where his family had few, if any, holdings.[3]

The earls would have expected Ealdgyth's eventual recognition as queen and that her son or sons would have prior claim to the succession, before Harold's sons by Edith, born when he was an earl rather than a king. Some have doubted the reality of the marriage, because she is recorded with little land in Domesday Book, although she could have held the lands recorded by the commissioners as still held by Earl Aelfgar. There are several discrepancies in the recording of late changes in land holding immediately before the Conquest. Her son Harold might have been used as a bargaining counter by Edwin and Morcar in their negotiations with the Conqueror. Sometime after 1070, she and Harold fled – Ealdgyth to Dublin and Harold, perhaps, eventually to Norway. William of Malmesbury says he was received by Olaf Haroldsson. He is said to have followed Magnus Olafsson to Anglesey in 1098.

Edith Swanneshals is recorded as Harold's unofficial wife in the *Waltham Chronicle*, in the passages about the recovery of Harold's body after Hastings. She was said to have been privy to the secrets of his private chamber. Less reliably, she is also recorded in the later and rather fanciful *Vita Haroldi*, which actually has her identify the wrong body in order to substantiate its claim that Harold, severely wounded, survived the battle and eventually died in old age as a hermit at Chester. This looks as though later writers had confused King Harold with his son by Aelfgar's daughter Ealdgyth. The *Waltham Chronicle*, more reliably, asserts that Edith Swanneshals was able to identify the king from certain secret marks on his body known only to her. The body had been stripped of all clothing, armour and royal insignia, which were taken to Duke William, who certainly had Harold's personal standard.[4]

Edith was termed Harold's concubine by the author of the *Waltham Chronicle*, in accord with the conventions of his own time, about 1180, but in her day she was accepted as having been his wife *more danico*. As at least two of Harold's sons were old enough to lead a raiding army against the Normans in 1068, he and Edith had probably been married for over twenty years, most likely in 1044 when he was made earl of East Anglia. He married her in order to enhance his standing with the people of his new earldom by marrying the daughter of a prominent local family, just as Edmund Ironside had married Sigeferth's widow and Cnut had married Aelfgifu. The marriage was frowned upon in the twelfth century, when attitudes towards marriage without the blessing of the Church had hardened, and was naturally attacked by Norman writers in order to blacken Harold's name, but to Anglo-Scandinavian laymen in pre-Conquest England, his marriage to Edith was perfectly legitimate and acceptable. It had the advantage for Harold that it would not prevent him from following Cnut's lead and contracting a later strictly Christian marriage for political reasons.[5]

More danico marriages were contracted by both parties in the knowledge that the first marriage could be ignored and the 'wife' repudiated, without the complexity of a Church divorce. Such marriages were increasingly regarded by churchmen as a form of concubinage, as the eleventh century wore on, akin to the 'marriage' of priests and clergy in major orders, contrary to the doctrine of priestly celibacy which was being enforced by the reformed papacy, then largely controlled by monks. Harold's mother was Danish, which perhaps explains his willingness to contract such a marriage. As it continued for over twenty years, until his death on the field of Hastings, it may even have been based on love, or the couple may have come to love each other after marriage and the birth of six children. These children were Godwine, Edmund, Magnus, Ulf, Gytha and Gunnhild, a mixture of Danish and English names. The fact that Harold's elder daughter (who fled to Russia and had her own son, Harold/Msistislav, Grand Prince of Kiev) was called Gytha is perhaps another indication that this might have been his sister Edith's original name.[6]

A concubine – and therefore perhaps a wife *more danico* – differed from a wife in having no defined legal status, with recognised rights for the woman and her children. There was no businesslike 'betrothal' and no dowry. Betrothal, involving consent to the marriage by the woman and her family, required an exchange of gifts and was a largely secular matter, a business contract between the groom and his future wife's family, the marriage being established by intercourse between the couple in the male partner's home. In practice, the difference was never a simple one, and a marriage *more danico* was much closer to Christian marriage than less formal forms of concubinage, which was how the Church regarded it. Harold's marriage to Edith might well have involved a betrothal and dowry, but lacked a church blessing. It was a stable but not indissoluble union.[7]

The more problematical question is the identity of Edith Swanneshals. That she was a beautiful woman, according to the canons of beauty of the time, is without doubt. She was *collum cygni* ('she with a swan's neck': that is, long and white). A white complexion was a desirable attribute for a woman of noble background. It indicated that she was no peasant woman who had to labour out of doors, where her skin became tanned and weatherbeaten. A great beauty was *blackleor* or 'white-cheeked' and that meant she could be called Fair (*Faira*) or Beautiful (*Pulchra*). There is, in fact, in Domesday Book a woman so wealthy that several entries call her Edith (Eddeva) '*Dives*', the Rich. She is also called Edith the Fair and Edith the Beautiful. In the nineteenth century, E.A. Freeman, in his *History of the Norman Conquest*, when rejecting a suggestion by Sir Henry Ellis, editor of Domesday Book, that Edith the Fair was Ealdgyth, daughter of Aelfgar (and Harold's queen), pointed out that Sharon Turner had suggested that Edith the Fair was Edith Swanneshals. He did not reject the suggestion, although he truthfully pointed out that there is no direct proof. He also raised the possibility that Edith the Fair was the 'Aelgyth' named as her daughter by Wulfgyth (mother of the thegn Ketel, in Norfolk, and sister of another thegn, Edwin) in her will. Wulfgyth had estates at Stisted, Walsingham and several other places, and granted an estate at Fritton to Earl Godwine and Earl Harold. Ketel, who granted land to Earl Harold at 'Moran' (now unidentifiable), was the 'man' of Archbishop Stigand. The modern published text of Wulfgyth's will identifies her daughter as 'Ealdgyth'. The names Eadgyth/Eadgifu and Ealdgyth/ Ealdgifu are frequently confused in Domesday Book and cannot always be distinguished one from another. The case for identifying Edith Swanneshals as Edith the Fair is unproven, but this was the kind of wealthy thegnly family from which she might have sprung and into which Harold might have chosen to marry.[8]

Modern historians have looked again at this question of the identity of Edith the Fair, and a consensus is emerging which tends to accept that she is indeed the Edith the 'swan-necked', as several arguments can be made in favour of it. Edith Swanneshals is also identified by several other entries in Domesday Book. At Stow, near Torksey in Lincolnshire, she owned three messuages (that is, houses with land attached to them) and had the sake and soke. She is said to have been a benefactor of St Benet at Holme, granting it an estate at Thurgaston. Also, a woman identified as 'Eadgyth' of Aisholt was one of those who had sake and soke in Kent, at Sutton Lathe and Aylesford. Aisholt was actually in Somerset, held in Domesday by the thegn Alweard. At Canterbury, Ralf de Courbepine held four messuages previously held by 'a certain concubine of Harold'. Norton, near Bury St Edmunds, was held by 'a certain freewoman, Edith' on lease from the abbot, with men commended to her. All or several of these women could have been Edith Swanneshals and/or Edith the Fair.[9]

As 'Eadgifu', Edith the Fair is found holding land in many shires: Kent, Hampshire, Hertfordshire (where she was 'the Fair' at Watton on Stone), Buckinghamshire (where a man of 'the Fair' held land at Hoggeston), Lincolnshire, Essex, Suffolk (where at Beyton she was 'Eadgifu the Rich'), as also in Norfolk, at Tostock and, as 'the Fair', at Darmsden, Sharpstone and Ashbocking. An 'Eadgifu' who just might be Edith the Fair also held land in the East Riding of Yorkshire, about 100 carucates, all held by Ralf Mortimer in 1086. It has been suggested that this woman was in fact the sister of Edwin and Morcar, though the spelling would seem to be against it. She was a substantial landowner in Cambridgeshire, where she is repeatedly cited as 'Eadgyth the Fair'. All of her lands in Cambridgeshire fell into the hands of Count Alan the Breton, Lord of Richmond.[10]

So Edith's lands in Hertfordshire, Buckinghamshire, Suffolk, Essex and Cambridgeshire, where her main holdings lay, are estimated at £366: that is, over 85,000 silver pennies. Harold had comparatively little land in Cambridgeshire, worth about £36, so if Edith the Fair was Edith Swanneshals, then she would have brought him land, money and, more importantly, men, to support him in his new role as earl. She had a large number of thegns and freemen commended to her or under her soke, estimated at almost 100 commended men, and many more sokemen. Another estimate of her holdings, taking in all relevant entries except Yorkshire, values her lands at £560 from over 410 hides, or over 175,000 silver pennies. She was indeed 'Edith the Rich'. She was the only woman in the top twenty people below the rank of earl; the others were mainly royal officials.[11]

One of the main arguments for identifying Edith Swanneshals with Edith the Fair lies in the claim that both were beautiful, in the evidence that she owned lands in just those shires where Harold had most need of support, and in the fact that Edith the Fair was prominent in East Anglia. In addition to land, she had messuages in Canterbury and Torksey, and was wealthy enough to employ her own goldsmiths. One was Grimbold the Goldsmith and, according to the Gospel Book of Thorney, a certain Wulfwine was also Edith's goldsmith. At Canterbury, a child born to Edith, who died in infancy, was buried near St Dunstan's tomb, and to do that required very influential support. Edith's daughter Gunnhild was educated at Wilton and was later said to have become a nun. It was common,

after the Conquest, for laywomen to take refuge in convents and
even pretend to have become a nun (or actually become one) in
order to escape being forcibly married off to a Norman lord. One
authority identifies Edith as 'Aedgeva Comitissa', with an estate in
Suffolk, although the same writer thinks of her as the widow of Ralf
de Gael, rather than of Harold. One of the problems in distinguishing
these women from one another is the variable manner in which the
Domesday scribes transcribed English names, so that it is sometimes
impossible to be sure which 'Edith' is being recorded. The name
appears in so many different guises that certainty is impossible.[12]

The strongest argument for identifying Edith 'the swan-necked'
with Edith the Fair lies in the eventual fate of Harold and Edith's
daughter, Gunnhild. She was certainly a nun at Wilton, although
she might not have taken formal vows, and is reported to have been
cured of a tumour of the eyes by Saint Wulfstan of Worcester, who
made the sign of the cross over her. She was still there under Abbess
Christina, daughter of Edward the Exile, along with Christina's
niece, Edith/Matilda, daughter of Queen Margaret of Scotland.
King Malcolm had wanted Edith/Matilda to marry Alan the Red,
son of Eudo of Penthièvre, Lord of Richmond, but Alan rejected
this idea and instead, in 1093, abducted Gunnhild, preferring her to
Edith/Matilda.[13]

Shortly after that, Alan died and Gunnhild, instead of returning
to the cloister, which was her only other alternative, 'married' his
brother, Alan the Black. This is known from the letters Archbishop
Anselm wrote to Gunnhild, demanding that she repent of her conduct and return to the cloister. She had argued with the archbishop,
insisting that she was not a nun, but in his second letter Anselm insists
that she had in fact willingly taken the veil and was indeed a nun. The
eventual outcome is not recorded. The point is that these two Breton
counts were probably using Gunnhild to legitimise their usurpation
of her mother's lands, and Count Alan is the recorded holder of Edith
the Fair's lands in Cambridgeshire. The move to return Gunnhild to
the cloister was intended to prevent this usurpation. Count Alan's
abduction of her only makes sense if he was trying to secure his East
Anglian lands by marrying the heiress, a tried and tested method

of doing so. Some of Edith the Fair's land in Suffolk (five estates, amounting to four carucates in all) was also held by Count Alan. He held five estates in Essex, totalling over five hides, which had also been hers. Another eight estates in Hertfordshire which had been held by Edith the Fair and her men were later held by Count Alan. If this argument is accepted, then Edith the Fair and Edith Swanneshals are the same person, and Edith the Fair is mother to Gunnhild and therefore wife of Harold Godwinson.[14]

Edith 'the swan-necked' disappears from the records after her identification of Harold's body for the canons of Waltham. As her lands in Domesday Book are all assigned to various Normans, many of them to Count Alan, she obviously suffered confiscation of all her property. What then happened to her is unknown, but a common tactic, adopted by her daughter Gunnhild, was to take refuge in a convent. There is a slim clue that this might be what she did. In the Hertfordshire Domesday, there is one solitary entry, for Pendley fol. 136v, where two hides, worth twenty shillings, were held by 'Eadgifu the Nun' from Ingelric and, in 1086, by the Count of Mortain, King William's half-brother. No connection can be established, but it is not impossible that Eadgyth became a nun. Alternatively, she may have fled abroad to her sons.

8

The English Succession

U
ntil now, the career of Earl Harold has been discussed with
scant reference to the burning question which loomed
upon the horizon of English politics during the last twelve
years of the reign of King Edward, and that is the succession. By
1054, it had become apparent that, for whatever reason, Queen Edith
was unlikely to provide an heir. Some of the reasons for that have
already been considered and need no further discussion. The major
issue confronting the king and his Witan was what to do about it.
Despite all arguments to the contrary, it does not appear from the
evidence of English sources, scanty in some respects though they
might appear, that there was any party in England advocating a
Norman succession. Those Normans, or Frenchmen, who might
have preferred such a solution had been expelled in 1052, and any
who were left were loyal servants of King Edward, who played little
if any observable part in politics.[1]

The approach adopted by the Witan in 1054 is clear enough and
includes no indication whatever that William of Normandy was
thought of. The decision recorded by the *Abingdon Chronicle* (C) was
that Bishop Ealdred of Worcester, recently promoted to the abbacy

of Winchcombe until a new permanent abbot could be appointed, was sent into Saxony, that is to the court of the German Emperor, where he was received (*underfeng*) with great honour, implying a diplomatic reception. The *Worcester Chronicle* (D) adds that he carried a message to the Emperor Henry III at Cologne and resided at court for a whole year. It is *Florence of Worcester*, whose author had access to a version of the *Chronicle* now lost, which states the purpose of Ealdred's mission. He was to ask the Emperor to send messengers into Hungary to recall the Aetheling Edward the Exile, son of Edmund Ironside, whom King Edward had apparently determined should succeed him. Nothing immediately resulted from this first initiative. Sending Ealdred to Cologne was the obvious course of action, given English ignorance of conditions in Hungary, but no progress was made because of difficulties between the Emperor and the king of Hungary. However, Ealdred does seem to have found out that Edward still lived, with an honoured position at the Magyar court, and that he was married to Agatha, probably the daughter of Henry II's brother Bruno and niece of Stephen of Hungary's queen, if not a daughter of Stephen and Queen Gisla. Ealdred had been unable to go to Hungary himself because the Magyars were in revolt against the Empire. That is much more probable than Körner's suggestion that it was not in the Emperor's interest to encourage co-operation between England and Hungary. Archbishop Herman of Cologne would have sympathised with Ealdred, since he was concerned over the Emperor Henry III' s own lack of an heir.[2]

It is unlikely that the Aetheling Edward, who had been separated from the land of his birth since infancy and was effectively a Hungarian, would have been particularly willing to return. He and his brother Edmund (of whom no more is heard) had been sent by Cnut to Sweden in 1017. The idea had been that the king there should eliminate them, but he proved unwilling to do so. From there, it is thought they might have gone to Denmark, or even Russia, but they ended up in Hungary. By 1054, Edward was a married man with three children, well established in Hungary, speaking little or no English. *Florence of Worcester* asserts that King Edward had 'decreed' that the Aetheling should be his heir, but it is unlikely that a definite decision had yet been reached about a man who was an unknown quantity. That there was a party favourable to the idea is more likely, and at the head of that party would most likely have been Earl Harold and the Godwinsons generally. Looking to the long term, Harold might well have envisaged a situation in which he and his brothers, as well as his sister Edith, would be the power behind the throne of a king with a limited grasp of English and no knowledge of the political situation. Most historians seem to agree that it was probably Harold who had inspired the idea of recalling the Aetheling, even if he did not actually put the idea forward himself. Ealdred was a friend of Harold, who had supported his attainment of a bishopric, and Ealdred had originally been instrumental in allowing Harold to escape the king's men in 1051. The negotiations over the Aetheling's return were protracted, and hampered by anti-German feelings among the Hungarians. In the event, nothing was achieved until after the Emperor's death, when the regent, Agnes, seems to have made peace with the rebels and permitted the Aetheling to return to England through her domains.[3]

Certainly no negotiations could have been undertaken without King Edward's consent, and the Aetheling did return in 1057, in obedience to the king's commands, according to *Florence of Worcester*. Unfortunately he died shortly after his arrival, lamented by the *Worcester Chronicle*: 'to the misfortune of this wretched nation'. Although the chronicler was dismayed that he was seemingly prevented from meeting the king, there is no real suspicion of foul play. Probably it was found on arrival that he had contracted some disease during the journey of over 800 miles. It was all too common for travellers to encounter strains of infection to which they had no immunity, or to die from accident or as a result of assault. Swein Godwinson did not survive his pilgrimage to Jerusalem, nor Aelfgar's son, Burgheard, his to Rome. The return of the Aetheling appears to have been accomplished by Earl Harold himself. Although no source says so, he is known to have visited the continent at the relevant time and in circumstances which would have provided him with the necessary opportunity. The *Vita Edwardi* confirms that he made a study in person of leading princes in Europe, and that he made a pilgrimage to Rome. The year 1056 provides the most likely opportunity for both of these things to have been accomplished, as it is known that he visited St Omer in Flanders. A charter exists, granted at St Omer by Count Baldwin V to St Peter's, Ghent, on 13 November 1056; it is witnessed by Baldwin's wife, Adela, his sons Baldwin of Hainault and Robert (the Frisian), and a number of prominent lords including Count Guy of Ponthieu, Count Manasses (probably Manasses the Old) of Guînes, Roger of St Pol and, most interestingly, Earl Harold (*Haroldi Ducis*).[4]

What happened next is more speculative, but it fits the circumstances very neatly. Three weeks after St Omer, Count Baldwin was in Cologne, on 6 December 1056, to witness the negotiations by which Pope Victor II, recently elected, brought about peace between Flanders and the Empire. The Emperor Henry IV, through his mother, the regent, granted a charter to St Bertin at St Omer on 6 December; Sigebert of Gembloux, in his *Chronicon*, puts Baldwin at Cologne early in 1057, recording the mediation by the Pope. There is no evidence that Harold was there, but given the close relations of his father to the count and the fact that his brother Tostig was married to Judith of Flanders, it would have been natural for Baldwin to have invited Harold to accompany him, given English interest in the affairs of Flanders and the Empire. Furthermore, Pope Victor was exactly the person to have given him assistance in the negotiations with the regent and with Hungary. (Before election as Pope Victor II, he was Gebhard of Eichstätt, Governor of Bavaria.)

From Cologne, the court moved to the Empire's centre of government at Regensburg, on the Danube, and after that the Pope went back to Rome for Easter. It is reasonable to assume that Harold accompanied the Pope and the Imperial court to Regensburg, from which it was easier to communicate with Hungary and King Andrew I, and that he then went to Rome with the Pope. From there, he could then have returned to Germany and escorted the Aetheling to England. A certain degree of corroboration for such a conjecture is available in the Relic List of Harold's foundation, Waltham Abbey. The *Vita Haroldi* refers to his zeal in collecting relics for his college and its church, and the Relic List appears to confirm this. The List can be interpreted as implying that Harold returned from Rome via Bavaria, thus allowing him to escort the Aetheling. It certainly suggests the possibility of visits by Harold to the sort of places a journey such as this would have involved. St Omer was the main route for merchants and others entering Europe from England, and the Relic List has relics from Ghent, St Ghislain near Mons, Aachen, Cologne, Worms and Regensburg, and also, for a possible return journey, from Rome followed by Metz, Rheims, Noyon, St Riquier and back to England. Of course, he could merely have sent agents to collect some of these relics, but his sister was noted for visiting monasteries and convents in search of relics, and so was Queen Emma. Harold might well have acted similarly, and would have been too busy at other stages of his career to have undertaken the journey. It is certain that he was not recorded as being anywhere else in England between his sojourn at St Omer and the return of the Aetheling to England in September 1057. The case rests on probability. The Aetheling's return is dated by Earl Leofric's death; the *Worcester Chronicle* (D) says it took place on 30 September 1057. Leofric's death was not the only significant death that year; Earl Ralf of Hereford also died (so removing another remote claimant to the throne), leaving a young son called Harold, who became a ward of Queen Edith. Then, from the death of the Aetheling to the eve of King Edward's own death, nothing more is said about the succession in English sources, which are very scanty. Nothing at all is recorded for 1064.[5]

It is possible that the Aetheling's children, Edgar, Christina and Margaret, also returned to England in 1057. However, they are not mentioned as present at the Aetheling's death, and it could be that they and their mother Agatha were brought back by Bishop Ealdred, the king's diplomatic man of affairs, in 1058, when he went on pilgrimage to Jerusalem and passed through Hungary. His companion, either then or earlier when he went to Cologne, was Abbot Aelfwine of Ramsey. Domesday Book mentions land in Huntingdonshire, five hides at Broughton, which King Edward granted to St Benedict, Ramsey, 'on account of the service which Abbot Aelfwine did for him in Saxony'. Freeman states that the Aetheling Edward's wife was called Ealdgyth, in which case her continental name was anglicised,

the usual practice. She could be one of the other 'Ealdgyths' mentioned in Domesday. The children now constituted a ready-made
family for Queen Edith:'how zealously she reared, educated, adorned
and showered with motherly love those children who were said
to be of royal stock' (*Vita*). Throughout the reign, Edith's maternal
instincts seem to have focused on children raised at the royal court.
This reference is also evidence that the children of the deceased
Aetheling were, in effect, adopted by Edward as his own, even if
only at the insistence of Edith, who was now exercising considerable influence as the childless king grew older. No one expected
the king to die as yet, and in ten years Edgar would be old enough
to succeed, with Queen Edith, supported by her 'devoted' brothers,
as his regent. That may, at least in part, be the policy for which the
Vita Edwardi Regis, under whatever title (now lost) it originally had,
was intended as a preparation. Edgar could be suitably educated and
trained for kingship under the benevolent guidance of the House of
Godwine. That would explain the attitude of the *Worcester Chronicle*.
It records that after the battle of Hastings Edwin and Morcar, along
with Archbishop Ealdred and the citizens of London, at first wanted
Edgar for king and promised to fight for him 'as was his undoubted
hereditary right'. Duke William found that 'the people would not
come to him' and submit, so set about harrying the countryside
around London. The Edgar party dithered, and 'always when it
should have been furthered, so from day to day the later it got the
worse it got', as the chronicler acidly remarked; eventually it was
decided to submit 'out of necessity'.[6]

   That was not quite the end of it. Edgar was adopted as a figurehead in the rebellions which followed over the next five years, in
East Anglia and in northern England, eventually escaping with his
sisters to Scotland. (He was later reconciled to King William.) Abbot
Brand of Peterborough, elected by the monks on the death of Abbot
Leofric, who returned home from Hastings to die, made the costly
mistake of seeking recognition of his election from Edgar. Duke
William (he had not yet been crowned) was incandescent, and was
only with difficulty persuaded by a number of 'good men' to accept
a bribe of forty marks of gold to grant the abbot his recognition. In

the Worcester text, Edgar is termed '*cild*', which, although rendered as 'prince' in modern translations, can also mean 'aetheling', that is 'thronerightworthy'. In 1058, it must have looked as though the succession problem had been solved and nothing more needed to be done.[7]

Another possible claimant was Eustace of Boulogne, second husband of Earl Ralf's mother, Edward's sister Godgifu. Ralf's elder brother Walter, Count of Mantes, still lived, though he never made any claim to the throne. He was to die in 1064, along with his wife, while a prisoner in the hands of Duke William; some said by poison. It is certainly true that William's rivals had a way of disappearing, either into endless captivity or into the grave. Harold Godwinson would have been well aware of that from his study of the politics of the region.

There were a number of potential rivals to Duke William within Normandy itself, cousins of King Edward on his mother's side such as Richard, Count of Evreux, Robert, Count of Eu and William of Corbeil, but all were quite unable to assert a claim to rival that of their overlord, the duke. In any case they, like William himself, had no English blood whatever. Therefore, during the next seven years, the three principal foreign claimants to the throne established themselves in positions of power from which an attack might be launched: Harald Sigurdson, called Hardrada, of Norway, Swein Estrithson of Denmark, and, of course, William the Bastard, Duke of Normandy. Harald achieved dominance in the north, at the battle of Nissa in 1062; Swein survived the battle, in which he was almost killed, and made peace with Harald, exchanging oaths and hostages, as was customary; and William freed himself from all obstacles, entrenched himself in power in Normandy, and married Matilda of Flanders to secure his northern border. The conquest of Maine in 1063 made him secure to the south, and the minority of Philip I, King of France, for whom Count Baldwin held the regency, prevented any other attack.[8]

As for Harold Godwinson, he continued to dominate politics and government as faithful right-hand man to King Edward. By a combination of military manoeuvring and diplomatic negotiation,

he had enabled the kingdom to survive the rebellious activities of
Earl Aelfgar of Mercia in alliance with Gruffydd of north Wales; he
had also built up the defences along the Herefordshire border, and
put in place a potential heir to the throne. His position was seen
by observers of the situation as that of 'Duke of the English' (*Dux
Anglorum*), this being seen by later writers as equivalent to that of a
'*subregulus*' (*Florence*): that is, 'under-king' – a word with overtones
which stressed his membership, albeit as a brother-in-law, of the royal
family itself. He certainly, even more than his father, stood for the
greater consolidation of the kingdom under the supremacy of his
family. There is no evidence that Harold was ever formally invested
as joint ruler of the kingdom, as Edward himself had been in 1040,
although *Florence of Worcester* claims that, presumably on his deathbed,
Edward had nominated him as his successor. But he was second only
to the king, seen by some historians as having attained the sort of
position attributed to Hugh Capet, as 'a new mayor of the palace'
(Capet was elected king in May 987, on the sudden death of Louis V).
A mayor of the palace was head of the royal administration, and
Harold would seem to have held a comparable position under King
Edward. Wace seems to acknowledge Harold's position; he says he
held the 'seneschalcy' of the kingdom, with control over lands, rents
and other wealth, and held England '*en sa baillie*': that is, he was the
agent of the king in charge of administrative and judicial functions.
The *Vita* uses the term '*bajulus*' of Earl Godwine, implying that he
was a sort of deputy to the king. It continues by saying that 'what he
decreed should be written was written and what he decreed should
be erased was erased'. Earl Harold seems to have held a similar or
even more important position. In France, the last descendants of
Pepin disappeared and were replaced by the Capetian dynasty. Hugh
Capet's actual title had been 'Duke of the Franks'. On the death of
King Edward, who had no direct heir, Harold, 'Duke of the English',
became king of England.[9]

The Bayeux Tapestry itself grants Harold the title of *Dux Anglorum*,
just as William, in response, is *Dux Normannorum*. The composer of
the Tapestry surtitles certainly seems to have had his own agenda. The
titles and captions can be read in a pro-Norman sense, but, equally,

fail to underline the Norman case when given an opportunity to do
so. The opening scene between King Edward and Earl Harold can
be read as showing the king sending Harold to Normandy, but fails
to establish that he did so. In the famous oath-taking scene, he could
easily have added a phrase such as 'concerning the crown' (*de corona*),
but does not do so. Throughout the work, Harold is presented as
the hierarchical equal of Duke William, and the impact of the oath-
taking is muted. The viewer is left to deduce that Duke William's
invasion is somehow connected to the swearing of the oath, but
nowhere is Harold actually accused of perjury.[10]

   Historians have noted Harold's position as 'mayor of the palace',
even those who are convinced by the Norman case. Eric John denies
the title to Earl Godwine while saying that the position of his son
Harold was much closer to it and that the return of the Aetheling
would not have disturbed Harold's position 'as Mayor of the Palace'.
Freeman compares the 'transfer of the English sceptre' to the House
of Godwine to that of the French sceptre to the House of Capet.
The *Waltham Chronicle* implies a comparison between the exaggerated position ascribed to Waltham's original founder, Tofi, and that of
Harold. Having described Harold as the king's right-hand man, the
writer claims that Earl Godwine succeeded Tofi 'in the control of
all England', describing Tofi, and thus by implication both Godwine
and Harold, as 'staller and standard-bearer of the King, accustomed
to advising the monarch... and... second only to the King', and then
saying that Harold was 'next to the King in his counsels' so that his
fellow countrymen 'fervently desired him as King... and chose him
in preference to all others'.[11]

   T.J. Oleson, writing about the Witanagemot in 1955, thought that
Edward's government was dominated by Earl Harold and that the
king resigned himself to a secondary position. He also argued that
Harold must at some time have begun to aim at the crown, while
satisfied at first to remain the power behind the throne. Of *Florence of
Worcester's* use of the term *subregulus*, Oleson argued that it might have
implied recognition, at some time, of Harold as successor-designate,
but that it probably meant that he was almost vice-regent. J.E.A.
Jolifffe likewise thought that an actual mayoralty of the palace might

have regularised Godwine's position and satisfied the ambitions of his son, so averting the dynastic quarrel of which Duke William took full advantage. Marjorie Chibnall thought that there might have been a custom which had developed during the tenth century of actually appointing the next heir as *subregulus*, and that this had been done on a number of occasions. There is no direct evidence that this was done in the case of Harold, but he does seem to have come close. Even William of Jumièges described Harold as 'the greatest of all the counts of his kingdom in wealth, dignity and power'. The *Vita Edwardi Regis*, on the other hand, can be read as presenting Queen Edith as Edward's real heir (even if only as regent for Edgar), and as suggesting that the king had, on his deathbed, decreed that Harold should be the protector of Edith and the kingdom, though the Witan does not seem to have even considered such an outcome, as there was no precedent for female rule in England.[12]

Despite all this, and despite any arguments for Edward having agreed that his eventual heir would be the Aetheling or, in the crisis of 1065, opting for Harold, account must now be taken of the Norman case and the assertions of both William of Jumièges and William of Poitiers that Edward had designated Duke William as his heir. It is a deceptively straightforward case as put by these two writers, and is widely accepted by historians, despite the glaring contradictions and omissions, the absence of any independent confirmation of their claims, and their vagueness and inconsistency as to time, place and motive. A typical presentation of the Norman argument as it presents itself to modern historians can be found in the writings of R. Allen Brown and Eric John. Others are less convinced, such as Frank Barlow and Emma Mason.[13]

As presented by William of Jumièges in the *Gesta Normannorum Ducum*, the claim was that King Edward had sent Archbishop Robert Champart to inform the duke that the king had designated him as his heir and that, following that, he had sent the greatest of his earls, Harold, to guarantee the crown and confirm the promise by oaths, sworn according to Christian rites. William of Jumièges asserts that Harold had fallen into the hands of Count Guy of Ponthieu, who threw him into prison, from which he was rescued by the intervention of Duke William. Harold then 'performed fealty' to the duke, 'in respect of the kingdom with many oaths', and returned to King Edward. Subsequently, after Edward died, Harold immediately seized the kingdom and thus violated his oath, refusing all demands from the duke that he keep his word, whereupon Duke William constructed a fleet, invaded England and defeated Harold at Hastings, where the latter was killed in the fighting. This was written shortly after the events described, in about 1070, by a man in a position to know what happened, but he did not apparently have much detailed information and his account represents Norman sentiment and Norman opinion about some of the most important events connecting the duchy with England at this crisis. It represents the basic Norman case, stripped of all later accretions.[14]

But there are problems even with this basic account. William of Jumièges did not work on the *Gesta* between the late 1050s and early 1067, and neither he nor his contemporary, the anonymous author at St Wandrille, mentioned at that time any promise made by King Edward to Duke William regarding the English throne. The claim only emerges after the Conquest was an accomplished fact (when both King Edward and Earl Harold, who might have contradicted it, were dead), when it was necessary to justify what William had done. The author of the *Inventio* does mention some of the arguments later used to support the Norman claim, emphasising the close family link between Duke Richard II and his nephews Edward and Alfred and claiming that he had educated them like his own sons. He refers to Alfred as having been murdered by Godwine (which is not true), and claims Norman support was given to ensure Edward's return to England, for which there is little evidence: Edward was recalled by Harthacnut. The Norman case here is at its weakest and requires much suspension of disbelief.

The story as it developed in Normandy was that it all began as long ago as 990, when an agreement was made between Aethelrede II and Richard I of Normandy, after the intervention of Pope John XV. It was made at Rouen between English thegns (Aethelsige of Sherborne, Leofstan, son of Aelfwold, and Aethelnoth, son of Wigstan) representing Aethelrede, on the one hand, and on the other hand

Duke Richard, supported by Roger of Lisieux, Rodulf fitz Hugh and Tursten fitz Turgeis. Each side was to cease committing wrongs against the other, and pay compensation if any wrongs were done, and neither ruler was to receive the other's enemies. Later, this is taken as a starting point for relations between England and Normandy which led the Normans to make boastful assertions that their Duke Richard II had subjected the English to his rule and the Scots and the Irish to his protection. The truth is that northern Europe regarded the Normans as pirates who tried, usually unsuccessfully, to bully others. The tale continues with the claim that Edward had promised to make William his heir when they were both boys together in Normandy – at a time when Edward had no prospect of ever becoming king of England. Furthermore, William was some twenty years Edward's junior. The idea is absurd.[15]

There does appear to have been some recognition in Normandy of Edward's royal status. There are charters which seem to support his claim to be king; one giving a church at Arques to St Wandrille, and another restoring land to the abbey of Fécamp, dated at the time when Duke Robert's alleged invasion fleet was waiting to set sail. They refer to the two aethelings and seem to call Edward a king (though that could have been added later), and they appear to belong to 1033–34, before Robert suddenly decided to go on the pilgrimage from which he never returned. This looks like evidence that Duke Robert, as some sources were to claim, had for a time intended to use force to restore Edward to England, but it may be better seen as evidence of Norman determination to intervene in the English succession. Robert never carried out his threat. One source suggests the fleet set sail but was immediately wrecked by a storm. William of Jumièges has a story of Robert sending envoys to Cnut demanding Edward's restoration (Cnut naturally ignored it) and assembling a fleet at Fécamp, which was wrecked at Mont St Michel. Robert then turned his attention to Brittany. William of Malmesbury reports an oral tradition of wrecks still visible at the mouth of the river near Rouen (but that could be an echo of an alleged battle at sea in 1066). A more natural explanation of the fleet would be that it had been part of a combined land and sea attack on Brittany (then confused with a threat against Britain?), and that references to Edward as a king derive from tales that he had been sworn in as king by his father when still a child. William of Poitiers then used all this to suggest that Duke William (then only a boy under the tutelage of his guardians) brokered Edward's return under Harthacnut. The most the duke could have done was permit Edward to return and provide him with a suitable escort.[16]

Like the *Vita Edwardi*, William of Jumièges asserts that Normans who accompanied Edward to England were rewarded with honours and gifts (unspecified). He knows nothing of any promise to Duke William. His information might well have emanated from the circle of Robert of Jumièges, who returned to the abbey in 1053 and remained there until his death sometime before 1055. No reason was given for King Edward's alleged decision, other than that he had no heir. Later writers were quick to add their own explanations.[17]

As time passed after the Conquest, various writers added their own embellishments to the story, but it must be said that the whole claim smacks of opportunism and that the various additional arguments, particularly about Harold's reason for arriving in Normandy, are none of them entirely satisfactory. The real cause will always remain unknown. The embellishments began with Archdeacon William of Poitiers. He concentrated at first on repeating the basic claim: that Edward had 'loved William as a brother or son' and now 'established him as his heir with a stronger pledge than ever before'. He paints a picture of Edward, a man of holy life, expecting to die at any time, longing for the 'celestial kingdom' and wishing to 'anticipate [his death's] inevitable consequences': that is, he implies, the English failure to accept the duke as their king. Edward is said to have sent Harold in order that he might confirm the promise already made. Harold was chosen, he says, so that he might use his authority to prevent the English, 'with their accustomed perfidy', from overturning what had been decided. There is no evidence of English perfidy towards Normandy until Harold rejected the Norman claim to the throne. William of Poitiers, in a rhetorical gambit, transferred Harold's alleged perfidy back in time and used it to vilify the English in advance. Already, the legend of 'perfidious Albion' had been born.[18]

Harold, on his way to Normandy, was forced by the weather to land instead in Ponthieu, where he was thrown into prison by the count. So far the two writers are in agreement. In a fulsome passage, William of Poitiers dwells on the possible fate of those who fell into the hands of 'the Gauls' and who, if rich, could be imprisoned, tortured and even die in captivity. All this to stress the duke's magnanimity in coming to Harold's rescue. In truth, Guy and Harold were acquainted; they had met in 1056 in the presence of Count Baldwin V. It is only the Normans who claim that Harold was in any danger in Ponthieu. It is useful to compare Harold's position with that of another well-known Englishman, Hereward, exiled son of a king's thegn, who similarly fell into the hands of one of Count Guy's neighbours, Manasses of Guînes. When Hereward had established his identity, he was released and treated honourably. It suited the purposes of the Norman duke to pose as the rescuer of Harold; it put Harold under an immediate obligation to Duke William. Having accounted for the way in which Harold fell into the duke's hands, stressing that he was honourably treated, the archdeacon then purports to know what happened next in great detail. Harold was taken to Bonneville-sur-Touques, where he 'swore fealty to the duke employing the sacred ritual recognized among Christian men'; William of Poitiers says this was witnessed by 'most honourable and truthful men who were there present', but whom he is quite unable to name: nameless witnesses! He then says, stressing that Harold acted 'of his own free will', that the earl swore to act as William's representative – '*vicarius*' – at Edward's court, to employ all his wealth and influence to ensure that the duke obtained the kingdom when the king died, to garrison a number of the duke's knights in the 'castle' at Dover, maintaining them at his own expense, and to maintain other garrisons at castles elsewhere in England. In return, the duke, having 'received ceremonial homage from him', confirmed him in 'all his lands and dignities at his own request'. All this is rhetorical embellishment of whatever undertaking Harold was required to give to the duke in return for his freedom. It is really too much! Certainly the archdeacon seems to have used legal terminology in making the most of his case, but the details are quite unacceptable and several historians reject them as they stand. There is no independent evidence for any of it. The straightforward account in William of Jumièges is far more acceptable, and even that lacks corroboration. The reference to garrisons in castles elsewhere in England looks as though it is derived from the knowledge on the part of the Normans that there had been castles with French garrisons in Herefordshire and probably at Clavering, in Essex. The archdeacon has simply made use of that fact to add some verisimilitude to his presentation. Harold, for his part, made no attempt whatsoever to import a Norman garrison into Dover, where the only fortification before the Conquest was the burh on the cliff top. Again, this looks like an echo of Eustace of Boulogne's attempt to occupy the burh in 1051.[19]

Later in his work, the archdeacon added further arguments, which he put into the mouth of the duke himself, claiming to be recording the duke's speech in his own words. This formed part of another rhetorical set piece, purporting to report negotiations between Harold and Duke William shortly before the battle of Hastings. This was a recognised literary device, used by historians ever since classical times. No one was expected to accept them as verbatim reports and no one did. They permitted writers to give a vivid rendering of what kind of exchanges might have taken place between rival commanders. The convention allowed the archdeacon to add more details to his account, and it may indeed have contained the substance of the propaganda put out by the duke before the invasion, and even part of Harold's own rebuttal. A monk appeared before William and told him what Harold had bidden him say, that he recalled that King Edward had appointed William as his heir and that he himself had been sent to Normandy 'to give you assurance of the succession', but that he also knew that King Edward, his lord, 'acting within his rights, bestowed on him [Harold] the kingdom of England when dying', and that such deathbed bequests were regarded by 'unbroken custom of the English as inviolable'. He bade William return to Normandy or he would 'break the friendship and the pacts he made with you in Normandy'. That Harold ever admitted that Edward had made any promise to William should be dismissed as unlikely, but this passage might well contain the substance of whatever reply Harold had

made to the duke earlier in the year, when it seems likely he first
received the duke's demand that he surrender the crown to him. It
is also of interest that Harold is made to admit that he had made a
pact of friendship with William while in Normandy. Significantly,
the archdeacon did not go so far as to make Harold admit that he
had sworn what the Normans claimed he had sworn.[20]

The duke then, apparently, sent his own messenger to Harold; there
is more rhetoric, and his message repeats and adds to the Norman
claim. William, in typical heroic vein, rebuts Harold's charge of
temerity and insists that he comes 'in defence of right'. He says that
Edward 'my lord and kinsman, made me the heir of his kingdom'.
Here begins the Norman stress on the relationship between king and
duke. Their insistence was always that the two were close relatives,
to negate the obvious counter-charge that William had not one
drop of English blood in his veins. He was only the great-nephew
of Edward's mother, Queen Emma, who had herself jettisoned her
Norman heritage and stressed her Danish ancestry, even pretending
that Edward was really a son of Cnut. That Edward was William's
lord perhaps recalls the true position in 1051, the only occasion when
the two met as adults, during William's visit to England, when he
might well have become Edward's vassal as part of the diplomatic
pact then agreed. It is noteworthy that neither of these two sources
ever mentioned that alleged visit, yet it would have suited their
purposes admirably to have been able to assign the king's promise
to that occasion. They were unable to do so, either because the visit
did not occur, or because that was not the occasion on which the
promise was made. William is never made to claim that he accepted
the offer in person. Another, somewhat groundless, suggestion is that
some kind of discussion of the succession question occurred in 1054,
when Abbot John of Fécamp visited England and was granted property in Sussex by King Edward. That he was sent by Duke William
is mere conjecture. There is no evidence for this, and the decision
of the Witan to send Bishop Ealdred on a mission to find Edward
the Exile would seem to rule it out.

The duke is then made to claim that the promise of the throne had
been made because Edward was grateful for benefits and honours

conferred on him by William himself and his great men. Yet Edward had last been in Normandy when William was a mere youth and not yet in command of his duchy. William had been born in 1027 or 1028 and became duke only in 1035, after his father went off on pilgrimage to Jerusalem and never returned. William had been supported by a number of powerful barons, led by Archbishop Robert, his great-uncle (who himself died in 1037), but his accession had been disputed and the situation grew worse after 1037. The period from then until 1047 was one of 'fell disorder': an evil time of violence and disaster. Edward would have been only too eager to leave Normandy when recalled by his half-brother. From 1041 down to 1052, at least, it was doubtful whether the duke would ever have beeen strong enough forcibly to assert any claim to England. From then until 1054, he faced one of the great crises of his reign, which was not ended until after the battle of Mortemer. That period coincides with the final triumph of the House of Godwine and the arrival in power of Harold Godwinson. The Normans in England had been reduced to political insignificance.[21]

The next claim of William of Poitiers – that Edward had required Archbishop Stigand and the three great earls, Godwine, Leofric and Siward, to confirm his choice of Duke William as his designated heir by swearing to do so 'in his hands', and that the king gave the son and nephew of Godwine as hostages – is simply unacceptable. Before his exile in 1051 and after his return in 1052, Godwine would not have agreed, and English sources make no reference to a debate over the succession as a cause of the exile. If the quarrel had been due to Godwine's opposition to William's nomination, then he had not agreed to it; if he had agreed to it, as the Norman claimed, there was no real reason for a quarrel over it. The dispute between Godwine and the king had other causes. Nor does it make sense that only Godwine had to provide hostages. Such arrangements required that hostages be exchanged, and William gave none. In any case, it would have required Edward to give hostages, not Godwine. The archbishop (who did not take the title until 1052, another inconsistency) and the earls are also said to have sworn *manibus junctis*, in feudal fashion. This was not the custom in England, where oaths were usually sworn on a Gospel Book.

Modern historians prefer William of Jumièges, who says that the promise was given to the duke through Archbishop Robert Champart, either in 1051, when on his way to Rome for his pallium, or after Godwine's return, when he fled abroad to Normandy. It has even been suggested that in the latter case the archbishop might actually have kidnapped the hostages. The *Chronicle* does record that the archbishop had to fight his way out of London. Godwine and the king had 'fixed hostages on either side and it was done...Archbishop Robert and Bishop Ulf and their companions turned out at the East Gate and killed and otherwise injured many young men'; they then fled abroad. If the archbishop had given William Edward's promise in 1051, then his visit in that year was in response to it; yet no Norman says so or even admits that the two rulers ever met in England. Some historians reject William's visit as unlikely. The view here is that William did come, on wholly unconnected business, to secure a treaty with Edward for mutual support; William was to close his ports to Viking raiders (and Earl Godwine) and the king was to give diplomatic support to Normandy during William's difficulties. It might even be the case that Edward used the opportunity given him by Godwine's absence to send the earl's son and nephew to Normandy. That he made any promise regarding the succession is made unlikely by Norman silence. But the manner in which William was treated and the sight of the opulence and riches of England could well have fired his ambition and avarice.[22]

The archdeacon, having made that part of his case, then repeated the assertion that Harold had been sent to swear what 'his father and others had sworn', that he had become William's 'man', his feudal vassal, and 'pledged the security of the English kingdom' to the duke. But if the earls had never sworn anything regarding the succession, and it is unlikely that they did so, then that cannot be the reason for Harold's arrival in Normandy, despite Norman assertions to the contrary. It simply suited William of Poitiers' brief to insist that Harold was sent to confirm Edward's bequest. As Eric John admits, William of Poitiers displays 'the arrogance of success and the brutality of triumph'.[23]

9

Harold in Normandy

While it is accepted that Harold Godwinson did indeed visit Normandy at some time between the end of his campaign in Wales, August 1063, and his presence at Portskewet, where he was constructing a hunting lodge in August 1065, the exact date cannot be identified. The consensus of opinion is that it was spring 1064. William of Poitiers' account puts it at a time when the corn was green and there was a dearth of food, which does point to spring, but he does not identify the year, other than that it was after events which occurred in 1063. That he mentions nothing of events after that year certainly suggests 1064. But by foreshortening his account, compressing events, he tries to cause the reader to assume it was 1065. This is done by stressing that King Edward was ill and not expected to live much longer at the time of Harold's return to England. That is true of autumn 1065, but not of 1064. *Florence of Worcester* maintains that the king's health only began to fail after Tostig's fall: that is, during November 1065. The *Anglo-Saxon Chronicle* is blank for the year 1064 and recommences its story with the building work at Portskewet, dated to Lammas 1065 (1 August). At that time Edward was not thought to be ill, and men's minds would have been on the prospects of the hunting season.[1]

The absence of any entry for 1064 in the *Chronicle* causes many historians to assume that the writers were silent out of embarass-ment and, rather than admit that Harold had been to Normandy and given some kind of undertaking to Duke William, preferred to say nothing. This assumes too much. The *Chronicle* during the last years of King Edward is full of chronological dislocations and brief entries. The *Peterborough Chronicle* (E), which for this period comes from a text of St Augustine's Canterbury, has only one line for 1062, about 'Count' William's conquest of Maine (in Latin not Old English); it puts the attack on Gruffydd in 1063 and, while omitting any events for 1064, attributes the events of 1065 to 1064. Many of the *Peterborough Chronicle's* earlier entries, between 1055 and 1061, are extremely brief. The *Worcester Chronicle* (D) starts the year 1063 at Christmas 1062 and, after describing the Welsh campaign, jumps from that date to Lammas 1065. The *Abingdon Chronicle* (C) gives the events from the appointment of Leofgar as bishop of Hereford to the death of Odda of Deerhust as 1056, and then records nothing until 1065, when Harold was at Portskewet, where he expected to receive King Edward and go hunting with him. The writers simply do not appear to have thought there was anything worth recording for 1064.[2]

There is a way of dating Harold's visit other than in 1064. This is the suggestion that it was actually made in autumn 1065 after Tostig's fall, on the basis that this fits the mention of the king being in his last illness and dying shortly afterwards. It is claimed that there was just enough time for Harold's journey, including the Breton cam-paign, between early November and Christmas 1065. It puts much weight on the idea that Edward hated the Godwinsons (as opposed to Godwine alone), and assumes that Edward was free to send the earl to Normandy after Tostig's fall had weakened Harold's power. The corn was still green because it had not ripened: hence the dearth of food, although November still seems rather late for harvest. There is no reference to famine in England at this time, and the alleged reduction in personal power did not prevent Harold from gaining the crown in January 1066. Nor is this view supported by others.[3]

That Harold was in Normandy is not disputed by later, mainly Anglo-Norman, writers. They confine their disagreements to discussions of the reason for his going there, or ending up there, and about exactly what agreement he made with the duke. No one account is preferable to any other. One can, as some historians do, accept William of Poitiers' story as basically true, or one can follow others and suggest that he was mistaken, misinformed or deceitful, and then make use of the later sources to provide an alternative explanation. None of the published accounts is at all watertight. To accept the Norman account as it stands is to believe what William of Poitiers' wants one to believe. He was putting a case forward to justify the fact of the Norman Conquest, which was not greeted with universal approval. On the other hand, none of the explanations offered by Anglo-Norman writers is satisfactory, especially as some affect to know more about what happened the further they are from the event. Some suggest that the real point of the disagreement between Harold and the duke was that Harold had promised to marry a daughter of the duke and failed to do so. That does not seem a sufficient *casus belli* even for the eleventh century. Others argue that Harold was seeking the release of hostages taken as long ago as 1052. Again, that looks unlikely. What could have inspired his sudden interest in doing so? William of Malmesbury's fanciful tale of a 'fishing trip' which went wrong is even more unlikely. A more modern suggestion, that Harold's visit to the continent was in connection with some other diplomatic purpose, and that he then fell into William's hands, suffers from the lack of even the slightest piece of supporting evidence, other than a suggestion by Henry of Huntingdon that he was going to Flanders. It depends on reading references in the *Vita Edwardi* to Harold's study of the princes of Gaul as being concerned with a visit to the continent in 1064, for which there is no evidence.[4]

There is no consensus of opinion on the matter, other than to agree that 'no convincing answer has ever been given', and scholars remain reluctant to accept that Edward required Harold to guarantee the Norman succession. What can be done is to subject the Norman claims to an untarnished reputation for honesty to more critical appraisal: that is, to concentrate attention on the case as presented

by William of Poitiers and William of Jumièges and largely ignore
the other versions presented by later writers, who were scarcely in
any position to know what happened. This might, though, have the
effect of deepening the mystery.[5]

It must be stated that the Norman writers, and indeed the Normans
in general, do not have an impeccable reputation for truthfulness.
Indeed, their track record for honesty and reliability needs more
thorough assessment than it has so far received. Sceptical voices have
been raised in recent accounts of the Conquest, but historians still
accept the basic premises on which the Norman case rests. There
is a tendency to accept the confident Norman assertion that King
Edward intended William of Normandy to be his successor, despite
the lack of any independent verification. It is not just English sources
which are silent; there is nothing elsewhere either.[6]

The truth is that the claim is only found in Norman sources,
written when the Conquest was an accomplished fact and no one
could safely deny it. The creator of the Bayeux Tapestry actually
avoids the issue. It merely shows King Edward in consultation with
some of his servants, one of whom may be Earl Harold, but it shows
nothing of what the king might have been saying. Subsequent scenes
show Earl Harold set off on his ill-fated voyage. No explanation
for it is offered. To a Norman audience, aware of William's claims,
the sequence would have had an obvious meaning, but it need not
be interpreted in that way. An alternative view would be that King
Edward is being informed of Harold's intention to go to sea and
that subsequent scenes show him doing so. There is no explanation
as to why.[7]

What Norman writers, and the creator of the Tapestry, seem to
have done is to combine a number of separate events which have
no actual or necessary connection, to form a superficially persuasive
case. They assert that King Edward promised the throne to Duke
William, but are not even consistent about when or how this is
supposed to have been done. One obviously suspect story has it that
Edward, while still in exile in Normandy, promised the young duke,
then a boy and some twenty or more years his junior, that after he,
Edward, had become king of England, the youth would be his heir.

Edward could not have done any such thing, as it was by no means certain that he would ever be a king. It also assumes that he had already decided that he would not father an heir himself. Nor were the two 'boys together'. William was born in 1027 or 1028, when Edward was already a man. Born in or shortly after 1002, certainly by 1005, Edward was at least twenty-two years older than William. In his youth, Edward started as only seventh in line to the throne and, even without the Danish conquest, was by no means certain to become king. He was an exile between 1016 and 1041. William was only a boy of thirteen when Edward was recalled to England at at least thirty-six years of age. At that time, William's future was hanging in the balance, as the political situation had deteriorated rapidly following the deaths of Archbishop Robert of Rouen in 1037, and Count Alan III in late 1039 or early 1040. Normandy was in a state of shocking disorder and no one could have exerted any influence on the situation in England.[8]

Yet it is in this period that Norman writers make their claim for a promise to William made by Edward in person, although William himself made no claim to having received the promise from Edward directly. The preferred version, offered by William of Jumièges, was that the promise was given to William through Archbishop Robert of Jumièges during his passage through Normandy on his way to Rome for his pallium, which would mean early 1051, though the writer, significantly, does not give a date. William of Poitiers adds that this was done with the consent of the three great earls, Godwine, Siward and Leofric, and of 'Archbishop' Stigand (as he was known when this was written; he was only a bishop in 1051), and that they had sworn in full feudal fashion, 'between King Edward's hands' (a usage unknown in England before the Conquest), to accept William as king after Edward's death. Yet in 1051 no one could have expected the king to die. Both writers then say that Harold was sent to confirm the promise and to 'guarantee the crown to the duke *by his fealty* and to confirm the same with an oath according to Christian usage' (Jumièges) or 'confirm his [Edward's] promise by an oath' (Poitiers). These texts are ambiguous. It looks as though Harold's pledge of fealty was being taken as an obligation to support his new lord's claim, which was based on a further claim that Edward had promised that William would be his heir. The oath at this point is presented as being sworn as confirmation of Edward's promise: the action of an ambassador speaking on his lord's behalf. If that is so, then Harold himself, according to William of Jumièges, was only making promises on Edward's behalf and, if that is the case, he was not personally bound to uphold it after Edward died. It is also likely that any oath of fealty to the duke taken by Harold, perhaps on the occasion of his being knighted by him, would have been seen by Harold as binding only in Normandy. In England, he was the vassal of a superior lord, a king. William was only a duke, and he and Harold were of equal status: *Dux Normannorum* and *Dux Anglorum* respectively.[9]

The claim about an agreement by the earls and Stigand can only be referred to 1051; after that, Godwine was in exile until September 1052, returned in triumph to his former position as premier earl, and died in 1053. It cannot have occurred later than 1051, and there is nothing to show that it actually happened even then. It might just be based on the claim in the *Carmen de Hastinge Proelio* (if it is earlier than William of Poitiers' work) that the promise was made with the consent of the English. There is no corroboration for this in English, or any other, sources, and the *Anglo-Saxon Chronicle* gives a very full account of the quarrel of 1051 which does not even hint at any concern over the succession. Nor does the version of events presented by the *Vita Edwardi* advert to it. There is no very convincing argument to suggest that Godwine and the earls would have agreed to such an offer in 1051, nor that Edward asked them to do so. This is all the product of fertile Norman minds. There is no sign that Leofric and Siward were at court in the spring and summer of 1051; Edward had to send for them after 8 September to come to him from the north when he summoned the Witan to confront Godwine.[10]

The solution advanced to explain all this is to suggest that the whole idea that Edward contemplated making William his heir stems from Archbishop Robert, who fled the country in 1052 and passed through Normandy then, before, in all likelihood, going to Rome to complain about his, as he saw it, uncanonical deposition. It is possible that it was then that he planted the idea in the duke's mind that Edward wanted him to be his heir. It might well have been in character for Robert to do this, in the same way as he had been poisoning the king's mind against Earl Godwine, and had persuaded him to put aside his wife, Godwine's daughter. If he could no longer ensure that Edward 'divorced' Edith, in order to marry again and secure an heir that way, Robert could at least do something to encourage a Norman succession. If Edward had shown unwillingness to contemplate another marriage, Robert might well have suggested the alternative of a Norman succession and Edward might not have rejected the idea out of hand, seeing William as one more among several 'possibles' before whom he seems to have dangled the succession, using it as a diplomatic bargaining counter, like a rich uncle with several nephews, playing one off against the other.[11]

The major objection to accepting a definite offer made to William in 1051 is the curious matter of William's alleged visit to England during 1052. The reality of this visit has been questioned, not least because William was heavily engaged in warfare on his frontier, where he was threatened by Geoffrey Martel of Anjou, who in summer 1052 had allied himself with Henry I of France. William himself hurriedly visited King Henry on 20 September 1052, but failed to prevent the alliance, which was followed by the rebellion of William, Count of Arques. The threat to the dukedom was lethal. At this time, William was certainly too preoccupied with the affairs of his duchy to risk leaving it. Earlier in the year the duke had been equally busy in the territory of Bellême, at Domfront and Alençon, which he beseiged and captured in order to strengthen his defences in that area. Any visit to England would have had to be very brief and aimed at securing an alliance with King Edward. Norman sources never present William as seeking anything from the king, as he could not be depicted as the petitioner in the situation. William needed something from Edward; the king did not need anything much from William other than the closure of Norman ports to Godwine's forces. The reality of the visit is accepted on the testimony of the *Worcester Chronicle* and *Florence of Worcester*. That it had nothing to do with the succession to the English throne is shown by the silence of Norman sources about it. If William had been visiting Edward in order to accept the promise of the sucession, the Norman writers would have boasted about it. Their silence is eloquent. On the contrary, William is made to assert that the promise had been made to him in his absence, and that was why Harold had been sent to confirm it to him personally. That puts William's knowledge of the promise to a time after his 1052 visit; Archbishop Robert went to Normandy in September 1052.[12]

The remarkable thing is that nothing more came of it for another twelve years. There were no further visits. Nor is there evidence of contact between England and Normandy. Not until Harold fell into William's hands in 1064 did anything further happen. On the contrary, the English took their own steps to provide for the succession. In 1054, the search for Edmund Ironside's heirs, the indisputable aethelings, had been initiated, ending in the dicovery of Edward the Aetheling and his consequent death.

Edward the Exile's children returned also, either with him or possibly in the following year, brought back by Bishop Ealdred, and they were then, effectively if not formally, adopted by the king and mothered by Queen Edith. Had there ever been any thought in Edward's mind of making Duke William his heir, then it must have been a transient fancy, inspired by Robert of Jumièges during his brief ascendancy, then forgotten for the rest of the reign. But it had done some damage; it had planted the seed of ambition in the heart of William of Normandy.[13]

Edward, from 1053 onwards, at least permitted and more likely encouraged the ascendancy of Harold Godwinson, who rose to a position comparable only with a Merovingian or Carolingian 'mayor of the palace', taking all the burden of the royal government and administration upon himself, leaving the king to his preferred pursuits, of religious devotions and hunting. The king at this time began his immense project, the building of Westminster Abbey. It is not known when the project was begun, only that it was finished just in time to become his resting place. How long it took to build a church depended on the wealth and attitude of the builder, as well as on the size required. If he began the project after Godwine's death, then it took about twelve years; if so, it was the king's major interest in life. Meanwhile, if the hints in the *Vita Edwardi* are accepted, Earl Harold in the south and his brother Earl Tostig in the north provided the king with the trusted counsellors he needed, having been groomed from childhood by their father to be the counsellors of kings.[14]

Harold's dominance provided the peace and unity the kingdom needed, marred only by the problem presented by Wales, until Tostig's misgovernment of Northumbria precipitated the crisis during which Harold again displayed the talent for diplomacy attributed to him by the *Vita Edwardi*. Sometime before that crisis erupted, during a period when English sources fail, Harold somehow ended up in Normandy, with ill-starred results. The gap in the *Chronicle* for 1064, and the total lack of any entries between 1056 and 1065 in the *Abingdon Chronicle*, means that there is no information available from English sources. The chroniclers seem to have thought there was nothing worth commenting on for 1064. Arguments that this somehow indicates embarassed silence simply do not convince. If Harold went to Normandy in 1064, then the chroniclers knew nothing of it. He himself would have been unlikely to say much to anyone.[15]

Those who are convinced by the Norman case, or who admit that there was 'something in it', are simply accepting, to a greater or lesser extent, what the Normans wanted people to believe, despite the contradictions and the absence of any independent corroboration. It has been remarked that in William's England there were not even any 'samizdat' or underground writings to contradict the Norman propaganda, simply because 'the feet of those who bark shall be cut off'. Later Anglo-Norman writers contradict what they know to be false, as when *Florence of Worcester* insists that it was Archbishop Ealdred, not Stigand, who anointed and crowned Harold. Not even the Bayeux Tapestry dared to show Stigand actually performing the ceremony.

A minimalist view accepts the unvarnished, unembroidered version of William of Jumièges: that Edward promised William the throne through Archbishop Robert and then sent Harold to renew or confirm it. This version alleges that Harold was blown by a strong wind onto the coast of Ponthieu, where Guy of Ponthieu, Count of Abbeville, imprisoned him. On learning of this, Duke William 'by force caused him to be released' (thus putting Harold in his debt). Harold was detained for some time, performed fealty to the duke 'in respect of the kingdom with many oaths', and was sent back to Edward loaded with gifts. Nothing of a campaign in Brittany, nor of swearing on relics, nor becoming William's representative in England and garrisoning Dover and other castles, as William of Poitiers asserts. That is the oldest and plainest account, stripped of the accretions it acquired at the hands of Duke William's 'talented propagandist', William of Poitiers. His version was never well received and only one copy survived, to be destroyed by fire in the seventeenth century; only a copy of a copy is extant. The William of Jumièges version was found more acceptable. It was widely copied, in an interpolated version, by Orderic Vitalis, from which scholars have been able to recover the original. It forms the basis on which Poitiers' version, and probably after that the Bayeux Tapestry version, was based.[16]

Before considering what might actually have happened to Harold, it is worth looking at the Norman record for veracity. They actually had a widespread reputation for chicanery and for making or inventing outrageous claims. Dudo of St Quentin, historian of the early dukes of Normandy, had the audacity to picture William Longsword and Richard the Fearless as reigning over half the world. Guy of Amiens described Robert the Devil as the actual conqueror of England. William of Poitiers charged Harold with the murder of the Aetheling Alfred. As Frank Barlow has maintained, the Norman case cannot be checked in detail. Many of the facts are correct but misleadingly explained. The account imposes a retrospective view of events on the England of 1051, which cannot be verified and makes use of the sort of designation ceremony used by Norman dukes to establish their heirs as a model for Edward's alleged designation of Duke William.

Orderic Vitalis testifies to the Norman reputation for a readiness to distort facts in their own interest. He says 'they strive to rule and often become *enemies to truth and loyalty* through the ardour of their ambition'. William of Malmesbury alleges that 'when they failed to get what they wanted by prowess they resorted to cunning to achieve their ends' and 'they weigh treachery by its chance of success'. Their writings are full of wonderfully fabricated accounts (note the story of Edward and William as 'boys together'). William of Poitiers boasts that Edward's accession was brought about under Norman influence by means of a letter sent by the Norman duke to the English, who were disputing Edward's election (he was in fact universally welcomed), threatening war if he was not received. Edward, he says, then returned to England with a small army of Norman knights. This cannot have happened in 1042, during William's minority, when he could not threaten anybody, and it is an embroidered, edited version of history, possibly based on Edward's abortive attempt to return in 1036. The anonymous author of the *Chronicle of St Wandrille* claims that Edward, already chosen and crowned as king, was excluded from the kingdom by a combination of Swein, Cnut and others, until restored with Norman help. This is simply not historical. All these stories were invented to justify the assertion that Edward had reason to be grateful for Norman help and therefore chose William as his heir.[17]

Other stories were propagated. Queen Emma, who was in fact only William's great-aunt, so that he had no drop of her blood in him, was presented as the 'genetrix', that is blood mother, of King Edward, and as the origin of William's claim by blood. As William of Poitiers expressed it: 'If a claim by blood be sought, it should be noted that King Edward was linked by the closest consanguinity to the son of Duke Robert whose aunt was Emma, sister of Richard II, daughter of Richard I, the genetrix of Edward'. So there was no real blood relationship at all, other than a remote one back in the time of Duke Richard I. Yet Emma is presented as the conduit through which Norman blood and its dukes entered England, so her marriage to King Aethelrede is seen as the origin of the Norman claim and therefore of the Conquest.

In his version, Orderic Vitalis, while asserting that Edward had informed the duke of his intention to make him his heir through

Robert of Jumièges and then, following that, 'through Harold himself', states that Harold had 'taken an oath of fidelity' to William,
so becoming his 'man' or vassal, and had 'sworn all that had been
demanded of him on holy relics'. He does not try to give the content
of the oath and admits that it was 'demanded' of him, which implies
duress. But his version still only makes Harold the emissary of the
king; his mouthpiece, as it were, confirming the decision on his
behalf. Then, in order to gain his freedom, he swore whatever was
necessary, as that was the only way out; he was driven, as William of
Malmesbury says, 'by the necessity of the time'. One further problem
is that when princes and kings communicated with each other they
did so by oral messages, and the messengers so sent needed a 'token
of credence', by which they could be accepted as the voice of their
master. This was an object such as a finger ring or a loose impression
of a seal; possibly, by the eleventh century, they might have 'letters of
credence' with the lordly or royal seal. If Edward had really intended
Harold to convey a confirmation of his promise of the succession,
surely he would have had either a token or a letter, but nothing is
heard of either. The mention of a ring and sword in the *Carmen de
Hastinge Proelio* might suffice, but why the sword? That over-eggs
the pudding.[18]

The *Vita Edwardi* presents Harold as an adroit man full of natural
cunning, who could not easily be deceived and possessed the ability
to dissemble his true thoughts. It is improbable that he could have
seen himself as bound by an oath given under duress. His problem
thereafter was that William was able to use what had happened to
present himself, to his Normans and to other interested parties, as a
lord wronged by a faithless vassal from perfidious Albion. The whole
affair enabled the duke to fulfil his ambition to become king of
England by persuading the Normans to back his planned conquest.
They were unable to avoid supporting their lord, even though some
of the greater magnates thought it would be too difficult and beyond
the resources of Normandy. The question now is whether what the
Norman writers claim occurred really happened exactly as they said.
The first part of the argument is without substance. There is no proof
that Edward had definitely marked William out as his successor. The

second strand, that he therefore sent Harold to confirm the promise, depends upon the first. If there was no promise, then there was no reason to send Harold to confirm it. Certainly, Edward had made no arrangements for William to succeed him, and there is no reason why he should suddenly decide to revive an alleged plan to make William his heir, in 1064, when Harold was at the height of his power, having recently defeated and tamed the Welsh. Edward did not then expect to die and Edgar the Aetheling would soon have been old enough to ascend the throne. It might even be suggested that the unknown agenda of the *Vita Edwardi* was to prepare the ground for Edgar's accession, with Queen Edith, supported by her brothers, as regent. She had before her the example of the Regent Agnes, widow of Henry III, the German Emperor.[19]

The most that can be said on William's behalf was that he had come to believe that Edward had designated him as the heir to the throne, and that he now set about making it come true. But Orderic Vitalis, in his account of King William's last moments, written as was his custom in the form of a speech by the king himself on his deathbed, gives his considered opinion of the Conqueror. He makes William deny that he had any hereditary right to the throne of England, which he had acquired 'by the grace of God'. He has King William say:

> I did not attain that high honour by hereditary right but wrested it from the perjured King Harold in a desperate battle with much shedding of human blood and it was by the slaughter and banishment of his adherents that I subjugated England to my rule.

The king is further made to say that he had made his way to the throne 'by so many crimes that I dare not leave it to anyone but God alone'. This is Orderic's considered judgement on the Conquest. He accepts the charge of perjury against Harold, seeing him as a faithless vassal, but attributes William's kingship to conquest rather than any right derived from King Edward. This is further substantiated by the letter that Pope Gregory VII (the former Archdeacon Hildebrand) wrote to William, which acknowledges that he had helped William attain the throne despite the misgivings of the cardinals over the shedding of Christian blood the invasion would cost.[20]

If this considered judgement is accepted, then the case presented by William of Jumièges, and even more so that put forward by William of Poitiers, becomes a matter of special pleading, put forward after the event, and perhaps based on the case presented at Rome, to justify what was in the end a brutal and bloody conquest. That, perhaps, is the real point of all this. Before launching an invasion, Duke William needed to be sure that the other princes of Europe would accept the *fait accompli*. In that, he was certainly successful. He launched an unparalleled propaganda campaign in 1066 to convince all the powers, including Pope Alexander II (who granted him a papal banner) and even the German Emperor, that he had right on his side. The case was most likely prepared by Lanfranc, who would have based his brief on the assertions of the duke himself and possibly those of his closest associates. It is probable that William had by then convinced himself of the righteousness of his cause, really believing that he was Edward's chosen heir, and that Harold, having betrayed his faith as his vassal, was therefore a perjured usurper. This enabled him to convince the Norman magnates that it was their duty to support him.

William of Jumièges presents a picture of the duke's actions as soon as it was known that Harold had become king. He launched a war of words. Messengers demanded that Harold 'desist from his mad policy and keep the faith which he had pledged with his oath'. Harold 'disdained to listen to this message' and 'seduced all the English people away from obedience to the Duke'. Of course, the English owed no obedience to Duke William; they had only just sworn their hold oaths to their new king, to whom they now owed allegiance, just as they had owed it to King Edward. Likewise, William of Poitiers accused the English of 'their accustomed perfidy' because they sought to 'overturn what had been determined' for them. Harold was accused of seizing the throne, with the assistance of 'a few ill-disposed persons', and of having been anointed and crowned by Stigand, 'who had been deprived of his priesthood by the zeal and anathema of the Apostolic See'.[21]

The account of Harold's sojourn in Normandy given by William of Poitiers and reflected to an extent in the Bayeux Tapestry, with significant variations and even more significant omissions, can be briefly summarised. Harold, having been released from imprisonment at the hands of Guy of Ponthieu, is treated as an honoured guest at Rouen, on the grounds that he has been sent by William's 'nearest and dearest friend' King Edward (whom he had not seen since 1052), and is taken to Bonneville-sur-Touques (in the Tapestry it is Bayeux, and in Orderic Vitalis' account Rouen itself) where he first swears fealty to the duke and then swears to accept a series of improbable conditions, of his own free will! He is then released and returns home, apparently being given one of the two hostages, Hacon, son of his brother Swein, as an earnest of the duke's good faith. Either before this, according to the Bayeux Tapestry, or afterwards, according to Orderic Vitalis, he accompanied the duke on campaign in Brittany, distinguished himself by rescuing several Normans from a quicksand, was renowned for his physical strength, and was knighted by the duke, if the scene in which the duke bestowed arms and armour on him is to be interpreted in that sense.[22]

There is much discussion of all this by historians, even about the nature and appearance of the relics upon which he is alleged to have sworn, but the Bayeux Tapestry is very circumspect in its treatment of the scenes it presents, and fails to spell out their significance. William of Jumièges is also somewhat ambiguous, and William of Poitiers just lays it on with a trowel. A minimalist view would be that Harold did become the duke's vassal, possibly by accepting arms and armour in a ceremonial manner, while no doubt assuming that it applied only while he was in Normandy, and that he swore what was demanded of him, partly in the role of Edward's representative (perhaps the source of Poitiers' use of the word *vicarius*) and partly in order to escape from a dangerous predicament.

In the event, it made no difference to his conduct in England. The scene in the Bayeux Tapestry in which a suitably chastened and embarassed Harold reports to King Edward may be mere embellishment. After all, if Edward had in fact sent him and did in truth want William to be his heir, then Harold had done what the king wanted and should have been thanked, whereas the scene looks more as though Edward is saying 'I told you so!' It does look more like an acknowledgement that Harold had put himself in a false position, in which case it is more Norman propaganda. In practice, Harold's recorded actions during 1065 consist of an invasion of South Wales, arising probably from the alleged ill treatment of English traders at Newport. They had apparently refused to pay the customary toll, and Rhiryd, son of Ifor, a *nepos* of King Gruffydd, cut their anchor and offered it to the shrine of St Gwnllyw in Newport. They complained to Harold, who ravaged Glamorgan in retaliation. His men violently entered the church, failed to find the anchor and were frightened by an ominous sign: some cheeses they found there began to bleed when cut open. Harold made an offering to the saint in reparation. The text then says that because of this wickedness Harold was defeated and killed by King William at Hastings, a clear case of hindsight. Harold, however, went on to begin building a hunting lodge, with the intention of inviting the king to hunt there, at Portskewet near Chepstow. But Caradoc ap Gruffydd ap Rhydderch attacked the site, slew the workmen and carried off stores and equipment. The Worcester chronicler thought there was a plot against Harold in this, but he was known for such gnomic comments and little significance can be attached to his dark saying. As the Northumbrian rebellion blew up in the autumn, Harold never took action against Caradoc. He certainly never accepted any Norman garrisons into England, nor is there any sign that he did anything to ensure William's right to succeed to the throne.[23]

The Bayeux Tapestry version of events has significant omissions. It leaves the viewer to work out what the scenes really mean. In plate 1, King Edward speaks to several servants, one of whom could be Harold, but there is no hint of what he is saying. In succeeding plates, Harold, Duke of the English, rides to Bosham, dines in a house nearby, boards ship and sets sail, whereupon he is blown by a strong wind to Ponthieu. No purpose is given for the journey. He is arrested by Guy and they talk, but nothing is said as to the subject matter. It might have been a discussion about the size of a ransom. After this comes Harold's release into William's custody, but nothing is said about the content of any discussion between the two. Viewers are left to assume that it concerns a message from King Edward to William, but if so there is no hint as to its content.

There follows the campaign in Brittany, ending with the bestowal of arms on Harold by William. Again viewers are left to assume that this is a knighting ceremony or that Harold has become William's vassal. That is what Norman viewers would think. (It can be pointed out here that if the Tapestry alone had survived and not the works of Jumièges and Poitiers, it would be very difficult to work out what was going on.) Harold then swears the notorious oath, but the viewer is not told what the substance of that oath was. Harold then returns to England and seems to be apologising to Edward for what has happened. If that is indeed the case, it does not look as though Edward had approved of Harold's journey, nor that he approved of its outcome.

The Tapestry was certainly of English workmanship, though of Norman instigation, and those who did the stitching and whoever was responsible for the legends, a sort of surtitles, left a great deal to the imagination of the viewer. Normans could interpret it one way and others, especially the English, in quite a different way. It has been suggested that the birds and beasts found in the upper and lower borders are derived from fables, such as 'The Fox and the Crow', similar to those of the fables of Marie de France from the twelfth century. If so, it is argued, then they comment on the action shown, pointing to hidden danger for the crafty and deceitful or the unwary. Thus Harold's fine appearance conceals an inner man who is flawed and false. Normans might certainly have interpreted it that way, but other observers might equally well think that it is a warning about the deceit implicit in the Norman presentation of events.[24]

In his account, Orderic Vitalis is very dependent on William of Jumièges, to whose text he added his own interpolations. He differs from his source, yet he too is unable actually to name the witnesses to the taking of the oath. The Bayeux Tapestry seems to show it taking place in the open air, permitting it to be witnessed by a large audience (who are not shown). There is some doubt about how public the ceremony really was. Orderic adds his own insistence that King

Edward was at that time 'on the point of death', which cannot be true for 1064. He then has a passage in which he accuses Harold of making a 'fraudulent claim' that he had been given William's daughter in marriage, and he is represented as telling King Edward that thus, as son-in-law to the duke, he had been given the duke's rights in England. This is a piece of pure fiction, designed to underline the picture of Harold as deceitful, and allows Orderic to claim that he stole 'the honour of the diadem' after Edward died. The English are said to have been angered by this and Harold opposed by 'powerful lords'; he is accused of being a tyrant and of having 'soiled the throne which he had wickedly seized with horrible crimes'. There is no substance to these wild, almost hysterical, accusations, and they are contradicted by *Florence of Worcester*'s account of Harold's brief reign. Even Orderic has to admit that the other surviving earls, Edwin and Morcar, 'attached themselves' to Harold, who married their sister 'Edgiva'. Of course he could not have done that if he had indeed previously married or been betrothed to a daughter of the duke. Orderic contradicts himself. He makes his case even worse by accusing Harold of depriving Tostig of the earldom of Wessex.[25]

That Orderic calls Harold's new wife 'Edgiva' casts a possible light on a mysterious scene in the Tapestry, never yet satisfactorily explained. Plate 18 shows a lady named as 'Aelfgiva' within a rectangular building, being touched on the face by a cleric, and the text says 'Where a cleric and Aelfgiva...'. The accompanying border shows a naked phallic figure of a man gesturing at them. Some sort of scandal is implied, but it cannot be simply some notorious scandal included for amusement. All the other scenes in the Tapestry are relevant to the story being told; therefore this must be relevant also, but the significance is a mystery to modern viewers. One faint possibility might be that it somehow refers to the recurrent claim of later writers that during his sojourn in Normandy Harold was involved in some sort of marriage offer suggested by William: either that he should marry a daughter of the duke, and/or that his sister should marry a high-ranking Norman. There are several variations on the theme, which even got into Snorri Sturluson's *Harald's Saga* and the *Chronicle* of St Andreas of Cambrai, which attribute William's invasion to his anger at Harold's refusal to

Above: 1 Oldest ruins of the residence of the bishops of Winchester.

Right: 2 Wall paintings from a side chapel in Winchester Cathedral. These were the work of Saxon artists, not Normans. Saxon churches would have been similarly decorated throughout.

3 Memorial to Harthacnut, son of Cnut the Great and Emma. Winchester Cathedral.

4 Site of the New Minster, Winchester. Built by one of the early kings after the invading Danes had sacked the Old Minster. The Norman cathedral was built on the site of the Old Minster. In this area, opposite the New Minster, stood the Royal Palace.

5 Memorial stone commemorating the battle of Stamford Bridge, North Yorkshire.

6 King Edward enthroned is told of Harold's departure. (Plate 1)

7 Harold, 'Duke of the English', rides to Bosham. A fine picture of an earl and his retinue. (Plate 2)

8 The earl feasts in his hall. (Plate 3)

9 The earl sets sail, destination unknown. (Plate 4)

10 He crosses the Channel and arrives in Ponthieu. (Plate 6)

11 He is taken prisoner by the count. (Plate 7)

Above: 12 They discuss Harold's position. (Plate 10)

Left: 13 After the campaign in Brittany, Duke William bestows arms on Earl Harold. (Plate 25)

14 The army
returns to Bayeux.
(Plate 26)

15 At Bayeux,
Harold takes an
oath and then
returns home.
(Plate 27)

16 Harold
reports to King
Edward. (Plate
30)

17 King Edward's funeral. (Plate 31)

18 The death of King Edward. (Plate 32)

19 The coronation of King Harold. (Plate 33)

20 The comet appears and Duke William decides to build a fleet. (Plate 34)

Above: 21 and 22 Note that the Norman knights carry their spears raised for throwing or stabbing downwards. (Plates 63 and 64)

23 The shield wall. (Plate 65)

24 The turmoil of battle. (Plates 70 and 71)

25 The battle reaches its final stages. (Plate 72)

26 Consecration of a
Saxon church.

27 Tower of Earl's Barton church,
Northamptonshire.

Top: 28 Cnut and his queen.

Above: 29 Impressions from the Great Seal of Edward the Confessor.

Above: 30 The
Witanagemot, the
king presiding.

Left: 31 Remains
of the shrine
of Edward
the Confessor,
Westminster
Abbey.

32 Only known and extant portrait of King Harold II, taken from coinage of his reign.

33 Edward the Confessor. A painting from Ludham, Norfolk, c.1500, showing Edward in similar fashion and manner to later pictures of the saintly Henry VI.

34 Seal of Battle Abbey.

35 Page from Simeon of Durham's *Historia Regum* (twelfth-century) describing the Norman Conquest.

marry his daughter. The names 'Aelfgiva', 'Aelfgyth', 'Edgiva', 'Eadgyth' and 'Ealdgyth' are frequently confused in post-Conquest sources. It might just be that the scene relates to a scurrilous Norman jest about Harold's sister, or his (future) English wife, or even about his concubine (as she was to Norman writers), Eadgyth Swanneshals.[26]

Other Anglo-Norman writers have various theories about Harold's motive in going to Normandy, including a suggestion that he had intended to recover the hostages. William of Malmesbury in fact conceded that the true reason was unknown, and resorted to suggesting that Harold was on a fishing trip! One may doubt whether high-ranking eleventh-century nobles ever did that. What the confusion of these writers actually shows is that they found it difficult, if not impossible, to accept that Harold had been sent to Normandy to confirm a hypothetical promise of the throne by King Edward to Duke William. Perhaps they too were aware that there was no independent corroboration for the idea. The *Brevis Relatio* (an account of Norman history in the eleventh century written at Battle Abbey in the early twelfth century) simply says that Harold took an oath 'as many say', a medieval writer's code for admitting that he himself has no access to any proof. Others resort to allegations of duress used against Harold and, by the twelfth century, claim that the Normans resorted to trickery, covering up the relics so that Harold was unaware he was swearing on them.[27]

Some modern writers are attracted to the idea that Harold was on some other mission, possibly diplomatic, of his own; that he was forced to put in to Ponthieu by strong winds, fell into Guy's hands and ended up in William's power. There is some support for this in Henry of Huntingdon (*Historia Anglorum*), who suggests, without adducing any specific motive, that Harold was on his way to Flanders. *Harald's Saga* suggests he was aiming for Wales but ran into bad weather, and even claims that storms prevented an early return to England. The *Saga* almost always interprets events as the result of the personal relations between opposing rulers, and here it alleges that Duchess Matilda was responsible for the marriage proposal. That allows the writer to attribute the Norman attack to William's claim simply to have a better right to the crown because he was closely related to King Edward (no promise of succession is mentioned), and because Harold had insulted him by refusing to go through with the marriage. All that this really proves is that the Norman claims were not universally accepted.[28]

As for the question of duress, Harold was William's 'guest': effectively in his custody, and unable to leave without his permission. The detention might well have been accomplished with velvet gloves, but Harold was no doubt aware that those who opposed William's wishes suffered for it. He had studied 'the princes of Gaul' and knew their reputations. He would have known of the fate of King Edward's nephew, Walter of Mantes, elder brother of Earl Ralf, who, with his wife Biota, had died in William's custody amidst rumours of poison. That had removed a potential claimant to the English throne. If Harold, as seems probable, swore to whatever was demanded of him, then he did so, as William of Malmesbury admits, driven by the needs of the time. Modern historians suggest that he could easily have been released from an oath given under duress, which was not recognised as valid by the Church, by his ally the saintly Bishop Wulfstan or even by Archbishop Ealdred. The real significance of the oath lies not in what Harold actually promised but in the fact that William could exploit the fact that he had sworn an oath, even if only of general fealty, so could paint him as a faithless vassal who had betrayed his lord. William went on to blacken Harold further, by saying that he had been anointed king by an uncanonical and schismatic archbishop. It was probably that latter argument that won the day at Rome.[29]

To sum up, it suffices to say that there was probably never any definite promise made directly to the duke by King Edward. He would not have seen the designation of a bastard duke with no English blood as compatible with his own honour. There are too many improbabilities about this and no independent corroboration. It was probably Robert Champart who planted the idea in William's mind, and the lucky accident that put Harold in his power allowed the duke to exploit the situation to the full, enabling him to convince his own adherents – the Pope, the German Emperor and the rest of the princes of Europe – that he had a case and should be allowed to pursue it on the field of battle. In the last analysis, he became king by conquest, rather than by any legal abstract right as designated heir of King Edward. Edward's own attitude was very different.[30]

10

Discord and Downfall

Following on from the renewed Welsh attacks came the rebellion of the north. The reasons for it lay in the manner in which Earl Tostig had conducted his government of the province. The appointment had been decided upon by the king and his Witan despite the objections of Aelfgar, Earl of East Anglia and son of Earl Leofric of Mercia. Aelfgar, as son of the next most senior earl, perhaps thought that he should have had the northern earldom. He had been earl of East Anglia since 1054, when Harold surrendered East Anglia to him. But, as Earl Leofric was now growing old, it was no doubt thought inadvisable to move Aelfgar, as his turn would soon come.[1]

Tostig, like his brother Harold, had been groomed by his father to serve the king. As he was of Anglo-Danish parentage, it was probably thought he would be acceptable in Northumbria, and Tostig's government of the north seems to have been accepted without protest. His most pressing problem was dealing with King Malcolm Canmore of Scotland, who had seized on Siward's death as a signal that he need no longer keep his Scots in check out of gratitude for Northumbrian assistance in overcoming Macbeth. So Malcolm ceased to act like a client king and became a threat. It could even be that fear of him lay behind the selection of Tostig as earl.[2]

Raiding was renewed in 1058. Malcolm had secured his position in Scotland by killing Macbeth and his successor Lulach, and now turned his men south. One aim seems to have been to enforce his claim to his father's territory in Cumbria. There are signs of Scottish control over the upper waters of the Tyne valley, and Cumbria was certainly in Scottish hands after the Norman Conquest, though it is not known exactly how or when it was taken. But in his response to Malcolm, Tostig, remarkably, never attempted to use force. There is no evidence of any attempt to invade Scotland, as Siward had done, in order to punish Malcolm. Instead, Tostig adopted a policy of pacification, seeking to placate him. It might be that he did not feel secure enough in his earldom to leave it and take his troops north. Perhaps he feared the Northumbrians could not be trusted to support him against Scotland. Yet he left his earldom in 1061, on pilgrimage to Rome, and to go to war against the Welsh in 1063. He spent long periods at court in the south.[3]

He seems to have adopted a diplomatic approach to Malcolm, seeing it as more effective. He reminded Malcolm of his debt to King Edward, an approach which seemed to work, as the raids ceased until 1061, resuming only during Tostig's absence in Rome. What Tostig did, in 1058, with the assistance of Archbishop Cynsige of York and Aethelwine, Bishop of Durham, was to persuade Malcolm to come to England and attend Edward's court, where a renewed treaty was negotiated, possibly at York rather than Winchester or Gloucester. The intention would have been to demonstrate that Edward was king even in the north and to impress Malcolm, the Yorkshire thegns and any Northumbrian visitors with the splendour and majesty of a king of England. Malcolm and Tostig swore brotherhood, the usual northern procedure for cementing a treaty, and Malcolm returned to Scotland. He might even have met his future wife, Margaret, sister of Edgar the Aetheling. Both English and Scottish sources suggest that a marriage was offered but that Malcolm then preferred to marry Ingibiorg, daughter of Thorfinn the Mighty, Earl of the Orkneys.[4]

The essence of Tostig's policy towards the Scots is described as aiming 'to wear them down as much by cunning schemes as by martial courage or military campaigns', and the result was that 'they and their king preferred to serve him and King Edward rather than to continue fighting, and moreover, to confirm the peace by giving hostages'. Such a policy would have shown that Tostig could use diplomacy as a technique of government, in contrast to the more active policy of Harold against the Welsh. Even in Wales, however, Harold preferred negotiation to outright warfare, at least while Aelfgar of Mercia still lived. Both were using the preferred techniques of their father, Earl Godwine.[5]

His policy brought Tostig the admiration of the author of the *Vita Edwardi*, reflecting perhaps the views of his sister Edith. The *Vita* describes Tostig as 'a man of courage and endowed with a great wisdom and shrewdness of mind'. 'Lavish with liberal bounty', he might have used bribery to influence the Scots. There was no problem while Tostig was absent at court in Winchester, which he frequently was, but in 1061, during Tostig's absence on pilgrimage, Malcolm invaded Northumbria and ravaged Lindisfarne. Tostig again negotiated, renewing his 'brotherhood'. The affair cannot have won Tostig much credit in Northumbria. Despite his reputation for being vigorous and warlike, he had preferred negotiation, and there was no military reprisal.[6]

Perhaps he had not trusted the Northumbrians to support military action in Scotland. Some of their interests lay on both sides of the border, and they could by now have been starting to resent Tostig's severe rule. The Bernician aristocracy certainly resented Scottish control of the upper Tyne valley, conceded by Tostig. From this moment on, Tostig's control over his earldom began to slip, and a downward spiral was initiated. This period coincides with renewed demands that the Northumbrian earldom be financially self-supporting, and an insistence that Northumbrian levels of taxation be brought more in line with those in the rest of England.[7]

The pilgrimage to Rome had other consequences. Ealdred, recently elected to the see of York in succession to Cynsige, accompanied the earl's party, to seek a pallium as archbishop-elect. On arrival, he found himself questioned by the Pope, because he wished to go on holding Worcester, as had been the custom for the archbishops in the tenth century. The Pope refused a pallium to Ealdred. The earl's party made representations on Ealdred's behalf, but in vain.

When the party left Rome, it was ambushed by the count of Galeria, a nobleman opposed to the reform movement at Rome. This was when Gospatrick, of the House of Bamburgh, saved the day by allowing the ambushers to believe that he was Earl Tostig. After the rest of the party had been released, Gospatrick revealed his true identity. His courage and chivalry impressed Count Gerard and he was released unharmed. The rest of the party returned to Rome, to replace their lost belongings and supplies. The embarassed Pope excommunicated Gerard, and Tostig was able to use the affair to secure a pallium for Ealdred.

Two legates accompanied the earl to England, where they were taken on a tour of inspection of the English Church and introduced to Prior Wulfstan of Worcester, whose spirituality so impressed them that they nominated him as bishop of Worcester. The archbishop then left Wulfstan at York as his deputy, while he went off to secure control of the episcopal estates of Worcester to generate income for himself and the new bishop. That enforced stay at York proved very useful to Wulfstan in early 1066, when he accompanied King Harold to York to win over the Northumbrians to the new monarch, making use of the contacts he had made in 1062 and no doubt at other times, when he acted as Ealdred's suffragan at York.

It is noteworthy that the legates did not seek to do anything about Stigand's anomalous position.[8]

For the first ten years of Tostig's rule in the north, all had apparently gone well, though resentments were festering beneath the surface. He was regarded as a West Saxon, despite his Anglo-Danish descent, and the 'smack of firm government' was insupportable to some, but it was the earl himself who became the target of resentment, not King Edward and his government. To the explosion which came in 1065, Tostig himself in no small measure contributed. At Christmas 1064, Gospatrick of Allerdale, youngest son of Earl Uhtred, was murdered while in attendance at court. The murder was part of a pattern of action by Tostig which had resulted in several other murders, perhaps part of an effort by the earl to stifle developing opposition to his rule. The reason for these murders is nowhere made explicit, but their effect was to trigger the Northumbrian revolt.[9]

Tostig's appointment as earl had been unusual, since he had no territorial or hereditary links with the north, and he lacked any power base there, other than such lands as went with the earldom. To make up the shortfall, he was endowed with estates in the Midlands. Tostig's vulnerability is illustrated by his need to employ a personal bodyguard, a household of 200 housecarls. Nonetheless he had evolved a two-fold plan of action. He enforced justice in a rigorous manner and, certainly after 1061, raised taxes. This earned him a reputation as tyrannical and bloodthirsty, a great raiser of tolls and taxes who yet spent a great deal of his time absent at court, where he was King Edward's favourite. This precipitated the crisis.[10]

Soon after his appointment, Tostig had acquired a 'man of business' who could deputise for him during his absences, Copsige. Between them, Tostig and Copsige levied an enormous tax which 'oppressed the nobles with the heavy yoke of his rule because of their misdeeds'. This led to accusations that he was 'punishing wrongdoers more from a wish to confiscate their property than for the love of justice'. Tostig is recorded as a pious man according to the conventions of the time, donating offerings to St Cuthbert: a large crucifix and a New Testament decorated in silver. The canons of St Cuthbert were able to invoke the awe inspired by his cult to secure pardon for offenders and to gain Tostig's patronage.[11]

Tostig was not entirely without approval in some quarters. He and Earl Godwine are both remembered in letters of gold in the Durham *Liber Vitae* and Tostig's name is on the sundial at St Gregory's Church, Kirkdale. In itself, this testifies to the establishment of more settled conditions. So Tostig had begun well, seeking to enforce law and order in a lawless province. It is recorded that he 'so reduced the number of robbers and cleared the country of them by mutilating or killing them so that any man… could travel at will even alone without fear of attack'. A similar testimony is attached to the Conqueror's name: that a man of property could travel the country safely, even carrying a purse of gold. Nonetheless, Tostig was also accused of exploiting the situation to enrich himself.[12]

There was a reform of the royal household in the interests of efficiency early in the 1060s. Offices in the household seem to have been more clearly defined. There could also have been a move, possibly inspired by Earl Harold, to require that the north pay more towards the upkeep of its own government. Tostig's rule was then seen as tightening royal control over the north at a time when the Witan in England was dominated by Harold, which would explain why Tostig blamed Harold for the revolt and accused him of conspiring against him. Tostig's promotion can then be seen not as an element in the aggrandisement, political and territorial, of the Godwinsons, but as part of a more rigorous approach to government. Siward's success, followed by ten years of relative calm under Tostig, had persuaded the Witan that the north was ready for closer incorporation into the rest of England.[13]

For most of his time in the north, Tostig had derived his resources from Midland estates, so funding his household of 200 housecarls. It was an overgrown establishment, mirroring that of the Scandinavian kings. The promotion of Ealdred of Worcester to archbishop of York – an obvious choice, as he had great administrative experience in Worcestershire and Herefordshire – could be seen as an effort to heighten control over the north. His appointment was probably intended to strengthen Tostig's government, but might have been seen by him as interference on the part of Earl Harold. If the pressure to tighten control of the north emanated from a Witan controlled by Harold, that could explain Tostig's attitude to Harold in 1065. But this policy of integration echoed that of previous kings; it was not new. What was new was Tostig's appointment, as previous kings had appointed as earl men with interests in northern Mercia, sensitive to local claims. That, perhaps, was why the rebels wanted Morcar for earl – a return to the earlier policy breached by the appointment of Tostig, and not evidence of so-called 'Northumbrian separatism'.[14]

An early indication of the problems that would arise was the matter of Aethelric, Bishop of Durham. He had been in a weak position, lacking local support. He was a monk from Peterborough and had upset the canons or clerks of St Cuthbert. A year after Siward's death, the bishop had resigned and taken with him to Peterborough a great deal of treasure, which was seen by the clerks as robbing St Cuthbert. Tostig made no attempt to defend the bishop, whose 'robbery' might well have been his reaction to being driven out by the rebellious clerks. Tostig unhappily chose as replacement another Peterborough monk, Aethelric's brother Aethelwine. He too became unpopular, was seen as an outsider, and later branded a thief.[15]

Tostig was now increasingly being seen as a severe and unpopular defender of 'justice', who levied fines and raised taxes arbitrarily, supported unpopular bishops and collected taxes in a manner which was contrary to established custom, overtaxing the north and transgressing against the privileges of the thegns. The most significant change, after 1063, was an alteration in the rate at which the geld was levied in those areas which were rated for it. The north had been beneficially rated before Tostig's time. For example, six carucates in Lancashire equalled one hide or carucate elsewhere, for tax purposes. Some other areas paid two shillings on six carucates, when the rest of England paid two shillings on one hide or carucate. Northumbria might not have paid the geld at all. The result was a fifty per cent increase in the rate of tax, raising both the king's income and that of the earl. Tax rose from two shillings on six carucates to two shillings on four carucates. That meant that thegns like Gamalbearn, with sixty carucates, saw tax rise from twenty to thirty shillings. Dunstan, with forty-eight carucates, paid twenty-four shillings instead of sixteen, and Gleniarain nineteen shillings and sixpence instead of thirteen shillings on thirty-nine carucates. These three were to be leaders of the revolt.[16]

In 1064, Tostig made a pre-emptive strike. Allowing them to believe that he intended to open negotiations, and having given them safe conduct, Tostig had two leading thegns murdered in his own house in York. He had now involved himself in a feud. *Florence of Worcester* puts the murders as occurring before the murder of Gospatrick, son of

Uhtred, at Christmas 1064, and in the year before the rebellion. Tostig
might well have been attempting to eliminate opposition at its roots,
apparently acting against the descendants of Ealdorman Waltheof
and his son Earl Uhtred. The murdered men were Ulf, probably the
grandson of Thorfinn MacThore, and Gamal Ormson, grandson of
Orm Gamelson. Then Gospatrick was killed at Christmas, allegedly
at the instigation of Queen Edith.[17]

These murders, rather than Tostig's repression of robbers, taken in
conjunction with resentment over the increase in taxation and the
levying of punitive fines, led to a well planned and co-ordinated
rising, led by the three Yorkshire thegns who had been particularly
hard hit by the rise in taxation. The real architect of the trouble was
probably Eadwulf's son, Oswulf, one of the three men most eligible
to be earl in Northumbria along with another Gospatrick, son of
Maldred (not acceptable to everyone), and Waltheof Siwardsson. But
in 1065 the thegns asked for Morcar. All the murdered magnates
were kin to Eadwulf. The murders are shrouded in mystery and the
responsibility could have rested with Edward himself, while Edith
was allowed to take the blame. But the most obvious person to have
benefited from them was Tostig.[18]

Then, as the *Vita* testifies, while Tostig was at court:

> …about some palace business which had been put upon him… a
> party of nobles whom he had repressed with the heavy yoke of his
> rule because of their misdeeds, conspired among themselves against
> him. Without delay they broke into his house, at York, killed those of
> his soldiers [*milites*, meaning housecarls] who were taken by surprise
> and could not get away and finally with fire and sword laid waste all
> his possessions and seized his treasures.

Tostig was at Britford with the king shortly after Michaelmas when
the revolt began, on St Bartholomew's day, 24 August. Tostig was
alleged to have robbed God, that is, the Church, and to have acted
against the law, contrary to established custom. The event was so
shocking that the Abingdon chronicler was moved to resume writing the *Chronicle*, left blank since 1057. The rebels accused Tostig

of having 'despoiled of life and land all those over whom he could tyrannize'. *Florence of Worcester* charges Queen Edith with the death of Gospatrick. The chronicler names two of Tostig's murdered house-carls as Amund and Reavenswart, and puts the number killed at 200. In addition, a number of the earl's men made a stand on the north bank of the Humber and more than 200 of them were slain.[19]

Some assume Harold was with Tostig in Wiltshire when the revolt began, or in Wales. He was not involved in any feud and had either married or was contemplating marrying Ealdgyth, Aelfgar's daughter, widow of Gruffydd of Wales. Wherever he was, he now had to deal with a highly dangerous situation. Having marched down from Yorkshire, the rebels sought to legitimise their actions. They outlawed Tostig, in what was probably the first of several proclamations, and sent for Morcar, Earl Edwin's brother. Under his nominal leadership, they marched on Lincoln and then came by way of Derby and Nottingham to Northampton. Earl Edwin joined forces with them, with the army of Mercia and some of his father's Welsh troops. Some part of the rebel force even seems to have threatened Oxford. At Northampton they went on the rampage and laid waste Tostig's estates. Just as in 1035 and 1051, the revolt had split the country. But it was not some kind of separatist movement. The rebels were protesting against the misrule of Tostig, not against the sovereignty of King Edward.

The king was at Britford, and the *Vita* gives some idea of what went on at court, though its account is partial and perhaps one-sided. Arguments were heated and men sought to apportion blame and find a scapegoat. Some accused Tostig and his misgovernment; he countered this by accusing Earl Harold of fomenting the rebellion. The *Vita* asserts that the rebels had 'undertaken this madness against their earl at the artful persuasion of his brother, Earl Harold', who had to clear himself of the charge on oath. It is noteworthy that his oath was accepted, despite the author of the *Vita*'s sly remark that he was 'too free with oaths'. The author of the *Vita* tries to distance himself, and Edith his patron, from the accusations by saying 'I dare not and would not believe that such a prince was guilty of this detestable wickedness against his brother'. No one wanted to resort to force; the constant distaste for anything resembling civil war dominated men's minds. It was decided to negotiate with the rebels, and Harold, as the king's strong right arm, was instructed to do so.[20]

So Morcar was chosen 'as leader and lord in their mad conspiracy'. Many inhabitants had been slaughtered in York and Lincoln, and anyone identified as a member of Tostig's household 'was dragged to the torments of death without trial'. King Edward tried to appease them, sending messengers, but the rebels rejected all reconciliation and demanded Tostig's dismissal; otherwise the king himself would be treated as an enemy. Edward tried a second and a third time 'to turn them from their mad purpose', and failed. The court was at Britford. The arguments at Britford were bitter.[21]

As Edith is thought to have sided with Tostig, she is also thought unlikely to have concealed anything detrimental to Harold. But the negotiations failed and a stalemate was reached, neither side being willing to budge. The ravaging continued and Edward was forced to consider action. He issued a royal edict summoning up the fyrd to his assistance, stirring up the population, with the intention of crushing the rebellion by force and so punishing the 'impudent contumacy' of the rebels. But others, especially Earl Harold, had second thoughts. They no doubt remembered 1051, and there was little enthusiasm for Edward's command. Winter was approaching and it proved impossible to raise enough troops, which suggests some sympathy for the rebel cause. Many felt instinctive horror 'at what seemed like civil war' and recoiled from it as they had in 1051. Efforts were made to calm the king and his 'raging spirit'. More in sorrow than in anger, the king relapsed into mental and perhaps physical decline, protesting to God with deep sorrow and complaining almost petulantly that he had been deprived of the obedience due to him from his men. He cursed them all, calling down God's vengeance upon them. Later, after the events of 1066, this was to be seen as prophetic frenzy on the part of a holy king. The *Vita* records it because of its ambivalent attitude to the succession of Earl Harold, reflecting Edith's dismay at the fratricidal discord between her brothers.[22]

Harold now assumed the role of chief negotiator, seeking to mediate between the king and the rebels. This move was to stand him in good stead, after he became king, in securing the acceptance of his rule in Northumbria. While all this went on, the rebels had 'sent for' Morcar, brother of Earl Edwin, choosing him as their earl. He had marched south with all the men of the shire, together with others from Nottingham, Derby and Lincoln. Neither side showed any sign of compromise, but Harold was determined to secure an agreement and seems to have realised that Tostig, being no longer acceptable in the north, would have to be removed. Harold also wished to avoid civil war, as that would provide an open invitation to England's enemies to intervene, perhaps especially the Normans. It was not that he saw Tostig as an obstacle to his own designs on the throne; there is no sign of such ambition on Harold's part. It is not known exactly when he began to contemplate a bid for the throne; it might not really have occurred to him until the king entered his last illness and it became apparent that the country would need a strong leader after his death. To suggest that Harold had already thought of the succession before the Northumbrian revolt is to assume something that needs more proof than the sources afford. It assumes, for instance, that Tostig and Edith would have opposed such a move, though there is no sign of dissension until Tostig lost control of his earldom.[23]

Harold concluded that his brother could not remain earl of Northumbria, and he sought to confine concessions to the rebels to something acceptable to the Witan. He therefore prevailed upon the ailing king to accept the rebels' minimum terms. The king and Witan were now faced with two great earldoms in opposition. Earl Edwin had willingly gone to his brother's support with his own troops, including some Welshmen, and had joined forces with the Northumbrians. They posed a threat too powerful to be outfaced by the king. Some historians have seen all this as evidence of a demand for self-government on the part of the north, but it was nothing of the sort. Had that been their intention, they could quite easily have held a coronation at York and defied the southern government to do anything about it. What they demanded was a more acceptable earl and a return to the status quo, as it was before Tostig began to make changes; thus they demanded the renewal of the 'Laws of Cnut'. Harold abandoned any effort to insist that they accept Tostig, and

conceded their demands. He was ready to see the northern earldom
in the hands of a Mercian who might prove to be only a figurehead,
rather than lose men in a civil war – men who might be needed if
the king were to die and Duke William or some other pretender
pressed his claims by force.[24]

So, at Northampton, Harold, on behalf of the king, accepted two
fundamental demands of the insurgents: Morcar was recognised as
earl of Northumbria and Harold reaffirmed the Laws of Cnut. Tostig,
driven out of his earldom and without support, chose to go into exile
in Flanders. Harold had done all he could short of outright war and
saw that Tostig was a lost cause. But the key to peace, other than the
removal of Tostig and the acceptance of Morcar, was the demand for
the re-enactment of the Laws of Cnut. Tostig had signally failed to
rule in the traditional manner, so the Northumbrians had successfully
outlawed him and secured confirmation of Cnut's laws. Tostig had
'turned all the thegns of Yorkshire and Northumbria' against him,
and they were the men who bore the burden of geld payments. Such
a body of thegnly opinion could not be ignored. Earls who prompted
the thegns to unite and act as a group risked ruin. But it was not
opposition to the rule of King Edward himself. England in the eleventh century was a face-to-face society. The collective body of great
lords, together with their vassals, to use feudal terminology, could not
function without a single head, a king. Such a man had to be at least
competent in personal relations with the small number of men who
enjoyed real territorial and political power. In addition, for decision-
making there had to be a primitive bureaucracy, of which the king
was the head, and there had to be a competent military leader. That
not only explains the later acceptance of Duke William, but also
the readiness with which Harold was accepted as king. In 1065 the
northern thegns recognised all this and were content to demand a
representative of their king who was acceptable to them.[25]

There has also been speculation (without further evidence, that is
all it can be) that Tostig had incited Caradog to make his attack in
south Wales in order to provoke Harold into retaliation, but this is
to assume friction between the brothers, of which there is no sign.
Some suggest a plot by Earl Harold to engineer the removal of Tostig

as a potential rival, but this again asserts something which would need some definite proof. Harold only revealed the extent of his ambition after the fall of Tostig and the death of King Edward. The *Vita Edwardi* is seen as evidence for the events at court during the rising, but its evidence must be treated with caution when it goes beyond known fact. It is a literary construct, a set piece, and in it the leading actors all play the parts assigned to them by the author, biased in Edith's favour. She is pictured as one who ensures that 'peace wraps the kingdom round', and might well have envisioned some sort of peaceful succession, perhaps with Edgar on the throne and Edith herself as regent, supported by her faithful brothers. After Tostig's removal, this was no longer feasible. From Edith's point of view, everything had been ruined (which explains the dire forebodings reported in the text), and the king had fallen into decline.

He had suffered paroxysms of rage, and it is not entirely improbable that these had triggered a series of strokes. The *Vita* speaks of his 'raging spirit' and 'sickness of mind', and by Christmas he was unable to attend the consecration of his beloved Westminster Abbey. He fell into periods of coma from which he roused just long enough to speak. He was then able to relate the dreams and visions he had experienced during his illness, and he made his will. Men in the eleventh century, particularly great lords and kings, died in public, as they had lived. Those present at Edward's deathbed were not a hand-picked group favourable to Earl Harold. Edith was present (weeping at the king's feet as she warmed them), as were Earl Harold, Archbishop Stigand and Robert fitzWimarc·the Staller, who seems to have been responsible for running the palace and its household. There were also a number of the king's 'French' servants. Stigand's evidence, if the *Vita* is to be accepted, actually cast the shadow of doubt over the proceedings, by somewhat sceptically protesting that the king was not in his right mind and did not know what he was saying – the ravings of a sick man. By modern standards, the king was perhaps not entirely in a fit state to make a last will and testament, but in the eleventh century he was seen as inspired by a spirit of prophecy. (Those present are also represented around the dying king in the Bayeux Tapestry. It merely says that the king is addressing his vassals. As usual, it does not clarify

what he was actually saying. Unable directly to confirm or to deny
that Edward had designated Earl Harold as his successor, the Tapestry
took refuge in discreet silence.)[26]

The *Vita Edwardi* paints a portrait of a venerable royal saint, inspired
on his deathbed to prophesy. The content of the king's vision as
related in the *Vita* can be said to carry all the hallmarks of a post-1066
creation, heavily affected by hindsight. The author gives the king a
speech in which he narrates the vision of the Green Tree. This is a
parable of a tree which is felled halfway up its trunk, with the felled
section carried a distance of three furlongs; it then spontaneously
joins up again, bursts into leaf and bears fruit. It is said that when
this miraculous event actually occurs, God's anger will have been
appeased. It could not have been seen to have any obvious meaning
at the time of Edward's death and is recorded only as proof of his
sanctity, along with his denunciation of the earls, bishops, abbots and
clergy of England as servants of the devil. No doubt Edward did
prophesy that death and destruction would follow his death. The
parable was later interpreted as a prophecy about the royal kin, in
which the throne passed into other hands and was later 'grafted' back
onto the main stem, by the marriage of Henry I to Edith/Matilda,
daughter of Queen Margaret, the sister of Edgar the Aetheling. Thus
the Norman dynasty was rejoined to that of the West Saxon House
of Cerdic.

The parable would not have been understood to that effect in
1066.[27]

The king had fallen into a decline during November and December,
but preparations for the Christmas court would have continued, and
also for the dedication and consecration of St Peter's, Westminster.
Men began gathering at court for the ceremonies. It is inconceivable
that Earl Harold could have contemplated leaving court at that time
(as one historian has suggested) to sail the Channel, either for some
purpose of his own or even on some mission for King Edward. The
Vita Edwardi gives no hint of any such departure. Therefore, the court
continued its work and men gathered for Christmas. Some had come
as they usually did; others, perhaps, especially clerics, for the consecration

of Westminster; and even some simply because the king was ill and might die. It was a large gathering, perhaps larger than usual, and sources claim the guests came from the whole of Britain.

Two twelfth-century 'forged' charters from Westminster have genuine witness lists which might well have come from genuine documents (to add authenticity to the forgery). They permit the suggestion that they reflect the composition of the Christmas court of 1065. They list both the king and Queen Edith, both archbishops (adding weight to the idea that Ealdred officiated rather than Stigand), eight bishops according to one charter, twelve according to the other, eight abbots, three other clerics, the chancellor, five earls, seven thegns and five knights (either household retainers – *cniht* in Old English – or the king's Frenchmen). Of the bishops, only Aethelwine of Selsey, Aethelmaer of Elmham, Aethelwine of Durham and Leofwine of Lichfield were absent. Of the earls, only Waltheof is missing, strengthening the idea that he became an earl after Harold became king. The list of earls is Harold, Gyrth, Leofwine, Edwin and Morcar. The list of other nobles and officials is acceptable; it includes Ralf the Staller, Robert fitzWimarc, Esgar, Eadnoth, Bondi, Wigod and Aethelnoth. It is very similar to the witness lists of the Conqueror and to genuine charters of King Edward. The Aetheling Edgar is missing, but he does not appear on any extant charter of King Edward. The majority of those present all came from south of a line from the Wash to the Severn. Therefore, the gathering was not quite 'from the whole of Britain'. There are thirty-nine names in all. It was not a packed assembly full of Harold's supporters, and could not have been easily overawed. Their decision would readily have been seen as the decision of the kingdom.[28]

Most of these men would have been present for the celebration of Christmas. Edward managed to attend the Christmas Mass, and many men would have stayed on for the consecration of the abbey, fully aware of his grave condition and possibly expecting his death – particularly Abbot Baldwin, his doctor. The nobles would have remained in expectation of Edward's death and burial. It was natural that they should then constitute a Witanagemot, at which the endorsement of Earl Harold, nominee of the dying king, would have followed immediately, avoiding the necessity of summoning another meeting. If, as the *Vita* states, there were grave forebodings in men's minds as they contemplated the future ('all men deduced future calamities from the signs of the present'), then a rapid decision about the crown was essential. It would certainly have been known that Earl Tostig was recruiting ships and men for an attempt to return by force, and men knew quite well that a king was essential if law and order were to be maintained.[29]

As it was plain that Edward had not long to live, arrangements would have been made for his funeral (the *Vita* says he gave instructions for it himself) and for his burial, at Westminster rather than at Winchester like his predecessors. Edward had already told those around him of the content of his dreams and the visions in them. He said he had seen two monks whom he had known well as a boy in Normandy and who were long since dead, who told him that all the magnates of England, both laymen and clergy, were the devil's servants, and that therefore God had cursed England, delivering it a year and a day after his death to the Enemy, so that 'devils would come through all the land with fire and sword and the havoc of war'. Edward promised to bring his people to repentance, only to be told that it was too late, the people would not repent and God would punish them. No doubt Edward did have forebodings of disaster after his death, expecting any successor to be challenged, but the account, as it stands, has all the hallmarks of hindsight, applied after the event to cast the king in the role of an inspired prophet. His deathbed speeches no doubt struck terror into the hearts of his hearers, but need not have been quite as definite as the *Vita* claims. The events of 1066 have coloured even this, the earliest account of Edward's last days. Having, in one of his lucid moments, praised Edith for her 'dutiful and loving service', and commended her and the kingdom to Harold's protection, the king gave instructions for his grave to be prepared in Westminster and for the news of his imminent death to be broadcast 'promptly to all parts so that all the faithful can beseech the mercy of Almighty God on me a sinner'. The last rites were administered and he died. His last instructions took the form of a deathbed will of *verba novissima* and were taken as fully binding. The following morning, 6 January, he was buried, and Mass was said, during which Harold was installed as king by Archbishop Ealdred, possibly assisted by Stigand, who had been responsible for the funeral rites. *Florence of Worcester*, originating from the abbey where Ealdred had previously held the office of bishop, is certain that Ealdred officiated, despite Norman claims that Stigand anointed Harold. The earl would not have risked using Stigand's services for such a vital rite, any more than he allowed him to vitiate the consecration of his foundation at Waltham. The Normans claim otherwise, as part of their vilification of Harold, associating him with an uncanonical, simoniac schismatic. The Bayeux Tapestry carefully avoids a direct falsehood. It shows Stigand, wearing a maniple, presenting the enthroned Harold for the acclamation of the congregation. It does not dare show Stigand anointing or crowning him. Stigand wears a maniple, suggesting that he was acting as deacon to another prelate. He has no pallium.[30]

II

The Reign of King Harold

If, as seems to have been the case, Ealdred performed the ceremony, it is likely that he, expecting the king to die, prepared himself in advance, in expectation that his services would be needed for a coronation. It is certain that Ealdred crowned and anointed Duke William, when he 'gave a pledge on the Gospels and swore an oath besides, before Ealdred would place the crown on his head, that he would govern this nation according to the best practice of his pred-ecessors if they would be loyal to him'. It has been cogently argued that he used the same Ordo on both occasions; it would certainly have been the obvious thing to do. Most of the English who had witnessed William's coronation had most likely also witnessed that of Harold. William's intention was that his coronation should erase from men's minds all recollection of Harold's reign, so that he could pose as the direct successor of King Edward. What better way was there to do that than to ensure that his ceremony was a carbon copy, as it were, which would not be forgotten. That would have the effect of legitimising William's succession and coronation. Ealdred himself had carried out missions on the continent and, according to the sources, while there he 'heard, saw and committed to memory many things which pertain to the dignity of ecclesiastical observance and many to the rigour of ecclesiastical discipline, things which he subsequently caused to be observed in the Churches of England'. That in itself suggests that England under the Confessor was not entirely immune to the spirit of reform found on the continent. Archbishop Ealdred had, of course, been to Rome, and, more importantly perhaps, had witnessed the coronation of the infant Henry IV of Germany.[1]

If doubt over Stigand's canonicity is added to Ealdred's promotion to York, which had given England an undoubtedly canonical archbishop, and to Harold's decision to ask Ealdred to consecrate Waltham, then *Florence of Worcester*'s claim that Ealdred crowned Harold should be accepted. The scene of Harold's enthronement in the Bayeux Tapestry appears to have been designed by someone who knew the Ordo, as it conflates three stages of that rite: offer of the sword of state, enthronement with crown, orb and sceptre, and acclamation. Ealdred had been a supporter of Harold and owed him his elevation to the archbishopric. That he, in due course, performed Harold's coronation seems certain. By a neat piece of iconography, the Tapestry pictures Edward's burial before his speech to his vassals and actual death, at which a priest, not Stigand, gives him the last rites. The scenes of his last speech and death are presented one above the other, signifying near simultaneity. The design allows the juxtaposition of his deathbed speech with the following scene, in which the crown is presented to Harold. Two men do so: one holding out the crown and pointing back towards the death of King Edward, the other holding a (ceremonial?) axe. Harold is then shown enthroned in majesty, already crowned and anointed, holding orb and sceptre, while attendants offer him a sword of state and Stigand presents him to the congregation. This is a political rather than a religious moment. The following scenes condense time rapidly. The Halley's Comet of 1066 is shown as men wonder at it, and Harold, crowned and on a chair of state in his palace, is being told about it. Ghostly hulls of ships decorate the lower border, presaging an invasion fleet. The comet did not appear until 24 April, so Harold had been king for some months. He holds a spear, indicative of readiness for war. Ensuing plates show the news being delivered to Duke William and the beginning of his preparations for invasion.[2]

What now needs to be established is exactly how Harold came to be a candidate for the throne. Up until late 1065, there is no sign of Harold having seriously contemplated making a bid for the throne. Until that year, there was no urgency about the succession. There is no indication that Edward was in imminent danger of death. His routine of court ceremonial, religious observance and indulgence in hunting continued right up to the moment when the Northumbrian rebellion began. The *Vita Edwardi* gives no indication of infirmity or ill health. It was the catastrophic effects of the rebellion which brought on his unexpected demise. Queen Edith's propagandist in the *Vita* hints at some deep-laid design of hers to position her family in such a way that its hold on power would be unaffected when the king ultimately died, and shows clearly that the deep division between Harold and Tostig which resulted from the rebellion ruined whatever project she had in mind. There is no evidence that she envisaged a change of dynasty. Her brothers are described as pillars of the state, men trained and educated to serve whatever king there might be. That perhaps explains the ambiguity which some historians perceive in the *Vita's* account of Edward's last words. Edith could not bring herself to accept that Harold was to be king, and her propagandist presents Edward's words in a form which enhances Edith's position, at the expense of clarity about what Edward said concerning Harold. The mere fact that he was accepted by the Witan and anointed and crowned shows that the magnates present at court accepted Harold's claim to have been designated as King Edward's successor, and that none of the witnesses present at Edward's death-bed denied or questioned it. The various versions of the *Chronicle* are clear enough. The *Abingdon Chronicle* (C) and *Worcester Chronicle* (D) say 'yet did the wise king entrust his kingdom to a man of high rank, to Harold himself, the noble earl, who ever faithfully obeyed his noble lords in words and deeds, neglecting nothing whereof the national king stood in need'; in other words, Edward nominated the man who had earned his approval. The *Peterborough Chronicle*, which for this year derives its account from its source at St Augustine's, Canterbury, says bluntly 'Earl Harold succeeded to the Kingdom as the king granted it to him and he was elected thereto'. *Florence of Worcester*, derived from a now-lost version of the *Chronicle*, states that 'the subregulus, Harold, son of earl Godwine, whom the king had nominated as his successor, was elected king by the chief men of all England; and on the same day was crowned with great ceremony by Ealdred, Archbishop of York'.[3]

When Harold's claim is considered, his status needs to be clearly understood. *Florence of Worcester* calls him *subregulus* or 'under-king', hinting at some informal degree of association in the kingship. He is described as acting jointly with Edward in accepting the submission of Bleddyn and Rhiwallon, successors in North Wales to the dead Gruffydd; *Worcester Chronicle* (D) says 'And king Edward committed the land to his two brothers Bleddyn and Rhiwallon; they gave hostages to the king and the earl and swore oaths that they would be loyal to him in all things'. *Florence of Worcester* is equally interesting, saying 'the Welsh were thus compelled to give hostages and submit and promised to pay tribute to him' – to Harold, that is – because he and Tostig had laid waste the country, and they outlawed and renounced their king, Gruffydd. Other indications of Harold's special status are found in two rather suspect charters. They are witnessed by Ealdred, who is termed archbishop, although he was not so at the date of these documents. It may be that the copyist who preserved them added the title he knew Ealdred to have acquired. (This was something copyists tended to do.) Their importance here lies in the way in which they endorse a quasi-royal status for Harold. The first concerns lands belonging to Worcester, and Ealdred signs it *cum licentia Edwardi Regis et Haroldi Ducis* ('by permission of King Edward and of Earl Harold'). Yet Worcester was then in Mercia and not part of Harold's earldom of Wessex. (He is again very closely associated with the king.) The second, and earlier, charter is witnessed by Earl Leofric, who died in 1057, and Walter, who became a bishop only in 1061. It looks as though the bishop's title also has been added. It identifies Harold as *Dei Gratia Dux*, 'Earl by the Grace of God', just as the king was so also by God's grace. There is no reason why a forger should have invented anything so favourable to Harold, and that suggests that the charters are based on genuine originals.[4]

It could be argued, therefore, that King Edward had been moving towards the idea of designating Harold as his successor during his lifetime, though there is no proof that he had actually done so. What he can be said to have done, despite Norman claims about an alleged promise to Duke William, was to have designated Harold as his successor on his deathbed. His final utterances on that occasion took the form of *verba novissima*, or last and final words. This formed his last will and testament. Recent research has shown that written wills were only useful as evidence and were not essential, because it was a man's last words which mattered. Wills made in this manner were regarded as solemn and binding, and we have William of Poitiers to thank for testimony that Edward's designation of Harold was so made. He reports Harold as arguing, in rebuttal of Duke William's claims, that 'He recalls that... the same king, his lord, acting within his rights, bestowed on him the kingdom of England when dying. Moreover... it has been the unbroken custom of the English to treat deathbed bequests as inviolable.'[5]

Such wills by *verba novissima* are distinguished from *donationes irrevocabiles post obitum*, or irrevocable gifts made so as to come into effect after death, or from *cwide*, verbal agreements of a revocable kind, declared in the presence of witnesses by a testator, both of which could be negated by a deathbed declaration in the presence of a priest and preferably in the presence of the beneficiary, so that the 'property' could be handed over directly. Such declarations had to be more than a mere pious wish, and the *Vita*, by including in King Edward's statement his wishes for the disposal of his body, his request that Earl Harold treat Edith faithfully and with honour, leaving her in possession of all her property, and his request that Harold allow the king's foreign servants to take service with him or enable them to return home, shows that this was indeed Edward's last will. It can be compared to King Alfred's will, as recorded by Asser, which was a deathbed bequest that would invalidate all previous wills.

A *post obitum* bequest also had to be made in the presence of the beneficiary, who could be placed in actual possession of his inheritance. But that form of bequest could be annulled by *verba novissima*. Cnut the Great was said to have become king in virtue of his agreement with Edmund Ironside, whose supposed will then constituted Cnut's legal claim to the throne. Kings were treating the crown as the hereditary property of their kin, and stress was always laid on the last will of a dying ruler.[6]

The usual method of ensuring that the Witan took heed of such a bequest was to crown the heir in the lifetime of the king, as Harthacnut might have done for Edward, or to share the kingship to some degree with the intended heir. That is where what has been said about Harold's status becomes important. But none of this leaves any room for a bequest to Duke William. Nothing was done in 1052, the only occasion when the two met as adults, so that no bequest was made in the presence of the intended recipient. That rules out everything other than a vague promise to make William his heir, and he was not the only claimant to imagine that he had been given such a promise. The accounts given in the Norman sources simply do not fit the criteria even for a *post obitum* bequest, and the duke was never put in possession of the crown by Edward in person. The story in the *Carmen de Hastinge Proelio* of a gift of a ring and a sword is not enough (and looks more like tokens of credence for an ambassador). The claims by William of Poitiers that Archbishop (*sic*) Stigand and the three earls had agreed to William's succession, and by William of Jumièges that a promise was delivered by Archbishop Robert Champart, are all simply inadequate. Even the story of Harold's alleged oath provides William with no legally binding title to the throne, which simply could not be transferred in that way. If William of Poitiers was accurately reporting the content of exchanges between Harold and William, then Harold was certainly claiming a gift of the crown by *verba novissima*. The *Vita* account would seem to confirm this, and is supported by the scenes in the Bayeux Tapestry and the assertions of the chroniclers.[7]

What the *Vita* account did was to amalgamate Edith's commendation to Harold's protection with Edward's transfer of the crown to Harold. It reads: 'I commend this woman and all the Kingdom to your protection. Remember that she is your Lady [Queen] and sister and serve her faithfully and honour her as such for all the days of her life. Do not take away from her any honour that I have given her.' The following request, to offer the foreign servants the chance to serve him, clearly shows that it was the crown that was being transferred. No pressure was put upon the dying man and there is no reason to suppose that Edith or Robert fitzWimarc would have permitted it. Edith's propagandist is more concerned to safeguard his patron's position after Edward's death, which could only be done if the king's last will was made freely and without constraint. The crown is not his main concern. In any case, once the Witan had agreed and Harold had been anointed and crowned, he became the Lord's Anointed and was legitimately king. It was consecration that made a man a king. Edith needed to safeguard her position after Hastings, and her spokesman stressed the respect in which King Edward desired her to be held. He cannot, therefore, endorse Harold unequivocally without offending the audience which might read his work, after the Conquest, when the rest of the work was written. He is emphasising Edith's right, as Edward's widow, to be protected no matter who is king. She was in fact given a protected status by William. His apologist, William of Poitiers, sought to clear her of any involvement in what, to him, was Harold's usurpation. He never dares to use the one argument which could have refuted Harold's claim – that is, that Edward was out of his mind – as that would have cast doubt on his status as a holy king. His visions were taken as evidence of inspiration, prophetic utterances confirming the sinfulness of the English in general and Harold in particular. Nor could the author of the *Vita* suddenly vilify Harold, who had been the hero of the earlier part of his book. The work is not a preparatory manifesto for Harold; it is propaganda for Edith, daughter of Godwine and wife of King Edward. So he leaves the wording compatible with the Norman claims, by omission or careful editing. He would have been dependent upon Edith's version of what happened. Edward might well have been more explicit than this source suggests.[8]

The timing was rapid, but the chroniclers do not, unlike the Normans, complain of haste. It was simply convenient and logical that the coronation followed immediately after the interment, while

just about everybody who mattered was still present. It was impera-
tive that the country should have a new king as soon as possible, given
the fears of foreign invasion and perhaps of civil unrest. Edgar the
Aetheling, still a young boy without experience of government and
with no affinity to support him, was not even considered. No one
is described in any source as a 'man' of Edgar, although Edwin and
Morcar, young men though they were, were already earls with their
own men and estates. As Harold's visit to York shows, there were still
concerns that trouble could flare up in the north, especially if Tostig
made a comeback, so for that reason alone, a king was needed. Tostig
had taken refuge at St Omer, where Baldwin V of Flanders had made
him castellan or military governor and garrison commander, and he
was recruiting mercenaries for a return in force, like his father before
him. Other pretenders to the throne would soon be stirring. Swein of
Denmark skulked on the fringes, eventually contenting himself with
sending in raiding armies after the Conquest, to take advantage of the
unsettled conditions. Harald Hardrada of Norway was an unknown
quantity, but could make some sort of claim, as heir to Magnus the
Good. His long and eventually fruitless war with Swein had recently
ended and his treasury was exhausted. He might dream of replenish-
ing it with the rich pickings to be had in England.[9]

And then there was William the Bastard of Normandy. King
Harold would have been well aware that he posed a threat. The
Chronicle is positive about this, the Worcester version relating that
by 24 April, when the comet was seen, Harold had begun to gather
together 'greater naval and land hosts than any king had ever done in
this country because he was informed that William the Bastard [a rare
use of that appellation] was about to invade this land to conquer it'.
The *Abingdon Chronicle* (C) adds that Harold was 'credibly informed
that Duke William of Normandy, kinsman of King Edward, was
about to invade and conquer this land, just as it subsequently came
to pass'. These entries perhaps hint at the content of the exchanges
which passed between the two kings, William boasting of his kinship
with Edward and Harold defying him as a mere bastard. That usage
is a reminder that in English law a bastard had no title to the crown.
There is a reference to Harold as 'pseudo-King' in the *Chronicle* of

St Maixent, from Aquitaine – perhaps another hint of what was being said, in addition to the known claims on the Norman side that Harold was a perjuror and a faithless vassal. They were part of a Norman propaganda campaign, which still holds many scholars in thrall. It began in Normandy itself, as William had first to win over his vassals, which he did by claiming to be King Edward's heir. It might even be the case that the full claim was only unveiled in 1066, when Harold failed to keep whatever commitments he had entered into with William.

The duke vented his righteous indignation at Harold's alleged perjury, won over his men and began the construction of an invasion fleet. That had to be built from scratch, as Normandy had no fleet. Meanwhile, as that was being done, the campaign was extended to accomplish the recruitment of reinforcements from neighbouring states such as Flanders, France, Brittany, Aquitaine and Boulogne. It was remarkably successful. William also had to ensure that Normandy would not be attacked in his absence, and the propaganda campaign was widened to achieve that end. Again, his success was remarkable. Norman sources claimed the at least tacit support of the Emperor Henry IV, claiming that he and the duke 'entered into a new friendship so that an edict was issed by which Germany might come to his aid if he asked for it against any enemy', though there is no corresponding record of it in German sources. It may reflect only that William's father-in-law, Count Baldwin, had made such an agreement, and that by extension it applied to Normandy. They also claim that Swein of Denmark sent messengers pledging support. If so, he played a double game, aiding the duke's enemies by sending troops to England which, according to William of Poitiers, were present at Hastings. This might, in part, reflect the Anglo-Scandinavian character of the English army rather than any actual supply of men, or the intervention of Swein after the Conquest, in 1069 to 1071. The gambit paid off. No other power attempted to attack. Only Conan of Brittany made threatening noises, but he died before he was able to do anything. Some thought William had had him poisoned, but there is no real proof of that.[10]

The real centre of the Norman propaganda effort was focused on Rome. To secure the support of the papacy would guarantee the security of Normandy. William therefore sought endorsement of his claim from Pope Alexander II (Anselm of Lucca). William of Poitiers, the indefatigable, claims that the duke otained from him 'a banner as a pledge of the support of St Peter', which would protect his army. The duke had sent a legation headed by Archdeacon Gilbert of Lisieux in spring 1066. The archdeacon might well have been assisted in the drawing up of the brief to be presented to the Curia (which lies behind the account of William of Poitiers) by Lanfranc. He had known the Pope in his schooldays and knew how to approach him. They also won over the support of Archdeacon Hildebrand, the power behind the papal throne. No effort appears to have been made, as far as known sources are concerned, to summon Harold to Rome to answer Duke William's charges. William of Malmesbury, without giving any source, appeared to believe that Harold refused to send a counter-delegation because Duke William would have arrested it as it tried to pass through northern France, and also claimed that Harold was too proud to do so, as that would imply that he had doubts about the validity of his own position. This looks like speculation on the chronicler's part. William then mixed together his alleged bequest from King Edward, his claim to be his near kin and Harold's alleged perjury. One source does assert that William was granted the kingdom by reason of his nearness to King Edward by blood or, as Poitiers put it, by '*ratio sanguinis*' and '*proxima consanguinitate*' – a claim of nearness of blood through his great-aunt Emma, Edward's mother. Truth to tell, there was no real consanguinity between Edward and William; they merely shared a common ancestor, Richard I, great-grandfather to the duke and grandfather of Edward.

The papacy had little, if any, knowledge of English law, especially as regards the succession to the throne. It ignored the existence of Edgar the Aetheling and knew nothing of the role played by the Witan. It also chose to ignore Harold's coronation, accepting the Norman allegation that it had been performed by Archbishop Stigand, who was not recognised at Rome. Harold was presented as a 'pseudo-King', an impudent usurper, a perjuror and a faithless vassal. Even his coronation was probably regarded as almost blasphemous, because of Stigand's lack of jurisdiction (he would have retained his character as a bishop and priest in possession of holy orders, but had no authority to act as archbishop). So Harold was branded a despot and tyrant bent on reducing the English to slavery, a description which better fits William than Harold. Most of Europe by the mid-eleventh century either had already adopted the hereditary principle or was in the process of doing so, while England continued with the practices adopted in the tenth century, where the crown was the possession of the royal kin, in the widest sense of that word, and a king was selected from that kin according to his suitability for office and the needs of the time.[11]

The papacy had its own agenda. It had doubts about the state of the English Church. Candidates for bishoprics had been rejected at Rome on several occasions, on the grounds of pluralism or simony. Consider the cases of Spearhavoc, deprived of the bishopric of London in 1049, and Ealdred, who only managed to secure transfer to York by means of a compromise and the influence of Earl Tostig. The reformers at Rome were opposed to worldly prelates like Stigand, in any case, and they were led by Archdeacon Hildebrand, later Pope Gregory VII. Hildebrand was supported by Cardinal Peter Damian, who was a friend of Normandy. The duchy was in reality little better than England from the reform point of view, but the duke no doubt made all necessary promises of reform. The irregularity of Stigand's position was well known; every canonical Pope since his elevation had refused him a pallium, although his position otherwise had been tolerated. There had been no outright demands for his removal. In 1062, the legates from Rome had even sat in synod with Stigand without demur and there was to be no demand for his removal, even after the Conquest, until 1070. Perhaps Rome was aware that Odo, Bishop of Bayeux and William's half-brother, was just as worldly. After 1066, Remigius of Dorchester accepted consecration from Stigand, and William was in no hurry to remove him from office, perhaps because he had been appointed by King Edward and it would look like a slur on his memory. Rome had perhaps not wanted to offend the Confessor by barring Stigand, with the fear that he might cease to pay Peter's Pence, which had subsidised Rome since Alfred the Great's time.

According to a rather aggrieved letter from Hildebrand, dated 24 April 1080, when he had become Pope Gregory VII, Duke William had benefited mightily from Hildebrand's assistance. He writes: 'I had to bear from certain of my brethren the almost infamous charge of having lent my aid in bringing about so great a sacrifice of human life'. The cardinals had grumbled behind his back (*submurmurant*) to that effect. He goes on to argue: 'How diligently I laboured for your advancement to royal rank'. This points to efforts made in 1066 rather than later, before William had become a king. This whole matter might have been well known elsewhere in Europe. A letter from Wenric, Bishop of Verdun and Trier, to Gregory, dated 1080, accuses the Pope of giving his support to Rudolf of Swabia (against the Emperor) and accuses Rudolf himself of perjury (rather like Harold), homicide and adultery; Wenric argues 'There are others who have usurped kingdoms by the violence of a tyrant, who themselves paved the road to the throne with blood, placed a blood-stained crown on their heads and with murder, rape, butchery and torment established their rule'. The parallel with the actions of Duke William is exact, and shows that his conquest of England did not meet with universal approval.[12]

Some have argued that there was no banner given to William in 1066, or that it was bestowed on him in 1070. The suggestion is that it was given in connection with the Penitential of the legate Ermenfrid, Bishop of Sitten, in return for the imposition of various penances on the Norman army for its sins during the Conquest, and that William had agreed to be re-crowned by the papal legates, as well as to depose Stigand. There is no direct evidence for a second coronation, as distinct from a crown-wearing attended by the legates, and a date of 1070 does not fit the context of Pope Gregory's letter. Nor is there any reason to reject the bestowal of a papal banner, as a means of extending the protection of St Peter to the Norman army and showing the support of the papacy for the 'enterprise of England'. The letter proves that Hildebrand advanced William's cause and the gift of a banner would have been a natural way of displaying papal approval. It had the effect of converting the Conquest into a sort of holy war against the sinful English king and his sinful people, a precursor of the idea of a crusade.

Pope Alexander II had good reason not to support King Harold and to hope for the removal of an uncanonical archbishop who was regarded as a schismatic, a pluralist and a simoniac. There was a developing policy of bestowing such banners on those whose activities the papacy wished to endorse. Benedict IX, as early as 1043, had sent to Emperor Henry III, as an endorsement of his campaign against the Hungarians, a *Vexillum ex beati Petri parte*. During the expedition of Pope Leo IX against the Normans in the Papal States in 1053, to defend the Church's territories against their savagery, he had fought under the banner of St Peter. This was part of a trend towards increasing use of force, a kind of papal militarism according to some, which included the sending of papal legates and the bestowal of papal approval for military action in support of the papacy. Robert Guiscard was given a banner by Nicholas II in 1059, and others had gone to the Patarine leader Erlembald of Milan and to Roger of Sicily in 1063. Even the leaders of the Barbastro campaign in Spain had received one in 1064, so the gift of a banner to Duke William was by no means a singular event. The trend eventually culminated in the launching of the First Crusade. It was associated with a warlike rhetoric which referred to supporters of the papacy as 'Militia of St. Peter'; the faithful were regarded as soldiers in the service of St Peter. The arrival of the Reform Party at Rome had been the turning point; they stood for the idea of holy war and sought to put it into practice.[13]

The bestowal of a banner on William remained a little ambiguous, and he rejected the idea that he had thereby become a papal vassal. The Normans used the gift to promote the idea that the Conquest of England had been a sort of holy war, visiting God's verdict on Harold. There is a little evidence in the Bayeux Tapestry to support the grant of a banner, as one banner shows a cross and four blobs that might be smaller crosses, which could represent the papal arms. However, it might only be the arms of Boulogne, as shown on the county's coins, unless Eustace, who later claimed to have carried the banner at Hastings, had adopted the device afterwards. Against that is the statement of the *Carmen de Hastinge Proelio* that the banner was carried by Thurstin fitzRolf. Perhaps the Pope gave more than a banner. Later sources assert that William also received a ring containing a relic of St Peter, variously said to be either a hair or a tooth. Wace (*Roman de Rou*) claims that Harold and the English were excommunicated, and a Papal Bull issued to do so. He says the Pope 'let the whole world know that they were excommunicate [*escumengié*]'. He also says there was a banner. Other sources also mention the banner and the ring. The evidence is late and the fact is not impossible, although earlier sources would surely have boasted of Harold's excommunication if it were true. They may only be elaborating upon the gift of the banner. The overall effect was to ensure that other rulers stood aside.[14]

Other sources add more clues about the Norman propaganda war. One source claims that God had chosen William and destined him to be king because Harold had expelled 'Edward's cousin Aelfgar [*sic*]', an error perhaps for 'Edgar', and a confusion with Tostig's expulsion. This source also accuses Harold of unjustly making use of the power and insignia of the kingdom. Others say that Harold had refused to marry William's daughter and that this had enraged the duke. The Normans were probably pulling out all the stops in an effort to discredit Harold and to ensure that no other power intervened to prevent the duke's invasion. But Harold had been unanimously accepted as king as soon as Edward was dead, and had a great deal of support. His 'men' had been recruited to – and from – royal offi-cialdom; they were high reeves, military commanders such as holds, and royal envoys like Archbishop Ealdred. Others were stallers like Eadnoth and Aethelstan Cild of Canterbury, and many were power-ful king's thegns. Harold could employ the services of Eadric the Steersman, who held Brandiston, Norfolk, and many other estates 'under King Edward, freely from Harold'. He was '*Rector Navis Regis Edwardi*', commanding the king's own ship, and a benefactor of St Benet's, Holme, where the abbot, Aelfwold, was also given a naval command by Harold. The abbot was persecuted by King William and took refuge in Denmark. The abbey probably provided the royal ship, as it was the co-ordinator of a shipsoke (a number of hundreds which collectively provided and provisioned a fighting ship).

So Harold had ascended the throne only to find, as the *Chronicle* says, that he 'met with little quiet so long as he was king'. This is evidence of the constant state of emergency he faced, rather than of internal dissension. William of Malmesbury, without giving a source for his statement, claimed that Harold was resented in some parts of the kingdom, perhaps basing that on the evidence in Domesday Book about Harold having been guilty of depriving churches, and some individuals, of land 'unjustly' or 'by force'. But these entries seem to concern the time when he was earl, not king. The question was whether Harold could survive the turbulent first year of his reign. Had Edward died earlier, before that fateful journey which ended in Normandy, nothing could have prevented a more peaceful succession. But Duke William chose to take Harold's succession as a personal insult, as well as a political challenge.[15]

Harold, according to Florence of Worcester's encomium, began well and started governing firmly, as he no doubt intended to go on. The administration of the kingdom continued as it had done hitherto. One writ survives, for Giso of Wells, granting him full control of his lands, issued in regular form and addressed to Abbot Aethelnoth of Glastonbury, Tofi the Sheriff and all the thegns of Somerset. No doubt there were others which, for obvious reasons, have not survived; they would have been of little value after Hastings, and it does look as though some were 'edited' by copyists, to claim issue by King Edward rather than King Harold. This might be the case with one issued for Abbot Brand of Peterborough. No charters have survived at all, but, again, some might lie behind a few attributed to Edward in a similar manner. Others could lie behind confirmations of landholding issued by King William early in the reign.

Writs and charters would have been sought from Harold to confirm changes in land ownership during his nine months in office. Churches, in particular, would have sought such confirmations. There would not have been a great number, as the reign was so short, but writs were certain to have been issued appointing abbots to Ely and Abingdon. Harold would have had his own seal (and the coronation scene in the Bayeux Tapestry might be based on its design, just as other scenes are based on pre-existing texts in the library of St Augustine's, Canterbury.) It also resembles the seal of King Edward. For Edward, ninety-nine genuine writs or charters survive for a reign of twenty-four years, representing an average of about four a year. But William could not afford to recognise Harold's reign, even if he had wanted to, and, after a brief period of indecision, William decided to date his reign from 'the day King Edward was alive and dead'.[16]

Further evidence of the continuity of Harold's administration is the remarkably profuse survival of coins from his reign. They were struck at some forty-five mints, from York in the north to Exeter in the south-west, and from Chester in the north-west to Romney in Kent. The regularity of their execution reveals that all moneyers were required to obtain their dies from London, proving the continuation of centralised control established by his predecessors. Proportionately, as many coins have survived from Harold's nine months as from the years of Harold I and Harthacnut. *Florence of Worcester*'s tribute insists that he 'began to abolish unjust laws and make good ones', which may reflect his source, now thought to be a no-longer-extant version of the *Chronicle*. He goes on to assert that he began 'to patronise churches and monasteries; to pay particular attention and yield reverence to bishops, abbots, monks and clergy; to show himself pious, humble and affable to all good men; but he treated malefactors with the utmost severity and gave general orders to his earls, ealdormen [*satrapes*], sheriffs, and thegns to imprison all thieves, robbers and disturbers of the kingdom; and he himself laboured by sea and by land for the protection of his country'. Eulogy it may be, but it reflects some of what is said of him in the *Vita Edwardi* and in the *Waltham Chronicle*.

His approach to lawbreakers might be reflected in the evidence in Domesday Book that he deprived five men of minor importance of their lands in Hampshire and Gloucestershire. He filled two vacant abbacies, appointing Thurstan of Witchford to Ely on 19 August and Ealdred to Abingdon on 22 January. It looks as though Waltheof was finally given an earldom in the East Midlands. According to Domesday Book, King Edward held Tostig's lands before they passed to Waltheof and, as an appointment between October 1065 and the king's death, 5/6 January 1066, looks unlikely, he was probably promoted by Harold. Waltheof was not listed as an earl in the charter witness lists, which seem to reflect the Christmas court. Maerleswein, a 'procer' or major nobleman from Lincolnshire, with estates also in the south-west of England, became sheriff in Lincolnshire and was appointed to administer northern England after the battle of Fulford, either replacing Morcar or, more likely, as his deputy, as Copsige had been to Tostig. He also became a staller. Otherwise, Harold retained the same personnel as King Edward: Regenbald, not yet termed chancellor, ran the developing chancery, and the stallers (Ansgar, Bondi, Eadnoth, fitzWimarc, Ralf and Aelfstan) continued in office. The Norman sources admit that he 'grew daily from strength to strength'.[17]

The only immediate cloud on the horizon was whether Harold would be accepted in the north, although the endorsement he had given for the installation of Morcar as earl, as demanded by the rebels, must have improved his standing in Northumbria and Yorkshire. Domesday Book shows a sizeable quantity of land held by Harold in Yorkshire, though it is not known exactly when he acquired it. If he held it prior to 1065, then he had a foothold in the area. It is also possible that the 'Eadgyth' holding lands in Yorkshire was Edith Swanneshals. To cement his hold on the province, Harold, accompanied by his supporter and mentor, Bishop Wulfstan of Worcester, who had ruled the York diocese under Ealdred, visited York, where the two rapidly won over the support of the northern thegns. Harold would have been able to assure them that Morcar, and his brother Edwin, who were present at court when Edward died and had attended the coronation, had endorsed his accession to the throne, and that there was no question of permitting the return of Tostig. He might also have repeated his confirmation of the Laws of Cnut. There could even have been a crown-wearing at York. All this was done early in the year and Harold was back in London for Easter on 16 April. Eight days after that came the appearance of Halley's Comet on 24 April.

The Bayeux Tapestry appears to telescope events here, showing Harold crowned and enthroned, holding a spear to indicate readiness for combat, at the moment he was informed that the comet had been seen, as if it were still Easter – the comet having appeared the day after the Octave of Easter. So royal business had been carried on as

usual, with feasting, worship, receptions, all intended to reinforce the
image of Harold as lord king. Some foreign powers had no doubt sent
acknowledgement of his accession, as they had done for the Confessor
in 1043. Gifts would have been given and accepted, petitions heard
and pledges given. The coins issued show an image of Harold as he
wished to be seen: not a realistic portrait but an icon based on classical models, in the mode of a Greek warrior with aquiline features
and a small beard. The linking of Harold's eventual fall to the comet's
appearance is, of course, hindsight. Had he been the victor at Hastings,
men would have seen the comet as foretelling the ruin and death of
Duke William. Norman sources alleged that Harold had 'seduced all
the English people away from obedience to the Duke', as if the English
owed him any such obedience anyway.[18]

All sources, Norman included, agree that Harold called out an
'innumerable army' to guard the coast, and William of Poitiers alleges
that (as is probable) he sent spies across the Channel. William no
doubt did the same, making use of the services of Abbot John of
Fécamp, whose abbey held lands in Sussex given by King Edward.
Harold is said to have confiscated them 'at the end of King Edward's
reign'. The abbey also held Rye. Poitiers has a nice little story of the
capture of one of Harold's spies, which allows him to put a boast
into Duke William's mouth, probably again derived from exchanges
between the two adversaries, that 'quicker than he thinks he will
know our designs and he shall have more certain knowledge of them
than he wants for he shall see me in person'. William is then said
to have sent the spy back to tell Harold that if he had not arrived
in England within a year 'then he might rest quiet the rest of his
days and fear no harm from me'. That is obviously written with
hindsight. It all shows William stirring up the spirits of his vassals to
win their support for his adventure, which some saw as far too risky
and beyond the resources of Normandy.

As for William's own preparations, these are well described in most
accounts of the year 1066 and need no repetition. The focus is on the
threats to England and Harold's response to them. Soon after April,
Tostig made his move, gathering supplies and men from his estates on
the Isle of Wight and arriving at Sandwich, where he recruited some

butsecarls and press-ganged others ('some willingly and some unwillingly'). There he was driven off by the approach of Harold's forces by both land and sea, so sailed northwards towards the Humber, raiding coastal towns in East Anglia. He met up with seventeen ships from the Orkneys, recruited for him by Copsige, before meeting with Harald Hardrada at Thanet, raiding up the river Burnham in Norfolk. Geoffrey Gaimar (*L'Estorie des Engles*) claims that Tostig raided two unidentifiable places: 'Wardstane' (Waldestane?) and 'Brunemue' (possibly Burnham on Crouch?). Tostig is reported to have visited Duke William earlier in the year and received verbal encouragement from him. It was certainly in the duke's interest to have Tostig keep Harold's men in a state of constant alarm, simply for its nuisance value. The earl is alleged to have visited Swein of Denmark, who refused to help because his resources were still exhausted after the long war with Hardrada. He preferred to keep a watching brief on the situation, but is said to have offered Tostig a position in his own service, which was rejected.[19]

Arriving off the Humber, Tostig ravaged Lindsey 'and slew many good men', but Edwin and Morcar came up with the army of Mercia and drove him out so successfully that a large proportion of his forces, which had totalled sixty ships, deserted him and returned either to Sandwich or to Flanders. Gaimar says that it was the Flemings who deserted. Tostig now fled to Scotland with only twelve ships, his original mercenary force, perhaps, plus his own retainers. There he was received by his 'brother' King Malcolm and permitted to recuperate for most of the summer. At this point, the Scandinavian sources become useful. *Harald's Saga* alleges that Tostig had recruited in Flanders, Frisia and Denmark. King Harold was meanwhile gathering together as large a fleet and army as possible, which took him some considerable time. It could not be done rapidly. The royal fleet itself had been virtually decommissioned by King Edward and had to be built up by commandeering ships along the south coast. The fyrd from the shires was called up, probably in relays of periods of service of two months, the first from mid-April to mid-July and then another from mid-July to mid-September. Meanwhile, Tostig linked up with Harald Hardrada.

Harald's Saga says Tostig actually visited Harald in Oslo Fiord and persuaded him to assert his right to the throne of England, and that he raised an army throughout Norway. Only his marshal, Ulf, refused. This is said to have happened before Tostig returned to Flanders to recruit men from England and Flanders. Harald assembled his men at the Solund Isles, near Trondheim, where he opened the tomb of St Olaf and trimmed the saint's hair and nails, locking the shrine afterwards and throwing the key into the river Nid. This signified that he did not intend to return. There were omens of disaster. One man dreamed of an ogress who expected Harald's venture to 'fill England's graveyards', and another of an ogress riding a wolf, carrying a dead body in its jaws. She too prophesied doom for Harald. He himself dreamt that St Olaf predicted that 'death at last awaits you'. From there, Harald sailed for the Shetlands and then Orkney, where Paul and Erlend, sons of Thorfinn the Mighty (who had ruled the Orkneys and Shetlands, the Hebrides and north-west Scotland for fifty years), joined him. He then went to Scotland and joined his forces with those of Tostig.[20]

As a result of all this, King Harold Godwinsson was unable to relax his vigil, and the system for raising an army and keeping it in the field came under great strain. He stationed his fleet at the Isle of Wight, from where it could be despatched to counter any Norman move, and placed the fyrd on guard all along the coast, expecting the attack to come from France rather than from the north. The *Chronicle* laments, however, that 'in the end it was all to no purpose'. Some writers have criticised Harold's tactics, and his failure to maintain provisions for his men in the manner attributed to Duke William. It should be remembered that accounts of William's actions were written in the afterglow of success. They were right because he won. But what more could Harold have done? The country had been at peace for most of King Edward's reign; that is why he ceased to collect heregeld, the levy to support a standing army, and disbanded the fleet. Harold had only a matter of months to put the country back onto a war footing, whereas Normandy under the duke was permanently ready for war. Edward had permitted no preparations, part of his fatalistic attitude that God would provide. The system of burhs or fortified towns, begun under Alfred the Great and completed under Edmund and Aethelfleda, had long since been allowed to decay. If it had continued in being in Aethelrede's time, perhaps Cnut would have had a harder time of it. In the event, after Hastings, only London and Exeter seem to have made any sort of resistance. Harold was driven to rely upon the fleet to deter an invasion, and the weather in the Channel played its part there. The fyrd was there to repel any landings. Harold was unable to co-ordinate defence sufficiently to prevent a landing in the far north, though Edwin and Morcar had repelled Tostig and were to do their best against Hardrada. That led, inevitably, to Harold's absence from the south coast when William made his move, at the very end of what was normally regarded as the campaigning season, and when bad weather in the Channel might be expected to deter a seaborne attack. Had William left it much later, the autumn storms might well have destroyed him.[21]

As it was, by 8 September the provisions for the fyrd had been exhausted, men were needed at home to bring in the harvest, and in all likelihood their periods of service had been used up. Harold had to stand down both the fyrd and the fleet. He had been with the fleet while Tostig was off the Isle of Wight, and his approach had then driven Tostig away from Sandwich. Harold now, in early September, allowed the fleet to move to London to refit. As the Peterborough version of the *Chronicle* says, he had certainly 'sailed out against William with a naval force'. His move to the Isle of Wight had been part of that move, aimed at deterring William rather than Tostig, which may explain why there was no pursuit. William was seen as the much greater threat, and Harold, through his spies, would have been aware of the preparations being made. At some time during September, the duke moved his invasion fleet, which was in various harbours around the mouths of the Seine and the Dives, out to sea, where it certainly encountered bad weather, intending to use the harbour of St Valery. The duke had been waiting for a south wind and was himself beginning to run short of supplies. Having possibly deliberately waited throughout August, intending to exhaust Harold's patience and provisions, he was now compelled to make a move as he had intended, to St Valery. The west wind, a gale, caused a great loss of

men, supplies and ships, and there were even some deserters. William
of Poitiers' account lacks dates, as does that of William of Jumièges,
so the exact time is vague. The only certain dates are 8 September,
when Harold made his move, the date of the battle of Fulford on
20 September, followed by Stamford Bridge five days later; then
William left Normandy on 28 September. It looks as though William,
aware of conditions in England and that the fyrd was being stood
down, had ordered the move to St Valery. Received opinion is that
he moved the fleet around 12 September, only to encounter fierce
storms and lose large numbers of men; but dates are not exact for
the movements of either fleet, and it could have been the same
storm which damaged both. It is therefore not impossible that the
two fleets, scattered by the storm, encountered each other. There are
several references in the sources to an actual naval battle between
the two fleets. Henry of Huntingdon says that Harold 'with a naval
force (*navali exercitu*) went forward at sea against Duke William'. This
denotes more than merely keeping watch at sea. Domesday Book
records that the thegn Aethelric, of Kelvedon Hatch, Essex, 'went
away to a naval battle against King William and when he returned
fell ill', leaving his land to St Peter's, Westminster.[22]

There are two curious anecdotes. From Neider-Altach on the
Danube, the scribe relates that there was naval warfare between the
Aquitanians and the English in the year of the comet: 'That summer
the Aquitanians fought a naval battle with the Anglo-Saxons and,
having defeated them, subjected them to their rule'. In the *Gesta
Herewardi*, one of Hereward's supporters, Brumann, is said to have
been responsible for the sinking of a Norman vessel and its cargo of
Norman clerics. Although mentioned in a post-Conquest context,
the Brumann incident has been inserted into the text from another
source; it interrupts the flow of the narrative and need not come from
the same moment in time. Lastly, there is the tradition in William of
Malmesbury that in his day wrecked ships could be seen in the river
near Rouen. These might have been the wrecks from Duke Robert
the Magnificent's time (as related by William of Jumièges), from an
attempt by the duke to assemble a fleet to put Edward on the throne
of England after Cnut had refused to restore him to power. This was

assembled at Fécamp and wrecked at Mont St Michel, which hardly
fits the idea of wrecks at the mouth of the Seine. A better explanation
would be that the westerly gales had blown Norman ships into the
estuary and that the wrecks could still be seen there in the twelfth
century. William of Poitiers magnifies the size of the English fleet,
saying that Harold sent a fleet of 700 ships to cut off any chance of
a Norman retreat from Hastings. The *Carmen de Hastinge Proelio* also
says that the duke 'prepared for a battle by land and sea' and that he
sent 500 keels (*quingentas carinas*) to sea to prepare for the Norman
return journey – evidence of an expectation on William's part of
naval action by the English. At St Valery, William still had to await a
favourable wind. That which was blowing allowed Harald Hardrada
to descend on the north of England. The duke ordered prayers to
St Valery and shortly afterwards the wind changed, so he ordered a
rapid overnight launch on 28 September, landing at Pevensey the
following day. He had to anchor and wait in mid-Channel for his
fleet to catch up with him before he could land. There need not
have been an actual planned battle, but the two fleets could well have
encountered each other during the storm, and both sides suffered
casualties. The effect was to delay William's invasion until after the
battle of Stamford Bridge, and to allow Harold to take forces north
to confront the Norwegians, thinking that the campaigning season
was over and that William might not come that autumn.[23]

12

All Roads Lead to
Hastings

The year 1066 tested the Old English military system to destruction. Yet the English were able, nonetheless, to produce four armies in the space of less than three months and fight three battles, although, as the *Anglo-Saxon Chronicle* remarks, 'in the end it was of no profit'.[1]

Harold Godwinson, King Harold II of England, had raised an army to defend and stand guard along the south coast throughout the summer, in vain. Duke William simply chose not to come when expected. Perhaps if the English fleet had still been at sea when he came all would have been different, but the autumn gales in the Channel did not permit a decisive naval battle to take place, and Duke William's initial move from the mouth of the Seine to St Valery was not the disaster it might have been. Although his fleet suffered losses, some of which could have been due to a brush with units of the English fleet, the most damage was inflicted by the storms. The English fleet was driven, in parlous condition, to take refuge in London, while the Normans took refuge in and around St Valery.

The case might be that the conflicting reports about the size of the
Norman fleet are due to the losses sustained on the voyage. But the
duke was still able to await a suitable wind and make his decisive
sea-crossing at the moment of his own choosing.[2]

Earlier in the year, Earl Tostig had caused alarm along the East
Anglian coast and on into the Humber estuary, but his attempt to
effect a landing in force in Lindsey was a disaster for him. Edwin,
Earl of Mercia, and his brother, Earl Morcar of Northumbria, were
more than a match for Tostig and the forces he had at his disposal,
and drove him out. Not only that: the mercenaries he had hired
proved unreliable and deserted him, and so, most probably, did the
butsecarles he had press-ganged into joining him from the south
coast ports. It might just be that the earls had thwarted a plan for
Tostig to draw King Harold into defence of the south coast and then
to decoy the earls into Lincolnshire while Harald Hardrada came
in from the north. If that was the intention, it failed. Having taken
refuge in Scotland at the court of King Malcolm, Tostig joined forces
with the Norwegian king, and their joint forces descended on the
north-east of England. Emboldened by their initial success against
Tostig, the earls Edwin and Morcar took the field again but found,
probably to their horror, that they were opposed by Hardrada, not
Tostig. It must be counted to their credit that they did not shirk
the challenge, though they might have been wiser to wait for King
Harold to join them. They concentrated their forces at Gate Fulford,
then near but not in York – possibly because Morcar himself had
an estate there and knew the area. It is noteworthy that no attempt
was made to defend York itself, which may indicate that its defences
were unsound and it could not withstand a siege or assault. This was
to be demonstrated at least twice by its failure to withstand attack
by the Norman king.[3]

What little is known of this battle comes mainly from *Harald's
Saga*, though the account appears to confuse the fighting at Fulford
with events which occurred during the northern rebellion against
King William, notably by assigning a prominent role to Earl Waltheof
Siwardsson and omitting Earl Edwin. Despite the kind of errors to
which saga material is prone, based as it is on oral tradition and the

poems of the Scandinavian court poets (the skalds), *Harald's Saga* provides a succinct and credible account. As well as having Earl Waltheof fight alongside Earl Morcar, the *Saga* also believed that Earl Morcar was killed in the battle. Perhaps Morcar was sorely wounded and carried from the field, leaving the Norwegians with the impression that he had perished. That, as well as the extent of the defeat, would explain the absence of Edwin and Morcar from Hastings.[4]

But the basic facts do seem to have been preserved in the poetry of Stein Hardison and in poems attributed to Harald Hardrada himself. According to the *Saga*, Morcar and his brother earl had a 'huge army' at York and moved down the river Ouse to confront King Harald. He had landed at Riccall, some fifteen miles south of York, just below the junction of the Ouse and the Wharfe, and was advancing northwards towards York, probably along the line of what is now the A19 road. The Norwegians had successfully bottled up a portion of the Mercian fleet. Perhaps the earls had hoped to cut Hardrada off from his ships, but he had been too canny. The presence of the earls at York and a fleet on the Wharfe suggests that they had been sent by King Harold to deal with any further raids by Earl Tostig and to deter landings by any other hopeful pretenders to the throne. If so, King Harald had moved further towards York than had been expected.[5]

The English sources say little about the battle which followed, other than that there was great slaughter in which 'many of the English were slain, drowned or put to flight and the Northmen had possession of the place of slaughter' and that it took place on 20 September, a Wednesday. The *Chronicle* also implies that King Harold had learned of the arrival of the Norwegians and was already on his way north, but that the battle of Gate Fulford came before he could join the earls. However, *Harald's Saga* locates the actual site of the battleground. It lay between the river Ouse and a great dyke surrounded by 'a deep and wide swamp' (and 'Fulford' means dirty or foul ford). Either King Harald or the earls had chosen to fight there, because it was a confined space which might restrict the manoeuvres of the enemy. Hardrada drew up his army, with his right flank protected by the river and the other weaker flank by the dyke. The earls advanced downriver 'in close formation', no doubt having formed the Old English version of the phalanx or testudo, called the shield wall. Harald Hardrada had put his best men in the centre and on the right.[6]

The earls threw their weight against what seemed the weaker wing, which gave way before them, possibly just as King Harald had planned. The English, led by Earl Morcar, pursued the retreating Norwegians, thinking that the enemy was in flight. It would appear from this that the Normans were not the only warriors to make use of the tactic of a feigned flight. King Harald allowed the English van to draw level with his own position and immediately signalled the attack, probably by means of trumpets, and, leading a powerful counter-charge and accompanied by his famous banner 'Landwaster', outflanked the earls, delivering an assault too fierce to be resisted. The English left flank gave way, plunging their army into confusion and breaking up the shield wall, and a great number were killed. The English army broke up before the onslaught and fled, some up river towards York and others down, but the majority were driven over the dyke and into the swamp where 'the dead piled up so quickly that the Norwegians could cross the swamp dry-shod'.[7]

Stein Hardison's poetry paints a graphic picture of the scene:

> Many were the men lost in the water;
> Drowned men sank to the bottom.
> Warriors lay thickly fallen
> Around the young Earl Morcar.
> Harald's son, young Olaf,
> Pursued the fleeing Englishmen,
> Running before King Harald.
> Praise the brave Prince, Olaf.

Another poem, attributed to King Harald himself, contains the belief that Earl Waltheof fought at Fulford. He might possibly have been present with his household troops, but there is no corroboration. Harald's poem reads:

Earl Waltheof's men
They all lay fallen
In the swampy water,
Gashed by weapons.
And the hardy men of Norway
Could cross the marsh
on a causeway of corpses.[8]

The English then fled towards York, where there was further slaughter, and the citizens discreetly surrendered. The Earls Edwin and
Morcar escaped and retired to nurse their wounds. They had been
so thoroughly defeated that they were unable to take any further
part in the war, unable even to raise further levies of men to support
King Harold. The remnant of the Norwegian army which survived
the next battle at Stamford Bridge left England apparently unaware
that Morcar had survived. The brother earls are not heard of again
until after Hastings, when, in London, they at first took part in the
resistance and then capitulated to Duke William. Perhaps Fulford had
shattered their confidence as well as their army.[9]

The sagas are often criticised for their errors, especially concerning family relationships, and this is seen as grounds for rejecting
what they have to say. But they are not the only sources to contain such errors, and while the sagas are rejected other writers are
accepted, despite their errors. Orderic Vitalis makes errors of fact
and identification and so do the various versions of the *Anglo-Saxon
Chronicle*. The Worcester text (D) identifies the Norwegian king as
Harald Fairhair (Harfagr), who had been king in Norway 100 years
earlier, and the Abingdon text (C) wrongly identifies Harald's son
as 'Hetmund' (Edmund), not Olaf. But the *Saga* and the chronicles
are otherwise in substantial agreement and supplement each other.
They agree about the battle of Fulford, and the *Saga* explains why
so many Englishmen drowned, and goes on to confirm that King
Harold caught the Norwegians unawares while awaiting the deliv-
ery of the hostages. These sources agree about the number of King
Harald's ships, and also that the English destroyed the bulk of the
Norwegian army, except for those left to guard their ships at Riccall.

Finally, they agree that King Harold achieved his victory with the forces he brought with him by a lightning march from London, and the *Saga* shows how and why he was able to do it. The Norwegian forces were divided and incompletely armed.[10]

Snorri Sturluson, of whose great work, the *Heimskringla, Harald's Saga* forms a significant part, explains why the sagas are better evidence than some historians are prepared to admit (while accepting evidence from Norman writers, whose work is riddled with fabricated accounts and fantastic stories). He rests his work, he says:

> ...principally upon the songs which were sung in the presence of the chiefs themselves or their sons, and take all that to be true that is found in such poems about their feats and battles.

They should be accepted as true, he argues, because the skalds would not have dared

> ...to relate to a chief what he and all those who heard it, knew to be false and imaginary, not a true account of his deeds, would be mockery not praise.

So, although the *Saga* might not be entirely accurate about English affairs, it does give the traditional account of the battles of Fulford and Stamford Bridge, in the form in which the information was taken back to Scandinavia by the survivors. As yet another battle (also involving Scandinavians, or at least Anglo-Scandinavians, if William of Poitiers is to be believed) took place within a matter of days, it is not surprising that accounts of that battle, Hastings, became confused with Stamford Bridge, which had also involved a King called Harold. What, then, happened at Stamford Bridge?[11]

The Norwegians withdrew after Fulford to Stamford Bridge, some seven miles east of York, to await the surrender of hostages from York. They also apparently sent much of their war gear to Riccall, as they expected no further resistance. The Stamford Bridge site might well have been chosen because it was a well-known landmark. It lies where several Roman roads met as they crossed the Derwent, notably one which is now the A166, and also an ancient track from York to Beverley called 'Minster Way'. Stamford Bridge also marks the point where three wapentakes met, Picklington, Acklam and Bulmer, at the boundary between the East and North Ridings of Yorkshire. It is now known as Battle Flats. The bridge would have been quite large by eleventh-century standards. Fighting took place on both sides of the river, as the *Anglo-Saxon Chronicle* and Henry of Huntingdon both testify. It would appear that King Harold first dealt with those Norwegians he caught in the open on the west bank, and then had to get his men across the bridge in order to deal with the main body of King Harald's men, on the east bank.[12]

The exact timing of Harold's rapid march from London cannot be established. He had disbanded the fyrd and moved his fleet to London around 8 September; he then arrived at Tadcaster near York (seven miles south-west) on Sunday 24 September. Harald Hardrada had arrived on the Tyne shortly after the return of the English fleet to London, and had then moved down the coast and sailed up the Ouse to Riccall, intending to occupy York, former capital of a Viking king-dom. Gate Fulford was then fought on 20 September. King Harold had already left London when that battle took place, riding day and night, according to the *Chronicle*. Most historians seem agreed that his army was composed of mounted infantry, mainly house-carls, king's thegns (and their men) from the royal household, and Harold's own retainers as earl of Wessex, together with the retainers of Gyrth, his brother, earl of East Anglia. Other mounted levies were recruited from shires along the way, through which the king passed. Old English infantry rode to battle and then fought on foot.

There is no real reason to assume that Harold was in any way delayed or hampered by having to wait for foot soldiers to march to battle. Such mounted infantry could manage twenty-five miles a day. They were also expected to have at least two horses, riding one and allowing the other to proceed unburdened. Harold no doubt could also expect, as king, to commandeer fresh horses along the way. If he did literally ride day and night he could have made Tadcaster in four days, although that would mean without sleep. A more likely calculation, allowing men and horses to rest by night, would be eight

days, leaving London round about 16 September. He therefore had
from 8 September to 16 September to recover from the rough sea
passage from the south coast to London, be informed of Hardrada's
arrival, and send out messengers to summon men from surrounding
shires within two or three days' ride of London. To move an army
200 miles in something like eight days, and then fight a battle on
the ninth day, was a tremendous military feat.[13]

The earlier Harold heard of Hardrada's coming, the earlier he
could have left London, but the only certain fact is his arrival at
Tadcaster on 24 September. Having set his men in battle array, Harold
proceeded through York early the following day, learning there of
the Norwegian presence at Stamford Bridge, seven miles to the east,
and knowing that he was not expected. He quite possibly knew the
area himself, since he had an estate at Catton nearby, less than a mile
to the south. 'Then came Harold, King of the English, against them
unawares beyond the bridge; and they met and till far on in the day
they fought very sternly', as the *Abingdon Chronicle* states. As a result,
as the English sources report, Harald Sigurdsson and Earl Tostig were
killed, and 'a mighty host with them, both of Northmen and English'.
From an addition to the Abingdon text made possibly as late as the
twelfth century (it is in a different hand and uses later English than
the main text), it becomes plain that Harold had to dispose of the
Norwegians caught in the open on the west bank, then force a
crossing of the bridge to confront the main body commanded by
Hardrada on the east. The text describes how a lone Norwegian held
off the English army, like Horatius at Rome, until he was slain by an
Englishman, who speared him from below, having gone under the
bridge, possibly in a small boat. Then Harold 'came over the bridge
and his army with him'. The incident may be an apochryphal tale,
but it is not impossible and might, like some of the other stories from
this battle, have an element of truth in it. After the breaking up of
the Norwegian battle line, and the deaths of Hardrada and Tostig,
the enemy fled. Many were pursued as far as their ships at Riccall,
where Harold accepted the surrender of Prince Olaf, then allowed
the remnant to return to Norway in only twenty-four ships. Earl
Tostig's body (recognised, it is said, by a wart between his shoulder

blades) was taken to York and buried in the Minster, while Hardrada's was permitted to be returned to Norway. In victory, Harold proved magnanimous.[14]

The Worcester text adds that the Norwegians were pursued all the way back to their ships and that 'some were drowned, some were burned; so many ways destroyed that few were left'. A runestone found in 1897, and now in Slesvig Cathedral, bears an inscription to the memory of Halfdan, son of Sulki, who died in the battle: 'He rests in England at Skia' (that is, Skidby near Stamford Bridge). Hardrada's fleet had been immense, particularly when it is considered that Cnut's standing fleet amounted to sixteen ships and Harthacnut's to thirty-two. How Harold had achieved such a devastating victory over what must have been a formidably large army is explained in *Harald's Saga*. It reveals that the Norwegian army was not at full strength but divided into two portions, because part of the force had been left at Riccall to guard the ships. Furthermore, those at Stamford Bridge had left much of their war gear, especially their mail coats (though the king apparently had his hauberk, 'Emma'), behind at the ships, possibly because no further resistance was expected after the slaughter at Fulford and Harald was only expecting a deputation from York to hand over the hostages he had demanded. Certainly, they were surprised to see an approaching army.[15]

The skalds from whose work the account of the battle was drawn dramatise events in the customary manner. They provide accounts of the kind of things King Harald and Earl Tostig might have said on seeing the approaching dust cloud which marked the arrival of the English. They wonder whether this is the deputation from York, accompanied by further supporters of Earl Tostig, and then, as the army draws nearer, they realise that it is an enemy upon whose shields and armour the sun sparkles as from a 'field of ice'. King Harold is described as acting as his own herald and as granting Tostig a chance to avoid bloodshed, offering to restore him to his earldom with rule over a third of the kingdom – an offer which the earl proudly rejects, demanding to know what King Harald would be given. The famous reply came: 'Seven feet of earth or as much more as he is taller than other men'. Harald Sigurdsson grumbles that if he had known it was the English king 'this Harold would not have lived to tell the deaths of our men'. Tostig placates him, saying that he could not risk becoming his brother's murderer.[16]

That a very brief parley took place before the battle is possible but unlikely. The English accounts describe an immediate assault on those caught on the west bank of the Derwent. Possibly there were exchanges across the river, after the first phase ended and before the bridge was forced. Harold might well have endeavoured to persuade Tostig to end the slaughter while there was yet time, but if so he acted in vain. Far more likely is the idea that the skalds were attempting to illustrate the characters of the protagonists. So, just as Duke William of Normandy is said to have tripped and fallen as he disembarked in England, which was seen as an evil omen, and turned it to his advantage, saying 'Thus claim I England for myself', so Harald Hardrada is said to have fallen over the neck of his horse and turned that about by saying 'A fall is fortune on the way', while King Harold, seeing it, said 'Let us hope his good luck has now run out'. What does ring true is Harald's comment about the English king: 'What a little man that was; but he stood proudly in his stirrups!' As Harald Sigurdsson is reputed to have been well over six feet tall (five ells or seven feet six inches, according to the *Saga*), everyone was 'little' to him.[17]

Whatever the truth or falsity of the pre-battle exchanges, the Norwegians had been caught in the open on the wrong side of the bridge and had to make a fighting withdrawal. King Harald is said to have formed his shield wall with wings bent so far back as to form a circle. He is credited with reciting a poem about his predicament:

> Without our hauberks do we go in array
> To receive blows from the brown blades.
> Helmets shine. I have not my hauberk,
> Our gear is down by the ships.

Dissatisfied with this, he then recited another, in which he boasted that Norwegians never skulked low behind their shields in the storm of battle but relied on their courage and their skill of hand and eye to make up for any lack of ring-mail, helmet or shield.[18]

In this way, the skalds, by putting words into King Harald's mouth, painted a picture of the battle which would not easily be forgotten and which conveyed King Harald's fearlessness. The account which followed had been much affected by reports of the battle of Hastings which came so soon afterwards, and many of the details can better be applied to accounts of that later battle. The one thing which stands out as possible is the claim that the English attacked the Norwegians on horseback. That they made cavalry charges as such is unacceptable, but it is possible that, because the Norwegians were caught in the open on a plain without full armour and had to assume a defensive posture, some Englishmen, arriving pell-mell at the scene, rode straight in and threw spears, or slashed at the shield wall as it was forming. The *Saga* says that the fighting was 'loose and light as long as the Northmen kept their order of battle', but that once the shield wall was broken the Norwegians found themselves attacked on all sides.[19]

Even if the heroic defence of the bridge is discounted as mythical, it is still likely that there was stubborn fighting as the Norwegians retreated across the bridge, and that they reformed the shield wall on the eastern bank. It is not certain whether King Harald died before or after the crossing of the bridge, but it is said that he fell into a 'fury of battle', rushing forward ahead of his men and fighting two-handed, so fiercely that none could withstand him; the English were almost routed. At that point he was struck in the throat by an arrow, and that was his death wound. All those who had advanced with him were slain, except a small party which escaped bearing 'Landwaster'. That might well be the time when the retreat across the bridge was made, since there was a long lull in the fighting while both sides reformed their line of battle and Earl Tostig assumed command of the Norwegian army. King Harold used the lull to offer Tostig a chance to surrender, but the Norwegians refused, as they would rather die than accept quarter from the English. The 'war-shout' went up and battle resumed. King Harald's men made ready to die around their king's body in a 'corpse-ring'.[20]

At that point, Eystein Orri, Harald's prospective son-in-law, arrived from Riccall with reinforcements, having run all the way, a distance of over twenty miles. Although his men were exhausted, Eystein Orri took up 'Landwaster' and led a last desperate charge. His men fell into battle fury, as the famed berserkers (*berserkir* or 'bear shirts') were said to do, and threw off their mail-coats, fighting as long as they could stand on their feet. Some dropped dead from exhaustion, dying unwounded, and almost all of the leading Norwegians were slain. At some time during all this, Earl Tostig also was killed, though not necessarily by King Harold himself, as some sources alleged. The Norwegian army broke into disorderly retreat and many were pursued by Englishmen, some no doubt on horseback, all the way back to Riccall, where King Harold gave quarter to the survivors led by Prince Olaf and Paul of Orkney, allowing them to return to Norway. Other survivors were Harald's son Magnus, and Tostig's sons Skuli and Ketil.[21]

Archaeology confirms the location of these two battles. Mass graves from the eleventh century have been discovered both at Fulford and Riccall, where some sixty skeletons which show typical battle scars – slashed arm bones and spear thrusts – have been uncovered in the last 150 years. In the 1950s, thirty-nine individuals were found at Riccall, and another six in the 1980s. Archaeologists estimate the total buried there would have been in the region of 500 or 600.[22]

Henry of Huntingdon believed that the battle was fought on both sides of the river; he describes two stages, separated by the crossing of the bridge. Geoffrey Gaimar calls the location the *Punt de la bataille*, or 'the battle bridge', and he is echoed by the *Battle Chronicle*, which refers to it as *Pons Belli*. It is Gaimar who says that the booty from the battle, mainly ships and war gear, was left in the care of Archbishop Ealdred of York. That proved to be an unfortunate, if unavoidable, mistake by King Harold, as some men were dismayed that he did not share out the spoils and therefore deserted him, although it is doubtful that the number who did so affected the outcome of Hastings. Having rested for two days at York, Harold set off back to London and, either before he left or while he was on the way, news came of Duke William's arrival in Kent. The king apparently left the Lincolnshire magnate Maerleswein (who had much land also in the south-west of England, in Harold's earldom) to administer

Northumbria (another indication that Earl Morcar might have been out of action at the time), probably as assistant to the earl, rather as Copsige had been to Earl Tostig. [23]

Harold's route going north, as well as that for his return, would have been along the line of the Great North Road (Ermine Street, the Roman road), and it has been suggested that the list of shires contributing men to the battles at Stamford Bridge and Hastings is reflected in the list given by Wace (*Roman de Rou*). For the northward route his list runs: London and Kent; Hertford; Essex; Surrey and Sussex; St Edmunds and Suffolk; Norwich and Norfolk; Canterbury (*sic*) and Stamford; Bedford; Huntingdon; Northampton; York. Canterbury is out of place, but may be an error for Cambridge ('Cantwarabyrig' and 'Cantabrigiensis'). Then, on the return, Harold would have received or called for men as follows: Buckingham; Nottingham; Lindsey and Lincoln; Salisbury; Bath and Somerset; Gloucester; Worcester; Winchester and Hampshire; Berkshire.

Stamford Bridge had been a tremendous victory. It marked the end of the Viking era and has been called 'one of the most complete victories of the Middle Ages'. Harold had proved to be a notable commander and had defeated the Norwegians 'under one of the most renowned warriors of the age'. Had the battle been fought a little earlier, before Duke William left Normandy, the news of the decisive defeat of Harald Hardrada might well have deterred the Normans from setting out. The sources confirm that many barons thought the venture too risky. But once in England William was committed to battle, as the story of his rejection of a warning from Robert fitzWimarc reveals. The last word can be left to the author of the *Vita Edwardi*, who writes 'and who will write that Humber, vast and swollen with raging seas, where namesake Kings had fought, has dyed the ocean wave for miles around with Viking gore'. [24]

Harold now, in the view taken by most historians, decided to attempt to repeat his success at Stamford Bridge against William of Normandy: that is, to take him by surprise and annihilate him. If so, then he had mistaken his man, and William proved to be a much tougher proposition. The Norman duke did not repeat Hardrada's mistake of forgetting he was in hostile country, and he never relaxed his vigilance. Instead, he began a campaign of ravaging in Kent and Sussex, part of Harold's earldom, and sent out screens of foragers and scouts to guard against being taken by surprise, hoping to provoke Harold into what he believed might prove a premature conflict. Harold, for his part, returned with all speed to London, repeating the tactic of a rapid march carried out while summoning yet another army with which to face this new threat. In London, he remained four or five days, during which time messengers on horseback would have been sent out to shires within two or three days' march. The *Waltham Chronicle* claimed that Harold thought he would be attacking a weak and unprepared force of Normans, before they were reinforced from Normandy, but this proved false because 'the power of God was not with him.'[25]

Norman sources paint a picture of dissension within Harold's family. They allege that Gyrth urged Harold to allow him to lead the army against the duke because he was not burdened with any obligation to Duke William, and could wage war with a clear conscience, as he would not be breaking his word. He is also said to have argued that in the event of his losing the battle, Harold would still be in a position to continue the struggle. Harold's mother, Gytha, is represented as pleading with him also, and Harold as spurning her, even kicking her. This all looks quite out of character for Harold, and allows the chroniclers to blacken his reputation, insisting again on their depiction of him as a perjurer.[26]

On his way to London, Harold is said to have visited the Holy Cross at Waltham to pray for victory. In the light of his knowledge that Harold was defeated, the Waltham chronicler relates that the figure on the cross bowed its head in sorrow, an omen of defeat, despite Harold's promises to endow the church further and serve it in future 'like a purchased slave'. Harold himself is said to have dreamed of victory before Stamford Bridge, and Abbot Aelfwin of Ramsey is said to have seen a vision, in a dream, of King Edward promising victory against the Norwegians, but sources then comment that, because of his pride, God denied Harold victory over the Normans.[27]

Having completed his arrangements and allowed those men who had accompanied him down from the north to recover, Harold then made a sixty-mile forced march towards Hastings, hoping to find William as unprepared for his arrival as Hardrada had been. Perhaps he did not count on the efforts of those sympathetic to the duke. It might well be that the duke was alerted to Harold's arrival in London and told when to expect him. There were the former Norman and French courtiers who had served King Edward, and there were the monks at Steyning on the Sussex coast, the men of Abbot John of Fécamp, any of whom could have communicated with the duke; certainly Robert fitzWimarc did so. He is reported to have sent a messenger warning the duke that Harold had just defeated the Norwegian king, killing both him and Earl Tostig, and that he was headed towards the duke 'at the head of innumerable troops all well equipped for war', which was 'a vast host... gathered together... from all the provinces of the English'. He suggested that the duke should avoid battle and retreat behind entrenchments, presumably at the castle in Hastings. (Despite the language in which the warning was given, by no means complimentary to the Normans, Robert fitz-Wimarc benefited after the Conquest, becoming sheriff of Essex.) Immediately after this, according to William of Poitiers, Harold was said to have sent a monk to order William to leave the country. This allows the chronicler to repeat the arguments in favour of the duke's claims, and to attempt a rebuttal of Harold's argument, based on the deathbed grant by King Edward. He is probably making use of information derived from exchanges between the two protagonists earlier in the year. If Harold had intended to try to catch William unawares, he would hardly have given him warning of his approach in this manner.[28]

In fact, Harold set off as soon as his arrangements permitted, setting out to meet his men at the rallying point, identified as 'the hoary apple tree': probably a landmark well known in the area, perhaps marking a point where several hundreds met, and known to Harold, who held estates at Whatlington and Crowhurst, which lie north and south of the battlefield itself. Scouts would have reported on Duke William's movements and Harold would have been well aware of the ravaging carried out by the Normans. William of Poitiers states that 'the king was the more furious because he had heard that the

Normans had laid waste the neighbourhood of their camp'. He adds that Harold intended to catch the duke unawares by means of a night attack, and William of Jumièges actually thought that Harold and his men rode all night and then appeared on the battlefield at dawn. In fact, the English arrived on the evening of 13 October and took up their position after a night's rest. William of Malmesbury's story contrasting the behaviour of the two armies – the Normans spending the night in prayer while the English spent their time drinking heavily – is inherently improbable; both sides would have taken what sleep they could. The wasting of the area is confirmed in Domesday Book; of each of Harold's estates it says bluntly 'It was wasted', and it records a fall in the value of the estate at Crowhurst from £8 a year to £5.[29]

That Harold sent a fleet of 700 ships to blockade the Norman ships is gross exaggeration, though seventy is possible. But this might have been introduced to allow the Norman writer to report William, in his pre-battle address to his men, urging them to fight that much harder because their retreat was cut off. William of Jumièges says that the Normans were ordered to stand by until dawn, in case of a night attack, which means only that relays of sentries would have been posted. The duke, pictured as the champion of a righteous cause, is decribed as attending Mass and receiving Holy Communion, and hanging around his neck the relics upon which Harold was said to have sworn his oath. It is stressed that the duke was attended by two bishops, his half-brother, Odo of Bayeux, and his adviser, Geoffrey of Coutances, and many other secular and regular clergy. That is said to have led some of Harold's spies to conclude that, based on their lack of moustaches, the Norman army must be composed of priests and monks! Harold, of course, knew better.[30]

Despite his assertion that 'no one has reported to us in detail' what Duke William said to his men, William of Poitiers nevertheless takes it upon himself to report it, a point which should serve as a warning not to accept everything he says as based on direct evidence. In effect, Duke William is portrayed as warning his men to fight well and win, or perish, but that they are not to be dismayed 'by the number of your foes'. The Normans then advanced in good order, preceded by the papal banner carried before them. William of Poitiers repeatedly insists that the English forces were numerous and formidable, and William of Jumièges calls them a 'terrible enemy'. This suggests that the reports in English sources about the English army as not fully drawn up in battle array should not be taken to imply that Harold had insufficient forces; the chronicles do state that he had a large army. References to English unpreparedness look more like attempts to explain away the defeat than a realistic account of events. An inadequate force could not have resisted Norman attacks from 9a.m. until sunset (which would have been at 5.08p.m.) on 14 October 1066.[31]

The English accounts imply that William stole a march on Harold by moving forward from Hastings on 13 October and onto Telham Hill on the following morning. Thus he enforced a confrontation, when Harold might have preferred to occupy Telham Hill himself before advancing against a Norman army still encamped at Hastings. Nonetheless, William did not prevent Harold, who no doubt knew the area well, from occupying a strong defensible position. But the duke certainly came against Harold earlier than expected, while the English army was still moving forward and before Harold had put his men fully into battle array. As the chronicle vividly puts it, in the original Old English, *Wyllem him com ongean on unwaer aer his folc gefylced waere*, or 'William came against him unawares, before his army was in [battle] array.' Harold could not afford to refuse battle; he had been, and still was, the earl of that area, with a duty to come to the relief of his men who were at the mercy of the Norman – a point which may be difficult for some to comprehend, in an age which currently puts rights before obligations.[32]

Some have argued that Harold acted impetuously or rashly in giving battle, emphasising the chroniclers' comments about his army being unprepared to fight, but this again does not fit his character as described in the *Vita Edwardi Regis*, which insists that 'the fault of rashness or levity was not one that anyone could charge against him'. Nor does the Norman insistence on the size of the English army prevent some from concluding that some contemporaries thought Harold's army too small for the task before it. The Normans might,

of course, have exaggerated the size of the English army in order
to magnify Duke William's achievement, but the army cannot have
been as inadequate as this might imply.[33]

Harold, then, reached the Sussex Weald by 13 October, perhaps
following the ritual exchange of envoys while Harold was still in
London. One line from the exchanges before the battle rings true.
Harold in effect quotes Genesis xvi 5: 'the Lord judge between thee
and me'. He was by then on Caldbec Hill, with William occupying
Telham Hill opposite. William, having ordered his men to don their
hauberks, then descended the slope, offering battle on the valley
bottom, which Harold naturally refused. There was no way he would
deploy an army of infantry in the open, against cavalry, and suffer
the fate of Harald Sigurdsson. The Normans drew up in three ranks,
with archers and light infantry in the van, heavy infantry, wearing
hauberks, in the second line, and cavalry, divided into three cohorts, at
the rear. References in the sources to the manoeuvres of Bretons and
Frenchmen suggest that the three cohorts of cavalry were divided
into a Breton left wing, commanded by Count Alan the Red, a right
wing of mixed Frenchmen, commanded by Eustace of Boulogne, and
the centre Normans, under the direct command of the duke, assisted
by Odo of Bayeux. The latter is shown in the Bayeux Tapestry wielding a staff or baton of command (not a mace), as is the duke.[34]

There are few definite facts about the battle, and what there are
come from those who approved of the invasion. Historians tend to
accept William of Poitiers' account over the rather more colourful
version in the *Carmen de Hastinge Proelio*, possibly because the former
account has been around a long time, whereas the *Carmen* was only
discovered in 1826 and some still doubt its authority and authenticity.
Nor does the lack of fuller details prevent some writers from giving a
blow by blow – even an hourly or minute by minute – account.[35]

The opening stages of the battle are muddled. The rivals are said
to have exchanged threats and arguments, the usual ritual for a set
piece battle, modelled perhaps on classical exemplars and probably
representing the counter-arguments exchanged between the two
men across the Channel and while Harold was in London. The duke
marshalled his men as close to the enemy as he dared, putting light

infantry and archers, some with crossbows, in the vanguard. Trumpets were sounded and signals made, and they then assailed the shield wall of the English and were repulsed by a barrage of missiles of all kinds. The suggestion that the infantry were actually led by William is fanciful; he would not have exposed himself to danger at this early stage, but would have commanded them to advance and waited to see the effect. William would have been probing the English line to determine the depth and tenacity of the defence. King Harold, unable now to bottle Duke William up in Hastings, had taken up a defensive position on a ridge below Caldbec Hill, on which Battle Abbey was later built. He adopted the tried and tested formation of the shield wall, the English version of the phalanx, which can be compared to the later tactic of the British square. The Norman writers speak of a vast host, with 'copious reinforcements from the land of the Danes who were allied to them'. They are said to have been inspired by 'zeal for Harold' and 'love of their country which they desired, however unjustly, to defend against the foreigners'. Like Byrthnoth at Maldon, Harold no doubt rode around, arraying his men, instructing them how to keep in position and telling them to hold their shields firmly and not to be afraid. He would then dismount and take his stand where he knew his close retainers to be most loyal.[36]

These same writers state that the English 'took up their position on higher ground, on a hill abutting the forest through which they had just come. There, at once dismounting from their horses, they drew themselves up on foot and in very close order'. This again casts some doubt on laments about the English having been prevented from drawing up their battle array. The reference to the presence of Danes is interesting, though unsupported by other sources. There could have been men at Hastings sent by Swein Estrithson; he and Harold were related through Harold's mother Gytha, and the Normans might also have concluded from the presence of Anglo-Danes wielding battleaxes that they were actually confronted by Danes. Accordingly, the English had the advantage of the ground, and profited by remaining within their position in close order. As William of Poitiers reports: 'They gained further superiority from their numbers, from the impregnable front which they preserved, and most of all from the manner in which their weapons found easy passage through the shields and armour of their enemies'. They bravely withstood and successfully repulsed those who were engaging them at close quarters, especially the light infantry and archers. They inflicted losses on the men who were shooting missiles at them from a distance. Naturally, the Norman writer is seeking to magnify Duke William's achievement by emphasising the difficulties faced by the Normans, but this does suggest that the English sources wished to explain the defeat as due to English weakness rather than Norman strength. *Florence of Worcester* even suggests that the English were handicapped by the narrowness of their position, which caused some men to retire from the battle, claiming that 'very few remained true to him [Harold]'. As the battle lasted for eight hours, this cannot be true. Florence himself says it began at the third (canonical) hour of the day, 9a.m., and lasted until nightfall.[37]

If Harold was able to do this, despite having only a third of his army in battle array at the start, after some had deserted him, and when he was hampered by the confined space on the ridge, what might he have done if William had landed first of the two invading leaders and been caught while disembarking at Pevensey? Other writers, unable to account for what happened in any other way, attribute the result to the intervention of God himself.

Much has been written about the exact position of the English army on the ridge, partly in an effort to calculate the size of Harold's army. Such calculations have provided so many varying estimates that all is in confusion. The numbers given by the chroniclers simply amount to the statement that the forces on each side were, for the eleventh century, considered to be huge. Modern estimates have provided figures of anywhere between 5,000 and 10,000 on each side. These calculations make no use of the surprisingly reasonable figure provided by one source, the *Chronicle of St Maixent*, which might derive its figure from the Poitevin Lord Aimeri de Thouars, who was present at the battle. The *Chronicle* puts William's force at 14,000. If allowance is made for some men having been stationed in the castles, which had been constructed and set to guard the ships, then a figure of 12,000 for the Norman army would not be unreasonable; Harold could hardly have had fewer and might be allowed 15,000. That would account for the insistence by Norman sources that large numbers were involved and that 'thousands' died. The main difference lay in the contrasting composition of the two armies.[38]

The Normans had archers and light infantry, heavy infantry and cavalry. The English had no cavalry, few archers and mainly heavy infantry, possibly supported by some more lightly armed levies (probably border troops from Herefordshire). The heavy infantry were mainly king's or earl's thegns, and the household retainers or housecarls of King Harold and his brothers, with the household troops of several abbeys and the better armed levies of the fyrd, some of whom might have been 'select men', sent from some shires on the basis of one man from each five hides. Some were even well-armed ceorls: that is, free men owning less than the five hides required for thegnly status. That Harold was able to raise successive armies throughout the campaign does suggest some sort of ability to call up relays of men, rather than a levy *en masse*. The Norman heavy infantry would have used swords and spears, as did the cavalry. Harold's men were not only equipped, like their opponents, with chainmail (the hauberk), helmet and shield, spears/javelins, and swords, but also with the fearsome Danish battleaxe. The latter weapon, wielded two-handed, could cleave in two horse and rider in one blow.

What did William see of the English army, as he descended the slopes of Telham Hill to a point near Starr's Green and looked up at his foe? He saw the enemy emerging from the woods behind them, which gleamed with armour and arms (*Carmen*, 863). North of the present day Battle High Street, the ground rises to a considerable height, and William would have seen the English – to Norman eyes an immense host – pouring down along a narrow neck of land (now marked by the High Street) onto a little jutting promontory before them. Exactly how large it actually was in 1066 is now impossible to say. The whole area on which the English took their stand was flattened and altered after the battle, to permit the construction of Battle Abbey. The only certain point is that the high altar marked the site of Harold's own position and his standards, the 'Fighting

Man' (the figure of an English warrior picked out in precious stones and gold thread) and the 'Dragon of Wessex' (a two-legged upright winged dragon, or Wyvern, probably red).[39]

The promontory offered a plateau of bare, uncultivated ground some 440 yards wide (some suggest it might have been up to 800 yards) and half as much deep. It might even have been marked by the famous hoar apple tree. East and west of the promontory ran spurs of ground with ravines either side of them, quite steep, which protected the English flanks and rear. The area was afterwards marked by the precincts and walls of the abbey. The shape is described as that of a hammer-head ridge. Wace, whose account is not entirely reliable but might contain some genuine information, thought the English battle line took up three sides of a square, but he also thought they constructed earthworks with three entrances through which the Normans were forced to attack, which is unlikely. There would have been no time to construct anything other than rudimentary defences, no fences or palisades. Wace might be confused by Norman descriptions of the shield wall as being like a fortress. Henry of Huntingdon uses the metaphor of a castle. In this quite confined space, the English took up position in close order: they were *densius conglobati*, densely packed together – so tightly packed that it was said that the dead could scarcely find space to fall.[40]

The shield wall ('war hedge' is another name for it) was the equivalent of the classical phalanx or testudo, but in this case it was oblong or rectangular rather than wedge-shaped, because of the shape of the promontory. Harold, and his brothers Gyrth and Leofwine, took up a position in the centre ('in the front rank'), on the highest point of the ridge, from which orders could be given and an oversight of the battlefield taken. The ground before them was not entirely devoid of obstacles to the Norman attack. The flanks might have been further protected by woodland, and the front was an area of marshy ground intersected by streams. It should be remembered that the early autumn had been a wet one, as Norman sources testify, so the slope would still have been somewhat waterlogged. The ground was steep, especially towards the flanks, rough and unsuitable for horses. Wace insists that there was a fosse across the field of battle, protecting one flank of the English position. The *Carmen de Hastinge Proelio* says there was a detached small hill off to one side, which William of Malmesbury calls a 'tumulus'. No men were stationed on it, but it might be the hill shown in the Tapestry, on which some Englishmen took refuge when the Normans counter-attacked. English Heritage has located a concealed rampart about halfway down the slope, which would also have been an obstacle to the cavalry.[41]

The English position was a strong one, the strength of which has been reduced, but not concealed, by the changes made subsequently, especially by the monks of Battle. The crest of the hill shows little change from the time when the monastery was built, and indicates that the monks extended the original site with earthen mounds or clay platforms and by the use of undercrofts. The slope bears little resemblance to the much steeper affair up which the Normans would have had to charge. King Harold had chosen well. He was, as a result of his journeys on the continent and his sojourn in Normandy itself, familiar with continental methods of warfare. One source calls him the 'best rider of old or new time', as though recognising his knowledge of both English and Norman ways of using horses. It might well be that Harold never actually expected to take the duke by surprise. That assumption depends on the assertion of William of Poitiers, and on modern arguments that he had rushed into battle, yet no actual surprise attack by night was attempted, and Harold is clearly shown making use of spies and scouts who kept him informed of the duke's movements. It is not impossible that he deliberately chose the best available position, even if it is conceded that William, by advancing early that morning, had perhaps prevented Harold from using some other location.[42]

Precisely because the ridge was compact and well protected on its flanks, the Normans found it difficult to assail the English. Thus the account says: 'they could not without severe loss overcome an army massed so strongly in close formation' and 'they bravely withstood and successfully repulsed those who were engaging them at close quarters'. This was achieved by the shield wall. This was not, as is often thought, merely a line of overlapping shields. Such a formation would not allow the men in it to strike back at the enemy. The line had to be so set as to permit men to swing their shields to one side in order to strike with spear, sword or battleaxe, or perhaps to drop down onto one knee to allow those in the second row to strike with spear or axe. It is here that *Harald's Saga* is informative. Although it purports to be describing Stamford Bridge, the confusion which arose later in telling tales of the two battles suggests that some of what it says belongs to an account of Hastings. The king, Harald Sigurdsson, prepares his men for battle, just as King Harold would have given his men their orders and as Ealdorman Byrhtnoth did at Maldon. The king in the *Saga* is expecting to be attacked by cavalry, which better fits Hastings than Stamford Bridge, and tells his men that cavalry 'always attacked in small detachments and then wheeled away at once'. Therefore, in forming their shield wall they must:

> ...set their spearshafts into the ground and turn the points towards the riders' breasts when they charge us and those behind are to set their spears against the horses' chests.

This made it no easy matter for the cavalry to attack; so they kept charging, then falling back at once when they could make no headway. Nonetheless, they persisted, and eventually, seeing the shield wall broken:

> ...they rode... upon them from all sides, showering them with spears and arrows.

This certainly reads more like a summary of the battle of Hastings than the battle of Stamford Bridge.[43]

The image that results is of a war hedge composed of shields and naked blades: that is, spears and swords. Andrew Roberts, in his account of the cavalry charge at Waterloo, states categorically that horses will not charge massed steel bayonets as presented by the British squares. If that is so, then the whole picture of cavalry involvement at Hastings is wrong. There cannot have been any 'shock charge' against a hedge of spears, especially uphill, and this is confirmed by the *Saga*'s statement that cavalry rode up to the opposing line and wheeled away at once, presumably after launching spears or javelins or striking out with swords. The Bayeux Tapestry mainly shows the Normans carrying their spears into battle held aloft, as if to stab with them or throw them Only rarely are they shown in the underarm or 'couched' position, and then they are being used against isolated individuals. Plate 67 shows three men in line: the first two have raised their spears to strike, while the third, still advancing, has his couched. In Plate 65, one man leading an attack attempts to spear a shield with a couched lance which points off to his left, across his body, as his horse turns right.[44]

No fewer than twenty figures are shown holding their spears overarm, as if to stab downwards or throw them, and one man holds his out to his right, as if about to raise it above his head. In Plate 68, a knight attempts to spear Earl Gyrth, who stands alone with shield and raised spear. Nowhere is any knight shown attempting to shock charge the shield wall. This might be due to the artist's inability to portray such an action, but it seems unlikely. Even in the scenes of the Breton campaign, no one is shown delivering a shock charge. The thrust of this analysis is to argue that the Normans rode uphill, more slowly than was possible on an open plain against a hedge of spears. On reaching the English line, they showered spears upon their enemies or struck out with swords as they wheeled their horses away from the shield wall. The knights would naturally tend to shy away from a hedge of spear points levelled at horses and riders. Any spearing with couched lance would have been against isolated groups of men or individuals, caught in the open after breaking out of their line to pursue the Normans. That casts a new light on organised tactics such as the feigned retreat. Such a retreat would be a natural sequel to an attack in which the cavalry, having assaulted the shield wall, then wheeled away and rode back down the hill to regroup.[45]

Reports of the battle state that there were at least three, possibly four, waves of cavalry, followed by a retreat, two or three of which were feigned and one of which was a real panic-stricken flight, which threatened to become a full rout involving the whole Norman army. In addition to these full organised assaults, one might envisage that there were continuous attacks by conroys (small detachments), as suggested by the *Saga*. The reports of the *Carmen de Hastinge Proelio* and William of Poitiers conflict with each other. The *Carmen* insists that there was a successful first assault by the cavalry which included a feigned retreat; the second assault, possibly led by the Bretons, got out of hand and almost became a complete rout, and that was followed by other successful feigned retreats. William of Poitiers declares that it was the first cavalry attack which threatened to become a real disaster, until the duke himself intervened to stop it (as the *Carmen* also claims), and that subsequent attacks involved the successful use of the feigned retreat. If, as seems probable, William of Poitiers was making use of information drawn from the *Carmen*, then it looks as if he discreetly rearranged events, as was his wont, to enhance the reputation of his hero, the duke, who is shown heroically stemming the retreat and, later, craftily making use of the fact that some of the English could be tempted into rash pursuit by ordering feigned retreats. The writer also claims that the purpose of these retreats was indeed to provoke the English into pursuit, so that they could be cut down outside the shield wall as they, in turn, became the victims of a counter-attack.

Admittedly, some historians criticise the *Carmen*, believing it to be a twelfth-century product, but the balance of probability seems to favour an early date for this work, around 1068, and William of Poitiers can be shown to be drawing on it not only for information but for vocabulary. Unless a better candidate can be produced, the most probable author of the *Carmen* remains Guy, Bishop of Amiens. But it is poetry, not history, and its evidence must be used with care, especially when there is no corroboration for its statements.

The early phases of the battle, as given in the sources, run as follows. The battle commenced at the third canonical hour, 9 a.m., with trumpet calls and an advance by light infantry and archers. This was met by a terrific barrage of missiles of all descriptions, spears, javelins (which the English called '*ategar*') and throwing sticks (pieces of wood with stones lashed to one end), while the Norman archers and crossbowmen shot uphill towards the shielded English. The light infantry tried to tempt the English into breaking ranks to pursue them, but this gambit was refused. As the infantry retreated, William ordered in the cavalry and, if the *Carmen* is right, they were led by a knight called Taillefer (Cut-Iron), who advanced singing verses from a song about Roland at Roncesvalles. He rode somewhat ahead of the rest, into the English line, which seems to have deliberately opened to let him in so that he could be cut to pieces. This version would seem to be confirmed by William of Poitiers, who does in fact have the knights engaged at close quarters with the English immediately after the barrage of missiles, but he then claims that the Bretons, on the left wing, along with auxiliary troops, broke before the English barrage and fled, causing a real retreat. It looks as though he has conflated the first two attacks, as described in the *Carmen*, into one.

The retreat seemed about to involve the whole army when the duke, putting himself directly in their path, shouted at them and threatened them with his spear, successfully slowing and halting it. William of Poitiers and the Bayeux Tapestry both present the duke as raising his helmet to show his face, in order to disprove a rumour that he had been killed. The chronicler provides a suitable speech given by the duke, accusing his men of madness in flying from the enemy and allowing themselves to be pursued and killed 'by men whom you could slaughter like cattle'. That describes what actually happened next. So the duke restored their courage and turned a retreat into a counter-attack. Bishop Odo of Bayeux assisted William in rallying the army, especially by encouraging the younger knights. The duke then led his men against the pursuing English and cut them to pieces. So successful was this counter-move that the duke carried on the attack against the main body of the English 'which even after their losses scarcely seemed diminished in number'. The whole Norman army is described as joining in the attack, but 'the English fought confidently with all their strength' and the attack petered out.[46]

After this, the chronicler admits that the Normans could not 'without severe loss overcome an army massed so strongly in close formation'; they therefore resorted to the tactic of a feigned retreat, not once but at least twice more, remembering how the English had broken ranks to pursue the earlier retreat. Nonetheless, the English continued to strive to prevent the Normans from penetrating their ranks, despite their losses. It could be that the confined space of the ridge worked to their advantage as the day wore on. They were easily able to bring extra men forward to replace those who fell. The Norman writers saw the battle as being of a new type, with one side 'vigorously attacking; the other resisting as if rooted to the ground'. The accounts concentrate on the activities of the knights throughout the day, referring only to light infantry and archers at the beginning, and to more work by the archers towards the end. Little or nothing is said of the part played by the heavy infantry, which must have comprised at least half the Norman army. The clue lies in the fact that William of Poitiers lists ten prominent barons who fought with Duke William and praises the 'many other most renowned warriors whose names are worthy to be commemorated'. His work was intended to be read by the nobility of Normandy, the barons and their knights, rather than by the foot soldiers who made up the bulk of the army. It commemorates the part played by the baronage and their knightly retainers. But no account of the battle can be complete which does not stress that the Norman heavy infantry must have played a significant part. Infantry are the backbone of any army, and it has to be accepted that the Norman soldiery would have been sent up the hill to engage the enemy face to face, in order to keep up the pressure in between cavalry assaults, while the cavalry were regrouping and securing fresh spears. The cavalry spears were liable to shatter on contact with an enemy shield or to be lost when thrown. The infantry would have been used to wear down the English resistance and give the front line no rest.[47]

The duke was an able tactician and kept up the pressure all day. The battle saw alternating waves of cavalry and infantry assault the English line. Some have doubted the reality of the feigned attacks, seeing medieval warfare as a sort of organised chaos, a disorderly free for all over which commanders had little control. That is a travesty of the truth. Men were trained in warfare from an early age, and the Normans were reputed to be particularly martial. Heavy infantry were trained to attack in dense phalanxes, and cavalry practised their manoeuvres under the command of their officers and the overall authority of commanders called *magister militum* or 'master of knights'. Commands could be given by voice, but more often were made by trumpet calls and gestures such as the raising or lowering of 'gonfanons', spears with bannerets attached indicating rank. The duke and Bishop Odo are shown wielding staffs of office, and Eustace of Boulogne carries a spear with a flag attached, probably the ensign of Boulogne. On the English side, the fyrd was organised not only by shires but by hundreds, led by *scirgerefa* and *hundredesman*. The men of Kent and Essex were traditionally believed to claim the right to form the front line, and are reported to have pushed the Normans back; the men of Wiltshire, Devon and Cornwall formed the second line. The Londoners formed the king's bodyguard. The whole battle line was a much more disciplined affair than modern readers can envisage.[48]

There were heavy casualties on both sides; William himself had three horses killed under him and had at times to fight on foot. The *Carmen* credits him with personally dispatching Earl Gyrth, but this may be poetic licence. The earl was found after the battle with King Harold and his brother Earl Leofwine, around the English standards. If Gyrth did fall to the duke, then it was in the closing stages of the battle, after the shield wall had begun to crumble. Certainly, after the deaths of Harold and his brothers (William of Poitiers does not record the manner of their deaths), the English battle line gradually disintegrated, disheartened by those deaths and the continuous pressure of the Norman attacks. No doubt the infantry and archers kept up their assaults. It would have taken very little thought for William to order his archers to aim a little higher. They were already firing uphill so that arrows fell on the inner ranks of the English army. It is an obvious tactic in that situation.

The household troops, housecarls and thegns, some of whom William of Malmesbury believed to be mercenary or stipendiary troops employed by Harold, held out longer than the fyrd men, and the immediate commended men of Harold and his brothers might well have chosen to stand and die around the bodies of their lords. But the main body of the English army sought safety in flight. The Bayeux Tapestry ends with the English chased off the field, and the border below shows the victorious Normans stripping the bodies of the slain; it is strewn with various body parts, notably detached heads, trunks and arms.

The claim that Norman numbers were 'not much diminished' is overstated, but that the Norman fighting men were filled with renewed vigour at the sight of the flight of the English is acceptable. The disintegrating army fled by every available means, leaving the wounded to 'bathe the ground in blood', as the pursuing Normans rode them down in full flight. Even so, some did manage a rearguard action around a 'steep valley', forcing the duke to take command, under the impression that these were reinforcements arriving too late to affect the outcome. He prevented Eustace of Boulogne and his men from retreating, and the count is said to have been struck in the back, while speaking to the duke, so forcibly that blood gushed from his mouth. He had to retire from the pursuit, leaving the duke to overcome the rearguard. The sources have to admit that many Normans were slain there, an admission which shows that Norman casualties were greater than they wanted to admit. This affair might well be the foundation of the later story about the dreaded 'malfosse', or evil ditch, into which many Normans were said to have fallen in the gathering gloom of twilight, so that they filled the ditch with men and horses, all of whom lost their lives. The reality of the tale is much disputed, as is the location of the ditch, but there is an area north of the spur along which the English retreated, where there was a ravine on the western side, an area known as Oakwood Gill.

William of Poitiers talks only of an ancient causeway hidden by long grass, which caused some Normans to fall and be killed, and only the *Battle Chronicle* calls it a 'dreadful chasm'. Orderic Vitalis attempts to combine all the accounts, describing a labyrinth of ditches into which the Normans fell. Oakwood Gill is hidden by the construction of the modern road; it could have been much deeper and steeper than it is now and might be the reality behind the tales of a 'malfosse'. In the confusion after the battle, many Normans pursuing the English into the gathering darkness must have fallen into hidden ditches, and the extent of their losses no doubt lost nothing in the telling afterwards.[49]

13

Aftermath:
The Lost King

So ended the battle of Hastings – or Senlac ('sandlacu'), as Orderic Vitalis preferred to call it, from the sandy and marshy nature of the ground. (Even the local hundred might have been called Sandlake.) It had been a hotly contested and hard-fought conflict, as Norman sources admit, and had continued without ceasing from 9a.m. until sunset, shortly after 5p.m., with total darkness by 6.30p.m. It was a close-run thing, Waterloo without the Prussians. The final stages of the battle had seen the deaths of Harold's brothers, Gyrth and Leofwine, and, most decisively of all, the death of Harold himself. That death led to the rapid disintegration of the English army, as the warriors lost heart and sought safety in flight. Only the king's personal housecarls and thegns might have preferred death to dishonour and died defending him. They died around his body and his standards. His personal banner, the 'Fighting Man', was presented to the duke after the battle. The fate of the 'Dragon' or 'Wyvern' banner is less certain, but there is a curious story in Irish sources. King Diarmaid macMael na m-Bo of Dublin (Harold's ally in 1052) and his son Murchad supported Harold's sons in their attack on Norman England, possibly in return for money. As part of his payment, the Irish king received 'the Battle Standard of the King of the Saxons' and in turn gave it to Toirdelbach, King of Munster, in 1068. This was not the 'Fighting Man', but it could well have been the Wessex banner.[1]

Duke William returned to the battlefield to be shown Harold's body, which had been found near those of his brothers beneath the standards. It had been 'stripped of all badges of honour'. Harold was then identified, not by his face but by 'certain marks on his body'. William of Poitiers is very guarded in what he says. The body, he claims, was given to William Malet 'for burial'. The duke refused to accept Harold's weight in gold, offered by his mother, Gytha, in exchange for it, thinking it 'unseemly to receive money for such merchandise'. Perhaps also he did not wish to see the body buried by his mother, when 'so many men lay unburied because of his avarice', including many of the duke's own men. Some men then remarked 'in jest' that 'he who guarded the coast with such insensate zeal should be buried by the sea shore'. The writer does not say that this was actually done and, in effect, he contradicts the *Carmen de Hastinge Proelio*, which claimed that the body was buried under a cairn on the clifftop, in a manner reminiscent of Viking burials.[2]

It is inherently unlikely that the duke, who was presenting himself as a champion of the Church against a perjured usurper, would have permitted it. Such a burial site, if it once became known to the English, would have become a place of patriotic pilgrimage, just what William wanted to avoid. No later sources refer to any seashore or clifftop burial. Instead, William of Poitiers gives clues as to what might have happened. He states that Harold had to be identified from marks on his body, as his face was unrecognisable, and says further that it would only have been just to leave the English 'who had rightly incurred their doom' to be devoured by vultures and wolves, but that William deemed this to be too cruel 'and allowed all who wished to do so to collect the bodies for burial', while he arranged for the honourable interment of his own men. That, together with the stripping of arms and armour from the bodies, explains the lack of any evidence from the field of battle that any struggle ever took place there.[3]

It does look as though later writers are correct in claiming that, in common with those who fought with him, Harold's body was recovered by Englishmen and buried. William of Malmesbury thought that the refusal to accept Gytha's offer of gold meant that the duke gave her the body without accepting money, and he adds that she had it buried at Waltham. The *Roman de Rou* also says the body went to Waltham. Both sources pre-date the *Waltham Chronicle*, which, shortly before Henry II evicted the canons and replaced them with Augustinians, was written to ensure that the foundation legend of Waltham Holy Cross was not forgotten, and that the refoundation by Harold and his subsequent burial there would be remembered. The Waltham story explains what happened and accounts for William of Malmesbury's confusion. It says that two canons from Waltham, Osgod Cnoppe and Aethelric Childemaister, asked permission to recover Harold's body and, having been granted it, identified him with the help of his long-standing 'concubine', Edith Swanneck (*Edivva cognomento Swanneshals/collum cygni*). She recognised Harold by certain secret marks on his body, known only to her because she had been admitted to the secrets of his bedchamber. The body was probably in the hands of William Malet, who had been charged with seeing to its burial. There might also have been uncertainty about which body was that of Harold, since he was found alongside his brothers Gyrth and Leofwine; this explains the necessity of finding someone who could identify Harold for certain.[4]

Harold's mother Gytha might well have been known in English as 'Eadgyth' (which might also explain the name of her eldest daughter, Queen Eadgyth/Edith), and William of Malmesbury might well have confused Gytha with Eadgyth Swanneshals, since they were both involved in the recovery of the body. The author of the *Waltham Chronicle* claimed to have been told the story by older members of his community, such as the Sacristan Turketil, who remembered Harold's return from Stamford Bridge; he also claimed to have seen Harold's body at the time it was moved to a new grave. The two canons then took the body to Waltham, travelling by way of *Pontem Belli* or 'Bridge of Battle'. There is a Battlesbridge in Essex, near Billericay (off the present day A130). The canons might well have crossed the Thames east of London, travelling in an arc round the city, to avoid Duke William's army. Meanwhile, the duke set about consolidating his grip on England and making himelf king.[5]

During the late eleventh century, Waltham developed and encouraged the cult of the Holy Cross itself (which Harold had fostered), in order to distract official attention away from its possession of Harold's body. No effort was made to develop a cult around his tomb; instead it was concentrated on the further development of Harold's experiment in founding a house of secular canons, a revival of the earlier English system of collegiate or minster churches, as an alternative to monasteries. As king, Harold might well have further encouraged this trend. In doing so before 1066, he had in fact encouraged the idea of cathedral schools, and he might in time have integrated his new clergy into the ancient parochial structure.[6]

William of Jumièges claimed that Harold had been killed *in primo militum progressu* (or *congressu*, in Orderic Vitalis); this is perhaps best translated as 'amid the front rank of his army'. The writer probably meant that Harold died when he first had to move into the front rank, as the men in front of him had fallen. Most sources make it plain that Harold survived almost until nightfall, and William of Poitiers mentions his death as occurring as evening was falling, after the English had lost a great part of their army. Had he fallen earlier, the battle would have come to an end then and not later.[7]

There is similar confusion over the death of Earl Gyrth; some sources imply that he was killed by Duke William during the Norman counter-attack which followed their real flight, but this can be dismissed as part of the construction of the *res gestae*, or 'great deeds', of Duke William, who had to be shown playing a hero's part in battle. The fog of war would have ensured that men's memories of what happened and when would have been confused. Other sources reveal that the bodies of Gyrth and his brother Leofwine were found after the battle near the English standard, alongside the body of King

Harold, indicating that he and his brothers remained at the heart of English resistance until the end.[8]

It is the manner of Harold's death that remains the subject of conflicting opinions to this day. Eadmer, in his *History*, says that Harold fell after there had been heavy fighting and significant Norman casualties, a view supported by the account in William of Poitiers. Neither says how Harold died and neither says he was shot by an arrow. The Bayeux Tapestry, which in its present form appears to show Harold clutching an arrow which is sticking in his helmet, is less decisive in this matter than it seems.[9]

The earliest version of Harold's death (if, as most historians now tend to accept, it was written *circa* 1067) is that of the *Carmen de Hastinge Proelio*. It is suspiciously detailed, and it must be remembered that the work is poetry, not history. But it presents Duke William as leading the final assault against Harold in person, which is not supported by any other source. William of Poitiers wrote later than the writer of the *Carmen*, and comparison of the two suggests that he made use of it. But he did not accept everything in it. He omits much of its testimony and rearranges its order of events. He does not claim that the duke killed Harold. He clearly had other sources, which contradicted what the *Carmen* said. The latter also says nothing about an arrow in the eye. Instead, a group of knights led by the duke attacked Harold's position near the standard and killed him. It is inherently improbable that William was one of the four men who the *Carmen* claims attacked Harold. Had William really slain Harold, virtually in single combat, the rest of Europe would never have heard the last of it. Such a feat would have been broadcast the length and breadth of Christendom. It wasn't, probably because he didn't do it. It is more likely that the duke ordered in a 'hit squad' of four, led by Count Eustace of Boulogne, who had his own reasons for hating a son of Godwine.[10]

The *Carmen* says that the duke called Eustace to his side:

He handed over the fighting in that sector to the French and moved up to give all the relief that he possibly could to those who were being slaughtered. Ever keen to do his duty... Hugh, the noble heir to

Ponthieu, went with them. The fourth man was Gilfard who inherited his name from his father. By the use of their weapons these four between them encompassed the king's death.

This is only one possible translation of the poem. The list of names given, if it is accepted that William was one of the four, was thus Duke William, Eustace of Boulogne, Hugh, 'the noble heir of Ponthieu', and a knight called 'Gilfard', thought by some to have been Robert, son of Walter Giffard. As the *Carmen* was probably (though there are still doubts about this) written by Guy (Wido), Bishop of Amiens, it actually seems to have been intended to enhance the role in the battle of Eustace of Boulogne and the House of Ponthieu. Some therefore suggest that the four did not include the duke, and argue that the heir of Ponthieu was not named but that either Robert or Enguerronol (sons of Count Guy), was intended, and that the third knight was Hugh de Montfort-sur-Risle, with Robert, son of Walter Giffard, as the fourth. Another account names them as Walter Giffard, Guy de Montfort, Hugh of Ponthieu and Eustace of Boulogne. It is not possible to be certain. William of Poitiers names Walter Giffard and Hugh de Montfort-sur-Risle as present at the battle. Hugh de Grandmesnil was also present. The *Carmen* was a poem and the poet felt free to use fictitious elements to enliven his tale, while still making use of genuine facts, such as the roughness of the terrain, the English breaking out of their line of battle and the use of feigned retreats. Some commentators argue that the account of Harold's death is a literary invention, crediting the duke with Harold's death, and enhancing the role in the battle of Eustace of Boulogne, along with the family of the counts of Ponthieu and other prominent Normans. But the silence of all other sources, none of which claim that the duke killed Harold himself, lends weight to the second hypothesis of a hit squad of four knights which did not include the duke.[11]

Whichever four knights were involved, it is said that the first speared Harold through the chest (and also struck his shield and his helmet), the second beheaded him, the third split open his entrails, and the fourth hacked off his thigh, which might be a euphemism for castration. The *Carmen* lists these actions without naming those who took them, only implying that the four struck in the order in which he named them. But Benôit de St Maure in his *Chronicle* says:

> Before this slaying was over King Harold was struck dead, struck through the two sides by three great steel headed lances and in the head by two swords which entered as far as the ears.

He also has Harold 'wounded in more than thirteen places'. These details are not vouched for elsewhere, except in the way that Orderic Vitalis, confirming earlier accounts, admits that Harold was unrecognisable by his face and William of Jumièges says he was pierced with many deadly wounds.[12]

After stating that Harold died when an arrow pierced his brain, William of Malmesbury relates a tale about a knight who was dismissed ignominiously from the Norman army for striking Harold's body in the thigh; there was obviously something shameful about his action.

As for the arrow in the eye, that story only emerged *circa* 1085 in Amatus of Montecassino's *History of the Normans*; he thought William had 100,000 soldiers and 10,000 archers. How could he possibly have had any knowledge of how Harold died? Baudri of Bourgeuil, in the *Adela Comitissa*, *circa* 1100, only says he was killed by an arrow, and William of Malmesbury says it pierced his brain. All later writers are following these sources except one late source, Benôit de St Maure, who ignores the arrow and accepts an account similar to that in the *Carmen*.

There are two aspects of the arrow story that need to be explored. A question that has been raised concerns the evidence for references to blinding which are to be found in the Tapestry and elsewhere. Thus, for example, Hastings was seen by some as a punishment for the death of the Aetheling Alfred, who was blinded on the orders of Harold Harefoot. In the Tapestry, a theme of blindness seems to be deliberately stressed, inserted by the designer to confer legitimacy on Norman claims. It not only suited the purpose of the Normans but also addressed the emotions of the English themselves, who felt that they had suffered the effects of God's wrath. So blinding is central to the presentation of Harold as a perjuror. The scene in which he is shown swearing his oath is full of 'ocular' images − of brooches, bosses, the 'Bull's Eye' reliquary − all of which reflect the idea of an eye. The oath is taken out of doors under the eye of God. It was certainly held that perjury would bring blindness, as a punishment from God. It was known that in the Old Testament Zedekiah, King of Judah, violated his oath and was blinded by the Babylonians. It might be that it was the presence of this theme that led later writers to infer, from references to Harold having been struck in the head, together with references to the use of archery towards the end of the battle, that he was struck down by an arrow.[13]

The second aspect casts doubt on the whole story. According to *Harald's Saga*, Hardrada was struck in the throat by an arrow. If the arrow in the eye story is accepted, then King Harold, nineteen days later, also died from being struck by an arrow. Two kings called Harold, in two battles which were later confused with each other, both died from an arrow within three weeks. Might there not have been some confusion over the manner of their deaths? It is unlikely that the Scandinavian tradition of the skalds was wrong about Hardrada, whose body was certainly returned to Norway. The Bayeux Tapestry does not help to decide the issue.[14]

That the Normans were determined to kill Harold is supported by the *Waltham Chronicle*, which says that leading warriors were slain on both sides and that the Normans eventually broke the English line, 'thirsting above all for the blood of the King'. Perhaps the author knew an account similar to that in the *Carmen*. That work sets the scene by describing the conflict between Earl Gyrth and the duke. The earl kills the duke's horse and the duke seizes another from a nearby knight. That horse too is killed by 'the son of Hellox' (who has not been identified). Eustace of Boulogne gives his horse to the duke, who is then said to have slain that son of Hellox. The duke and Eustace fight on together and the duke, seeing Harold on the crest of the ridge, launches his final attack. Not only does the *Carmen* have William mistake Gyrth for Harold; it perhaps confuses the killing of the son of Hellox with that of Gyrth, who is described as a young man, although he was probably the same age as William. In this account, the final assault, in which Harold was killed, then followed, though it must have occurred much later in the day, as all other sources state. William of Poitiers recorded none of this, although he had access to the *Carmen*'s account. Perhaps he rejected what he saw as poetic embroidery, knowing from his other sources that it did not happen quite as the author of the *Carmen* described it. He might also have done this if there was something dishonourable about the action of the fourth man.[15]

What then, of the evidence of the Tapestry? It does seem, somewhat discreetly, to follow the account in the *Carmen*. There is a mêlée in which knights attack Harold's position. The text says 'Those who were with Harold fell'. A dismounted knight clutches an Englishman in civilian clothing and is about to behead him with his own sword. A knight attacks two mail-clad Englishmen, one of whom bears the 'Dragon' standard. They have arrows sticking in their shields. A third man in front of them falls, transfixed by a spear. Then, under the word 'Harold', a mail-clad figure, as the Tapestry currently shows, clutches an arrow which just touches the end of the figure's nose guard. The shield here has three arrows in it, each with triple flights. Immediately to the right, under the words *interfectus est* ('he is slain'), a mailed figure dropping a battleaxe falls to the ground, having been struck down by a single blow. This scene is the centre of heated controversy. Are the two figures successive images of the same man? If so, then it looks as though Harold was hit by an arrow and then struck down by a knight with a sword. There is no group of four and no sign of the use of lances. Lastly, a group of Englishmen is attacked by mounted Normans and the rest of the English are shown fleeing the battlefield. The end of the Tapestry is now missing. It should be noted that it condenses all the action in the battle into seventeen plates and makes no attempt to show the battle in full. It is thought that the end of the work originally showed a scene of Duke William crowned in state as king, which would balance the work; it opens with King Edward on his throne and also shows Harold enthroned as king. It would have been logical for it to end with a similar scene involving Duke William.[16]

Whether the two figures are intended to be successive representations of Harold is still a matter of debate. The first holds a spear and

a shield; the second a battleaxe. The whole scene is heavily restored
and minute details do not permit a safe interpretation. The restora-
tions differ from the drawings made of the Tapestry before it was
restored using what were thought to be stitch holes, marking where
the woollen threads had once been. As now presented, the scene
shows the 'arrow' passing outside a conical helmet, with no apparent
injury to head or eye. It should be compared with a nearby scene in
which an Englishman flees the battlefield clutching an arrow, which
is plainly sticking out of his eye. A body in the lower margin has an
arrow sticking out of the man's mouth. It has been suggested that the
figure, apparently labelled 'Harold', was originally shown holding a
spear but that the designer changed his mind, not wanting too many
horizontal lines, and turned it into an arrow, rather awkwardly, after
the raised arm had already been stitched and the 'arrow' was never in
the figure's eye. Too much weight cannot be put on such details; the
Tapestry shows other oddities such as bowstrings which pass behind
the shoulders of the archer – quite impossible. The execution of the
scenes was not always completely accurate. It is also possible that the
nineteenth-century restorers were too much influenced by the idea
that Harold was killed by an arrow in the eye.[17]

    A further problem is that the oldest drawings of the Tapestry do not
show a figure hit by an arrow at all. Dom Bernard de Montfaucon,
a Benedictine of St Maure, published '*Monuments de la Monarchie
Française*' in 1724 and sent a team of engravers to Bayeux, led by a
man called Benoît, to copy the entire Tapestry. The figure labelled
'Harold' is shown holding a long rod (perhaps originally a spear or
javelin?), the end of which extends across the bottom of the letter
'o' of 'Harold' and touches the nose guard of the figure's helmet.
It has no flights or feathers. Later reproductions of the Tapestry, by
Lancelot in 1730 and Ducarel in 1767, show the scene similarly.
Only after the 'restoration' do the flights appear, after Stothard had
been at work to create the impression of an effort to remove an
'arrow'. Of course, the engravers of 1724 might have been mistaken.
The figure is one of a group showing Harold's standard-bearer and
an unnamed warrior, and spears are being hurled at them. Nor is it
certain that the inscription following the name 'Harold' should read

Rex interfectus est. This too has been restored. One suggestion is that it could equally well have read *Rex in terra iactus est* or 'the king is thrown to the ground'. (The drawings show that 'inter' is followed by a 'p' [perhaps an incomplete 'r'] not an 'f', and then 'ius' or 'tus'.) If this is the case, the second figure is Harold and the others might be Gyrth and Leofwine. No early viewers of the Tapestry took the first figure to be Harold. Stothard's copy was made in the early nineteenth century, after some restoration had been carried out, and shows the words *interfectus est*. But the rod held by the figure labelled 'Harold' has no flights.[18]

It was William of Malmesbury who, having said that the fortunes of war at first smiled on the English, at Hastings, while Harold remained alive, stated that the battle was lost because Harold fell when his skull was pierced, by an arrow sent from a distance, causing the English to flee. The last word should be left to Wace:

> I know not who it was that slew him. I do not tell and indeed I do not know, for I was not there to see and have not heard say who it was that smote down King Harold.

The only certainty is that Harold died at Hastings and was buried at Waltham. The site of his tomb was destroyed at the Reformation and is marked by a slab and an upright stone, where the choir of the abbey church once stood. A now lost stone was found at Waltham by the philosopher David Hume, which read *Hic iacet Haroldus infelix* or 'Here lies Harold the ill-fated'.[19]

The Augustinian monks who replaced the canons at Waltham in Henry II's time did not want any suggestion of a connection with Harold, so they sponsored the production of the *Vita Haroldi*, which fostered the belief that Harold had not died at Hastings but survived to become a hermit, either at Chester or Canterbury, having recovered from his serious injuries. This is legend, and a common theme about the survival of a lost king or hero, like Arthur or Frederick Barbarossa. The reference to Chester might arise from the fact that his son, by Queen Ealdgyth, and also called Harold, had lived there after the Conquest.

A more fitting end to an account of his life and all too short reign (nine months and nine days) is to consider what sort of king he might have become had the Norman Conquest either failed or never happened. William the Bastard won in the end because he was that most fortunate of warriors, the lucky general. His *felicitas*, or luck, had begun when Robert of Jumièges allowed him to believe he was King Edward's chosen successor; it continued when Harold fell into his hands in 1064 or 1065, and it enabled him deliberately to delay his arrival in England until the autumn. This prolonged Harold's task of providing for the security of his realm until autumn gales wrecked the English fleet and opened the way for an invasion. Duke William's luck held yet again when, through the efforts of Earl Tostig, Harald of Norway landed first. King Harold therefore had to fight the Norwegians before he faced William, which fatally depleted his army. William's good fortune peaked towards the end of the day's fighting, when Harold himself was killed and the English fled leaderless into the darkness. Sigebert of Gembloux, quite credibly, reckoned the losses at Stamford Bridge alone were 1,000 men. He also put Harold's army at seven legions, which would mean 14,000, similar to the Poitevin estimate, in the *Chronicle of St Maixent*, for William's army. Yet had Harold survived the day, he would have been able to raise yet another English army to deal with a depleted Norman one on another occasion. He could simply have penned William in and starved him out, in which case Harold Godwinson, and not William of Normandy, might have ruled England for the next twenty years.[20]

If Edward the Confessor had died in 1063, when Harold was at the height of his power and influence and had not yet been a 'guest' in Normandy, and while his family was still united around him, nothing could have prevented him becoming king and founding a new dynasty. England at that point was strongly protected on her frontiers, free from civil war and far ahead of any other country in political unification. There is a sense in which it is true to say that William's triumph stemmed from the division in the House of Godwine, caused by the fall and banishment of Earl Tostig. The earl had failed in his attempt to govern Northumbria and Harold was unable to prevent his fall. That led directly to the battles of Gate Fulford and Stamford Bridge and, ultimately, to Harold's defeat at Hastings. So what kind of king might Harold have made, and how might the future of England in the eleventh century have unfolded?

He certainly began well in the nine months at his disposal. His assumption of power went virtually unchallenged, and he moved quickly to secure the acceptance of his rule in Northumbria. As he had readily renewed the Laws of Cnut in the autumn of 1065, and was the leading member of an Anglo-Danish family, it can be accepted that Cnut's law, as later embodied under the Normans under the name of *Laga Edwardi* (or 'Laws of Edward'), would have remained the basis of England's laws, although the Murdrum fine would not have become part of it. Harold would have inherited the same administrative system as William, and it can be suggested that he was just as capable of operating that system as William I. *Florence of Worcester* testifies that he began with the 'smack of firm government', enforcing good law and maintaining order.[21]

The monetary system remained intact, as witness the survival of Harold's coinage from some forty-four mints. He seems to have produced as much coin in nine months as Harold I and Harthacnut did in several years. It has been pointed out that the coinage of Edward and Harold was far superior to the shapeless, ill-struck issues of Henry I, Stephen and Henry II. Harold was able to raise several successive armies for the defence of his realm and, some sources imply, recruit stipendiary troops as well. That suggests also that he was able to continue to collect royal dues and taxes, which were enhanced by the addition of the resources of Harold's great earldom of Wessex. These were added to the royal demesne and made Harold an even richer king than Edward, quite the equal of King William I. As king, Harold would have been in receipt of millions of silver pennies. King Edward's income has been estimated at about £8,000 net, plus annual payments. Harold as earl received some £5,000. Together, these sums represent over 3 million silver pennies.[22]

Harold stood for the consolidation of the kingdom under the supremacy of his family, and that would have continued, had his rule survived. His combining of the royal lands of the monarchy with the

lands of Wessex would have recreated the kingdom as it was under
Alfred, and his assumption of the crown displaced the line of Cerdic
with a new house, just as the Carolingians were replaced by Hugh
Capet. The foundation of the Capetian house created a French
kingdom which became the most powerful kingdom in Europe. The
kingdom of England under the House of Godwine could have been
more than its equal, without suffering from the entanglement in the
affairs of Europe brought about by the union of the kingdom with
the Norman dukedom. Just as the Capetians avoided extinction at the
hands of powerful vassals to become a strong monarchy, so Harold
with his family behind him could have united England and perhaps
proceeded to subdue Wales and Scotland, much earlier than happened
in fact.[23]

By marrying the sister of Edwin and Morcar, Harold united the
Houses of Godwine and Leofric. Perhaps he would have married
off one of his sisters to Earl Waltheof and so included the House of
Siward. William of Poitiers, not known for his love of Harold, admits
that Harold 'abounded in riches whereby powerful kings and princes
were brought into his alliance', and one can envisage a continuation
of that policy of seeking European alliances. It would not have been
only under the Normans that England turned towards Europe. Could
it not have been the case that the real point of the journey which
ended in Normandy had in fact been aimed at arranging an alliance
with Normandy, or a renewal of the alliance made by Edward in 1052,
which would have included a diplomatic marriage to a daughter of the
duke, but that Harold repudiated the marriage and the alliance because
of the duress he suffered at William's hands, which led him to distrust
the Norman bastard? Unless, as *Harald's Saga* hints (confusing Wales
with Brittany, perhaps because the source said 'the Brittani', meaning
Bretons), Harold had aimed at an alliance with Duke Conan of Brittany.
After William's campaign in Brittany, he joined forces with Geoffrey of
Anjou and threatened the Norman border. Only his death prevented a
renewal of the war, as he had put in his own claim to the English throne,
just as William was preparing to invade England himself.[24]

But there are many other aspects of the way England developed after the Conquest which can be explored from a different

perspective on the assumption of Harold's survival as king. It might be thought, for instance, that England, without the Conquest, would have had neither castles nor Romanesque cathedrals. As for castles (that is, fortified noble residences), two points can be made. Firstly, the example of the building of motte and bailey castles had been set by Ralf of Hereford and his followers in Herefordshire, as well as the castle at Clavering in Essex. Secondly, almost all sign of fortified thegnly residences was destroyed by the incoming Normans. But evidence has survived of a few enclosures in the form of a simple ditch and bank, at Goltho in Lincolnshire, Sulgrave in Northamptonshire and Middleton Stoney in Oxfordshire. There might have been a link in other places between such pre-Conquest enclosures and later Norman structures such as castles and churches. In a number of places, it is thought that the Norman castle was superimposed on an already existing enclosure. It is thus not possible to be sure that castles would not have been built, especially along borders and in coastal areas, for defence. Harold, who had travelled on the continent, as Tostig and others had done, would have seen and admired such structures. Harold was prepared to copy European style in rebuilding his church at Waltham. He might well have decided to have a royal castle built for his own use, an example which would probably have been followed by many others. Along the route followed by the Conqueror after Hastings, a number of mottes and re-used mounds have been detected, and some might well have been pre-existing English thegnly residences, but all evidence of these was sytematically destroyed by the Norman works.[25]

As for churches and cathedrals, works in stone were not unknown in England. The Confessor had spent much treasure on the erection of Westminster Abbey, his queen, Edith, rebuilt Wilton in stone, and Harold built Waltham Holy Cross. The latter had a stone nave and side chambers and a portico, and was a minster built in stone. There is no reason to suppose that the example set by King Edward and Edith, as well as Harold, should not have been followed. There is no way of knowing how many stone churches had been built before the Conquest, as they were replaced or, as recent evidence suggests, remodelled and extended by the new Norman lords. But Repton in

Derbyshire reveals the impressive nature of late English foundations. King Edward had opened the door to continental influences, probably under the influence of Earl Harold and his sister, appointing a number of foreign, mainly Lotharingian, bishops, men from Flanders and the Holy Roman Empire. Harold had supported Archbishop Ealdred's elevation, and the bishop had visited the continent, bringing back with him many ideas for the improvement of English liturgical practice. Had these influences been allowed to continue under King Harold, they would undoubtedly have led to the development of the Romanesque style in England.[26]

But far more 'Saxon' fabric has survived in many parish churches than was once thought. Norfolk, for example, has over fifty, more than any other county. It has even been argued that all of the round-towered churches (120 standing, eight visible ruins,) are Saxon. For example, Haddiscoe St Mary, St Mary's Burnham Deepdale and All Saints Edingthorpe have what are probably late 'Saxon' round towers, at least in part, built just before the Conquest. St Andrew's Great Dunham has a Saxon square tower. In Oxfordshire, there are eight churches with 'Anglo-Saxon' architectural features. Others have put forward the point that the architects (masons?) who designed Earl's Barton in Northamptonshire and Bradford-on-Avon in Wiltshire would have been building something more advanced by the year 1100. Earl's Barton is largely of Saxon stone construction, but otherwise most churches were constructed of wood and have not survived. St Kenelm's, Minster Lovell, Oxfordshire, was a wooden church of cruciform plan, which was rebuilt in stone to the same plan.[27]

The Conquest is usually said to have improved art and architecture, providing a new impulse, but that impulse had already been given. The 'Winchester' style (found also at Glastonbury, Canterbury and Ely) continued after the Conquest and had its roots in Carolingian exemplars. Towards the middle of the eleventh century, church decoration was evolving towards the Romanesque style. Furthermore, there was the Scandinavian artistic language (the Ringerike style), involving the use of animals and foliage, which was very popular in England under Cnut. Under an Anglo-Danish king, that influence would certainly have persisted. Many 'Anglo-Saxon' artistic traditions survived during the twelfth century, especially the use of the Winchester style in several media – manuscript painting, ivory carving, metalwork and sculpture – and that included the Viking animal styles. They are found at Ipswich, Norwich and Southwell. The English love of ornament was too deeply rooted to be abandoned. Nonetheless, the Normans destroyed the existing churches and replaced them with their own pompous buildings. As soon as a new Norman bishop or abbot was appointed, he began a new church.

On a more prosaic note, it can be argued that the English Church was not in such a poor state as historians once believed. The Norman kings found themselves at odds with their archbishops in a manner foreign to the reign of the Confessor, and were in conflict with the reforming movement of Rome. Yet Rome had made no really determined effort to secure the removal of Archbishop Stigand, as the legatine visit of 1062 demonstrates. The cardinals were quite ready to sit in council with Archbishop Stigand. Rome had usually accepted King Edward's episcopal appointments without demur, and was won over to accept Ealdred in 1060. As king, Harold might have been able to obtain recognition for Stigand as archbishop, using the payment of Peter's Pence as a lever. Stigand, after all, was not a more hateful figure than William Rufus' chancellor, Rannulf Flambard, Bishop of Durham.[29]

There are other areas of English history under the Normans where there would have been similar developments if Harold had been king. The extent to which the Norman kings introduced extensive change in England can be overstated. William I and his successors used the Old English fiscal, legal and administrative systems to their full extent, extracting from them as much as they could, rather than changing them. There is no reason to conclude that Harold would have been less capable of doing so. He probably began as he meant to go on, and he would have been a more 'hands on' king than the Confessor ever was. He made sure that the coinage remained sound during his nine months, and was certainly running the administrative and judicial systems as they had been run when Edward was king and Harold himself was, *de facto*, running the administration.

The record of the chamberlain's holdings in Domesday Book suggests that there was no very great difference in the composition of the royal chamber or the treasury after 1066. The *Peterborough Chronicle* for 1085 reflects no radical change in the fiscal system. Humphrey and Alfric, William's chamberlains, succeeded Aluric, Edward's man, in his lands and office. Henry the treasurer is mentioned, but there is no certainty that he held office under the Confessor, though he could have been one of his 'Frenchmen'. The chamber in Edward's day had been the authority through which all the king's cash was safeguarded and spent, and it remained 'domestic' under King William. The treasury had, by the eleventh century, come to be located at Winchester, which would have attracted a regular attendance there of officers of the chamber, and had begun to develop its own identity. As the scant evidence for 1066 suggests, Harold had simply taken over the existing system, as William was to do in 1067, and if Harold, like his father, had been the king's *bajulus* (he was seen by Wace as a 'seneschal' and by *Harald's Saga* as 'in charge of all the royal treasuries') then he would have overseen the continuation of the development of both chamber and treasury during the Confessor's reign, possibly with the assistance of the queen, his sister. The chamberlains continued to develop under the Normans, becoming known as *cubicularii* under Rufus and Henry I, and such logical development might equally well have occurred under the rule of Harold.[30]

The early Norman kings used the specialised staff of clerks inherited from Edward and Harold, and they had imposed on them a governmental task which became increasingly elaborate as time went on. Such developments had been occurring before 1066, but the coming of the Normans caused the destruction of whatever records there were. Unquestionably, an almost automatic evolution of the administration would have gone on even without the stimulus of the Conquest. An office of receipt and account would have developed, though not perhaps called an exchequer, under Harold or his immediate successor. A body similar to the *curia regis*, but based more firmly on the Witanagemot, in its capacity as an accounting department, might well have evolved. What became known as the exchequer did eventually become more organised and centralised under the

Normans, but then the rest of Europe was developing its administration also. There is no evidence that developments in England
were inspired by the example of ducal administration in Normandy
which was a much more primitive system than that of England, so
the development must have had its roots in English practice before
1066. But the Norman kings loved money. King William 'took from
his subjects many a mark of gold and more hundred pounds of
silver... for little need. He was fallen into covetousness and he loved
greediness above all'. William Rufus and Henry I are also accused of
this vice. Harold, of course, was equally keen on the accumulation
of wealth. The Normans accuse him of avarice – a real case of the
pot calling the kettle black.[31]

The Norman exchequer's system of receipt of coinage, which
was then counted, weighed and blanched (to test for purity) before
being stored, was no great advance on the Old English procedure.
Under Edward, someone must have been responsible for receiving
and accounting for the sheriff's render of the *firma Comitatus* (his
'farming' of the shire), and some sort of record must have been kept,
possibly in the form of split tally sticks, which have not survived,
naturally. Under Henry I, the accounts were recorded on Pipe Rolls,
the use of which could well have evolved out of the recording of
geld on Geld Rolls.

King Edward, and, for that matter, his earls, were rich, accounting
for some 4 million silver pennies a year. They could not have managed to do this without record-keeping. But the Normans had no
interest in retaining past records, especially after the compilation of
Domesday Book, so nothing has survived. Records of some sort must
have been available to the Domesday commissioners, and it may be
that the juries they employed were asked to testify on oath to the
accuracy of those records. Eventually, sometime in the early twelfth
century, the upper exchequer began to use the device which gave it
the name 'exchequer': from the *scaccarium* or chequered cloth which
served as an abacus, so that receipts in tens of thousands, thousands,
hundreds and tens could be displayed before the sheriffs. The balance
of their accounts was worked out in their presence. The concept of
the abacus certainly reached England before the end of the eleventh

century, and, given Harold's interest in the coinage, it might well have developed sooner rather than later, had he been king.[32]

Harold, like William, would have inherited the *cynerhta*, or sovereign's rights, and surrendered none of them. The Norman kings eventually allowed many Old English rights to lapse, because they saw power as flowing from dominion over England by right of Conquest, importing continental ideas and feudal concepts of jurisdiction. Harold would doubtless have continued to develop royal powers along the lines on which he had inherited them, and in which he had been instructed by his father, Earl Godwine. Old English law and administration followed Carolingian or Frankish trends, taking from the Franks a general concept of law, its treatment, definition and function. Church and king worked in tandem as the dominant power. Written law was promoted in oral customary courts, and the accumulated result formed the core of what the Normans were to call the *Laga Edwardi*.[33]

King William took over an Anglo-Scandinavian kingdom which was changing and had already changed. Housecarls were performing many of the functions previously carried out by king's thegns. There was a heavy annual land tax, the geld, and kings maintained a military establishment like the household of Norman kings. Earls were becoming provincial governors with vice-regal powers. Harold had been seen as *Dux Anglorum* or 'Duke of the English', a kind of vice-regal title, just as Hugh Capet had been 'Duke of the Franks'. An England free of the Norman yoke, governed by its own king, might well have evolved a quasi-feudal society, earls (as members of the ruling house) probably being equated with counts and dukes, and housecarls and king's thegns becoming the equivalent of barons (as later Anglo-Norman writers described them).[34]

The Norman magnates, collectively, could not function without a single head, the king, and the Old English state could not do so either, which explains both the alacrity with which Harold was accepted as king and the equal rapidity with which the somewhat effete southern nobility accepted the Conqueror. A king had to be competent in personal relations with those who enjoyed real political power – as Harold wisely cultivated Edwin and Morcar by marrying their sister – but competent also in decision-making, as head of the nascent bureaucracy. He had to be a competent military leader, and Harold had certainly demonstrated that in Wales and again in his brilliant victory at Stamford Bridge. As Orderic Vitalis commented: 'The English are always loyal to their princes'. William of Poitiers said that when the English submitted to the duke they said, 'We are accustomed to obey a king and we desire to have a king as lord'. Harold took over the royal powers without difficulty and was an active king. William of Malmesbury said of him 'because of his character he would have ruled wisely and bravely'.[35]

Looking further to the future for England under a native English rather than a Norman king, detailed forecasts are, of course, impossible. One thing is certain. There would have been no entanglement with Normandy, or Anjou, and so ultimately no claim to be kings of France and no Hundred Years' War. England would not have suffered the destruction of its native aristocracy, slain, exiled or rendered penniless. Instead, England found itself under the rule of an alien aristocracy from Normandy. One result of that foreign importation was to be the division of English society between a mainly French-speaking upper class and the largely English-speaking middle (townsmen and merchants) and lower (yeomen, villeins and serfs) classes.

The 'Anglo-Saxon' state was a nation state with an effective central authority, uniformly organised institutions, a national language, a national Church and clearly defined frontiers. Above all, it had a strong sense of national identity; its inhabitants called themselves the English and their kingdom England. None of this was imported by the Normans. They brought a certain exploitative ruthlessness and their own interpretation of feudalism. But had Harold enjoyed a long reign he might well have been able to improve the situation in the north, so further uniting the kingdom. There could have been much more to Harold's reign and his government of the country than is to be found in the *Anglo-Saxon Chronicles*. It is not now possible to distinguish the originals available down to 1100. The Abingdon text (D) is immediately post-Conquest and has been interpolated. The Peterborough text (E) does not permit the reader to know exactly what his source contained in 1066. Both have been revised, perhaps

censored, at a time when England was firmly under Norman rule.
There might even have been a continuation of the Canterbury text
(C) which has now disappeared, and it is thought that a lost text
of the *Chronicle* lies behind the *Chronicle of Florence of Worcester*. The
Peterborough text conveys the anguish and frustration of the English
and focuses on the Aetheling rather than on Harold. Continental
sources express horror and moral indignation at the bloodshed and
loss of life, and English sources, had they not been stunned by defeat
and under Norman influence, might have said the same.[36]

The last word about Harold may perhaps be left to the epitaph
recorded in Harleian M.S. 3776 fol.62n–62v.

Blessed father of Our Country
Harold
Marked out by your merits
You our shield, fist and sword.

In this Tomb brave Harold Rests
Who Once famed King of England was
On Whom renown, mien, character and authority
Conferred Power and a Kingdom,
A Sceptre and a Crown as well.
Until He strove, a Famous Warrior,
To Defend his own People,
But died: slain by the Men of France.

14

Epilogue

Much important information has been omitted from the main chapters in order not to impede the flow of the narrative. This concerns aspects of the politics of the reign of Edward the Confessor and the proof of the contention that England between the reigns of Cnut the Great and Harold II was an Anglo-Scandinavian polity.

This situation had been established by the original Viking invasion and the ensuing recovery under Alfred and his successors. It was not fundamentally changed by the second onslaught by Swein Forkbeard and his son Cnut. Defeat was nationwide and caused neither political fragmentation nor any weakening of the monarchy, which was, if anything, strengthened. 'Anglo-Scandinavian' was perhaps a better description of Old English Society than 'Anglo-Danish', especially at the top, but there was no fundamental change either in that society or in its institutions.[1]

The inhabitants of England, whether of Anglo-Saxon, Danish or Norse stock, regarded themselves and spoke of themselves as 'Englishmen'. This is obvious from the pages of the *Anglo-Saxon Chronicles* and from those of Domesday Book, which speak of

Englishmen and Frenchmen and occasionally of Danes or Bretons, but never of Anglo-Saxons. The Danes, both descendants of the Viking invaders and of those who came with Cnut, learned to identify themselves with the land in which they had settled and, living in England under Cnut and his successors, lived under English law. Differences of racial origin ceased to be important when intermarriage became commonplace, even at the highest level. Aethelrede II married the great-granddaughter of the Viking Rollo; Edmund Ironside married the widow of the Danish thegn Sigeferth; and Cnut took an English wife, Aelfgifu of Northampton, daughter of Ealdorman Aelfhelm, before putting her aside to marry Aethelrede's widow. Even King Edward married Edith, the Anglo-Danish daughter of Earl Godwine and Gytha, sister-in-law/cousin of Cnut himself.[2]

The area north and east of a line running approximately from just north of London to Chester, along the line of the Roman Watling Street, but not including north-western Mercia, became known as the 'Danelagh' or Danelaw. It was a zone within which the Danes could decide on matters of law and politics for themselves, just as in the area of the former kingdoms of Wessex and Mercia, West Saxon and Mercian law predominated.[3]

Earlier kings had decreed that the Danes should have the right to live 'according to such good laws as they best prefer,' especially in the area known as the Five Boroughs (Lincoln, Derby, Nottingham, Leicester and Stamford), each of which had been the base of a Danish army. They had their own courts and officials, but accepted the kings of England as their lords. One distinguishing mark was the use of the Scandinavian term 'wapentake', from *vápnatak* or the shaking of weapons, rather than 'hundred', for the subdivisions of a shire with their own court.[4]

Then there is the Anglo-Scandinavian institution called a 'soke'. This was an estate made up of a main or central village and dependent pieces of property called variously berewicks or sokelands. The tenant of a soke, called a sokeman, held his land by attending the court of his lord, the holder of the soke, and by paying him a money rent and rendering various services of a non-military kind. The sokes were governed by a great body of custom requiring the sokemen to seek the lord's court, his mill, his sheepfold, his church and so on, to the exclusion of other competing institutions. The sokes in the Danelaw might have had a military purpose, in that they provided for the upkeep of the military followers of Danish lords.[5]

There is also the question of the fighting men known as house-carls. They are seen by some as a body of professional soldiers, maintained by kings and earls as a sort of standing army or house-hold bodyguard. It has been argued, on the basis of twelfth-century evidence which might not apply to the eleventh century, that they belonged to a highly organised guild, united by loyalty to the king and a code of behaviour intended to ensure honourable conduct. Cnut is thought to have introduced them into England, as he had a permanent body of soldiers in his personal service drawn from the crews of forty ships retained in England after he had disbanded most of his fleet and sent it back to Denmark. But there is evidence that it could have been Harthacnut who recruited them. The only certainty is that housecarls were never heard of in England before the reign of Cnut, and that King Edward retained some of them and granted them land.[6]

Only some two dozen men can confidently be identified as house-carls owning land before the Conquest, which does not suggest that there was such a large number of them as to justify the assumption that King Edward kept a standing army of them. After all, if he had such a force, why was it not used in 1051 when Edward confronted Earl Godwine? It seems far more likely that they formed the 'genge' or retinue of most great men, especially the earls, and a small body of household troops who guarded the king. If that were so, then there might have been, in total, some hundreds of these men available to fight for King Harold in 1066; most of them died in the battles or fled abroad after the defeat at Hastings. Some would have been the remnants of Cnut's military household, the 'milites... who are called housecarls in the Danish tongue'. Some of them were quite wealthy and were the equal of king's thegns and stallers who held office in Edward's reign. Even the Frenchman Richard fitzScrob could be called 'my housecarl' by the king. Like thegns, they were equipped for war with hauberks of chainmail and wore leggings to protect themselves, as they fought on foot, needing protection for groin and inside leg.[7]

The polity that was eleventh-century England was also culturally Anglo-Scandinavian. The influx of Danes and Norsemen caused a fusion of art and folklore. Men and women found themselves born into two worlds, one Viking, the other Christian. Kings and lords like Aethelrede, and indeed Edward the Confessor, were at home in the Viking world and earned a place in Norwegian and Icelandic saga. Aethelrede was visited by the famous Icelandic poet Gunlaug Serpent's Tooth, who sang his praises at court. King Edward spent his early youth in a world in which the Vikings were heroes, and he is said to have especially admired Olaf Tryggvason. Much of this can be shown from the poetry of the age. Edward figures in *Olaf's Saga*, Caps 16, 20 and 26. The decorative arts were also influenced by the Ringerike style, which flourished under the Danish kings. It is present in many places, especially on the sarcophagus from the eleventh-century church of St Paul's and on stones preserved at Winchester, as well as in the decoration of manuscripts. The Winchcombe Psalter has a Ringerike snake like that on the St Paul's stone. At Lincoln, the Anglo-Scandinavian élite owned Hiberno-Norse monuments, and Creeton, Lincolnshire, has more Anglo-Scandinavian monuments in its churchyard than any other unexcavated church in the county. In northern England, monuments show a blending of Christian and Norse mythology in which, for instance, Sigurd is portrayed as a counterpart to St Michael the Archangel. Pagan iconography was used to convey Christian ideas.[8]

Genealogical Tables
and Map

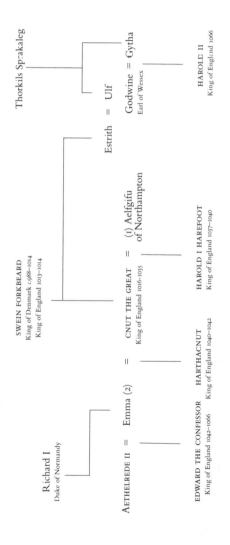

Thorkils Sprakaleg

SWEIN FORKBEARD
King of Denmark c.988–1014
King of England 1013–1014

Estrith = Ulf

Godwine = Gytha
Earl of Wessex

HAROLD II
King of England 1066

Richard I
Duke of Normandy

AETHELREDE II = Emma (2) = CNUT THE GREAT = (1) Aelfgifu
King of England 1016–1035   of Northampton

EDWARD THE CONFESSOR   HARTHACNUT
King of England 1042–1066   King of England 1040–1042

HAROLD I HAREFOOT
King of England 1037–1040

1 The Anglo-Danish Dynasty

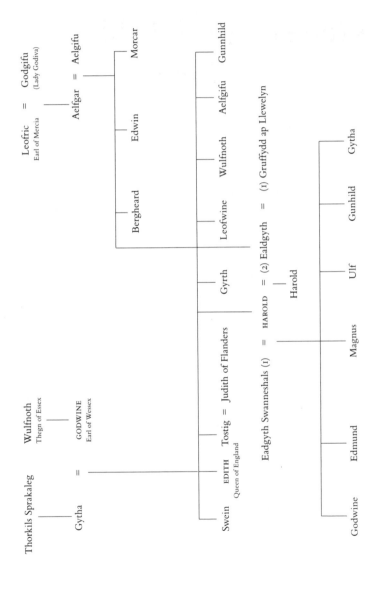

2 The House of Godwine

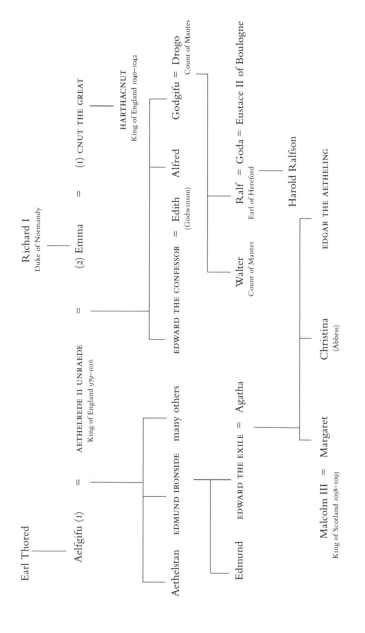

3 The Descendants of Aelthelred

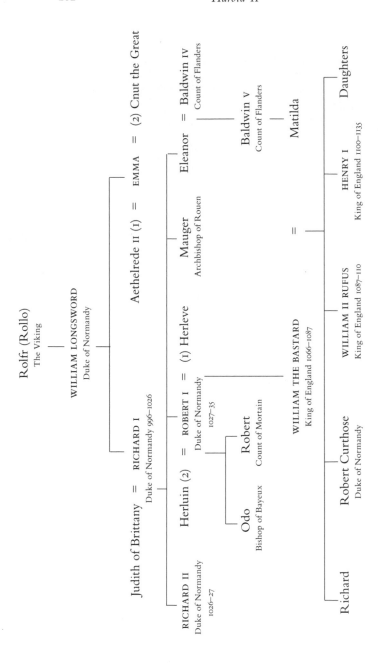

4 The Dukes of Normandy and Kings of England

The Journey of Earl Harold in 1056

Notes

1 The Anglo-Scandinavian Prologue

1   G.O. Sayles, *The Medieval Foundations of England*, p.145; E.A. Freeman. *History of the Norman Conquest*, vol. I pp.166ff; D.J.V. Fisher, *The Anglo-Saxon Age c.400 to 1042*, p.320.; S. Reynolds, *Kingdoms and Communities in Western Europe*, p.266; *Chronicles* C.D.E.F.1002 and 1015 (*Anglo-Saxon Chronicles*, ed. and trans. J. Stevenson, 1853 and M. Swanton, 2000).

2   Hadley and Richards, p.85; R. Fleming, *Kings and Lords in Conquest England*, p.21 and p.47; Ian W. Walker, *Harold, the Last Anglo-Saxon King*, p.1; K.Mack, 'Changing Thegns; Knut's Conquest of the English Aristocracy', *Albion* 16, 1984.

3   Campbell, pp.33-4 and 36; Eric John, *Edward the Confessor and the Norman Succession*, E.H.R. 94, 1979; Fleming, pp.40-1.

4   Fleming, p.42; Ann Williams, 'Thegnly Piety and Ecclesiastical Patronage in the Late Old English Kingdom', *A.N.S.* 23, 2000; R. Fleming, 'The Domesday Estates of the King and the Godwines; a study in late Saxon Politics', *Speculum* 58, 1983; E.H.R. 94; *Vita Edwardi Regis*, p.6; Hill, P., *The Road to Hastings; the Politics of Power in Anglo-Saxon England*. p.56.

5   Fleming, p.44.

6   Fleming, pp.48-51.

7   Fleming, p.53; G.O. Sayles, *The Medieval Foundations of England*, p.157

8   Michel de Boüard, *Guillaume Le Conquerant*, p.238.

9   Fisher, p.341; Freeman, vol. I p.583 and vol. II p.518; Chronicles and Florence 1042.

10   Campbell, p.225; D.J.A. Matthew, *The Norman Conquest*, p.36; F. Barlow, *Edward the Confessor*, p.53; P.G. Foote and D.M. Wilson, *The Viking Achievement*, p.11; *E.H.D.I.* p.428; J.R. Maddicott, 'Edward the Confessor's return to England in 1041', E.H.R. 109, 2004; *Quadripartitus* Ch. 9. *A.S.C.* C and D 1041.

11   Ian W. Walker, *Harold the Last Anglo-Saxon King*, p.153.

12   Walker, p.152; *Chronicles* D.1046 C.D. 1066.

13 Oman, p.624; Stenton, p.570; Barlow, p.202; Chronicles C.D. and Florence
1054; D.E.F. 1055.

14 Walker, pp.104-5; Stenton, p.570; Barlow p.203; Higham p.234; Chronicles
E.1064; C.D. 1065.

15 Higham, p.234; Oman, p.632; Barlow, p.203; Chronicles D.1061; Kapelle, p.94;
Oman, pp.632-3.

16 Stenton, p.560 and 572; Barlow, pp.207-209; Ormerod, p.51.

17 Ormerod, p.51; Oman, p.635 and 627; Stenton, pp.572-576; Barlow, pp.210-13.

2 The Rise of the House of Godwine

1 *Anglo-Saxon Chronicles*, ed. and trans. J. Stevenson, 1853 and M. Swanton,
2000, D, E and F 1009 (Swanton translates 'cild' as 'prince'); J. Stevenson, *The
Chronicle of Florence of Worcester*, 1853; Emma Mason, *The House of Godwine.
The History of a Dynasty*, Ch.3; Ian W. Walker, *Harold the Last Anglo-Saxon
King*, Ch.1; Sir Frank Stenton, *Anglo-Saxon England*, 3rd edn, pp.416-7; E.A.
Freeman, *The History of the Norman Conquest*, vol.1, note F; Oman, *England
Before the Norman Conquest*, p.570. D.G.J. Raraty, 'Earl Godwine of Wessex; the
Origin of his power and his political loyalties', *History* 74, 1989.

2 Freeman, note F; F. Barlow, *The Godwins*, pp.18-19; Swanton, Chronicles
D.E.F.1009 Florence, Stevenson 1007-8; Oman, p.570; M.K. Lawson, *Cnut; the
Danes in England in the Early Eleventh Century*; Raraty, *op. cit.* above; Williams,
op.cit. p.116.

3 Mason, p.31; Walker, p.9; Freeman, note F, above.

4 Walker, p.5; Freeman, note F, above; Lawson, *Cnut*; R. Fleming, *Kings and Lords
in Conquest England*; A. Rumble, ed., 'The Reign of Cnut', *Albion* 16, 1984;
K. Mack, 'Changing Thegns; Knut's Conquest and the English Aristocracy',
Midland History 11 A; Williams, 'Cockles among the Wheat; Danes and
Englishmen in the Western Midlands in the first half of the Eleventh
Century', D.B.I 21;26 and 24;34.

5 Freeman, note F, above; Walker, pp.10-12; Mason, pp.30 and 34; Oman, p.585;
P.Stafford, *Queen Emma and Queen Edith*, Blackwell 1997, pp.41 and 256.

6 Walker, pp.6-7; Mason, pp.27-8; Oman, p.576; Chronicles C.D.E.F. and
Florence 1015.

7 Barlow, *The Godwins*, p.21; Freeman, note F; Walker, pp.6-7; Chronicles
C.D.E.F. and Florence 1017.

8 Freeman, note F; Hill, *op.cit.* p.64; Geoffrey Gaimar 'L'Estorie des Engles',
p.155.

9 Barlow, *The Godwins*, p.28; Chronicles E.F. 1025; Hill *op.cit.* p.65; Runestenen
ved Oddernes Kirke, p.8; M. Olsen, 1908.

10 English Historical Documents vol. II, 1042–1189, ed. D.C. Douglas, no.131;
Walker, pp.9 and 11; Williams, *Midland History*, 11.

11 F. Barlow, ed. and trans., *The Life of King Edward who rests at Westminster*; Walker,
p.11; Chronicles E.F. 1025.

12 Chronicles C.D.E.F. and Florence 1018 and 1020.

13 Harmer, Writs no.116; Walker, Ch.I; Mason, Ch.III; Chronicles 1026 to 1036;

Oman, Ch.27; Stenton, Ch.12.

14   Chronicles E.F. 1039; C.D.E.F. 1040 and Florence 1040.

15   Barlow, *Life of King Edward*; Walker, p.16; Mason, p.41; Stenton, p.423; Chronicles C.D. and Florence 1040.

16   Chronicles C.D. and Florence 1041.

17   Walker, p.16; Mason, p.42; Oman, p.609; F. Barlow, *Edward the Confessor*, p.56; *Encomium Emmae Reginae*, ed. and trans. A. Campbell; *Saxo Grammaticus Gesta Danorum*, p.360; Chronicles C.D. and Florence 1041-42; Hill, p.74; William of Malmesbury, *Gesta Regum* I 197.

18   Barlow, *Edward*, pp.20-21; Mason, p.43.

19   Mason, p.44; Barlow, *Edward*, p.57; Walker, p.18; Oman, p.613; Chronicles D.E.F. and Florence 1043/44; K.J. Leyser, *Communications and Power in Medieval Europe*, p.109; Ann Williams, *Aethelrede the Unready: The Ill-Counselled King*, p.151ff; J. Le Patourel, *The Norman Empire*.

20   Freeman, note F; Walker, p.12; Mason, p.35.

21   Walker, pp.18-20; Barlow, *Edward*, p.91; Oman, pp.613-4.

22   Walker, pp.23-4; Stenton, p.428; Chronicles E. and Florence 1045/1046.

23   Stenton, pp.547-49.

24   Walker, p.19; *E.H.D.* vol.II, no.187 and no.183.

25   Walker, p.61 and pp.127-8; Mason, 138-41 and 198-99.

26   T.J. Oleson, *The Witanagemot in the Reign of Edward the Confessor*; Walker, p.20; Stenton, p.547; Chronicles C.D. 1046.

27   Stenton, p.430; Walker, p.21; Oman, p.615; Chronicles D.E. and Florence 1049.

28   Barlow, *Life of King Edward*, pp.19-22; Oman, pp.611-12; Stenton, p.565; Mason, p.51; Fleming, p.89, for Wroxall; M.W. Campbell, 'A Pre-Conquest Occupation of England?', *Speculum* 46 1971.

29   Oman, p.618; Stenton, pp.569-70; Mason, pp.89-92; Walker, p.78; Barlow, *Edward*, p.94; Chronicles C.1055 D. 1052 (for 1051).

30   Walker, p.40; F. Barlow, *The English Church 1000-1066*, London 1979; P.A. Clarke, *The English Nobility under Edward the Confessor*, Oxford 1994.

31   Barlow, *Edward*, p.86; Mason, p.57.

32   Mason, p.54; Walker, p.22; Oman, p.615; Chronicles C. 1044/1046; Florence 1049.

33   Oman, p.614; Barlow, *Edward*, p.92; Stenton, p.427; Chronicles D 1048, Florence 1047.

34   Stenton, p.428; Oman, p.614; Barlow, *Edward*, pp.97-98; Chronicles C.D. 1047–1050, Florence 1049.

35   Chronicles C.D. 1049–1050 and E 1046 (for 1049), Florence 1049.

36   Stenton, p.429; Chronicles C.D. 1049–1050 E 1046 (for 1049).

37   Mason, pp.56-7; Walker, p.25; Chronicles A. 1050. C. 1049–50, Florence 1049.

38   Barlow, *Edward*, pp.102-3; Walker, p.27; Mason, p.53; Stenton, p.425.

39   Stenton, p.650; Oman, p.615; Barlow, *Edward*, p.141; Chronicles E 1047 (for 1050) C 1049 D 1050 (for 1051), Florence 1051.

40   Barlow, *Edward*, p.63 and p.80; Mason, p.46; The Leofric Missal ed. F. Warren, Oxford 1883, p.99.

3 Arrivals and Departures

1   *The Chronicle of John of Worcester*, vol.II, ed. R.R. Darlington and P.J. McGurk, Oxford 1995; previously known as *Florence of Worcester Chronicle of Chronicles*; and the edition ed. and trans. by J. Stevenson, London 1853, from which most citations are derived.

2   *Anglo-Saxon Chronicles*, ed. and trans. M. Swanton, and other translations; J. Stevenson, London 1853, S.I. Tucker, in *English Historical Documents* vol.2, G.N. Garmonsway, 1955. See R. Fleming, *Speculum* 58, 1983; Sayles *op.cit.* p.158. Introductions to these translations provide a useful guide to the form and nature of the chronicles.

3   *Vita Edwardi Regis* (hereinafter *Vita*); *The Life of King Edward who rests at Westminster.*

4   *Vita*, pp.31-39 for Godwine and the archbishop; Walker, Ch.3; Mason, Ch.4; F. Barlow, *The Godwins*; Oman, Ch.28; Stenton, Ch.15; R. Huscroft, *Ruling England*, p.25; Frank Barlow, *Edward the Confessor*, Ch.5; Michel de Boüard, *Guillaume le Conquerant*, pp.240-53; Eric John, *Reassessing Anglo-Saxon England*, Ch.11.

5   *Vita*, p.41; Mason, *op.cit.* pp.54-5 and 69; Walker, *op.cit.*, p.43; De Boüard, *op.cit.*, p.208; John, *op.cit.*, p.176; Barlow, E.H.R. 80, 1965.

6   *Vita* pp.29-31; Barlow, p 50, 76, 125, 164-5.

7   *Vita*, p.37.

8   Freeman, *passim*; G.O. Sayles, *The Foundations of Medieval England*, p.157; D.C. Douglas, *William the* Conqueror, pp.166-70; Oman, *op.cit.* p.620; Stenton, *op.cit.* p.567 and 560-1; John, *op.cit.* p.127 and 179; *A.N.S.*17 1995; C.P. Lewis, *The French in England before the Norman Conquest*; E.H.R. 94 1979; Worcester Chron. D 1052; Hill p.104. Some accept that Edward wanted William as his successor; others are sceptical. Some put an offer of succession before the breach with Godwine, others after it.

9   *Vita*, p.37; *Peterborough Chronicle* E for 1048 (actually 1051); Barlow, p.77, 79 and 86; Mason, p.50; D.J.A. Matthew, *The Norman Conquest*, p.30.

10 Charter for Godwine K.C.D. 793; all three chronicles C,D,E for 1049.

11 Worcester D 1052 (for 1051) as against Peterborough E 1048 (for 1051); Oman, p.617; Stenton, p.562ff; Mason, p.61; Walker, p.30; De Boüard, p.24; Barlow, pp.110-11.

12 D under 1052 (1051), E under 1048 (1051), Florence of Worcester 1051.

13 Stenton, pp.599-600; John, p.178; H.W.C. Davis, *England under the Normans and Angevins*; R.A. Brown, *The Normans*, p.123; Douglas, pp.212-3; William of Poitiers G.N.D., p.264; De Boüard, p.340. Hill, p.104, thinks Edward gave Dover to William in 1051 when he promised him the throne. That, if true, might mean that Eustace was taking control of it for William. A likely story!

14 D and E for 1051 plus Florence of Worcester; Oman, pp.618-9; *Anglo-Saxon Chronicle* version F in Latin and Old English, B.Mus. Cott. M.S. Domit. A viii.

15 E 1048 (1051); Florence of Worcester 1051.D 1052 (1051); Stenton, p.561; Mason pp.52-3; R. Fleming, 'The New Wealth, the New Rich and the New Political Style in late Anglo-Saxon England', *A.N.S.* 23, 2001.

16 E, D and Florence of Worcester 1051. For 'genge' meaning 'retinue' or band of

retainers, see C for 1043 – the three earls and their band 'mid heora genge' –
then E and D 1051 for Siward and Leofric and 'heora genges'; also Hereward
and his genge in E 1070.

17   Mason, p.33; E and D for 1051; Oman, p.618; Stenton, pp.563-4; Barlow, p.111.

18   E and D 1051 and Florence of Worcester.

19   D and E 1051; Eric John in *The Anglo-Saxons*, ed. J. Campbell, p.225. For King
      Diairmaid, *Vita*, p.25 and 41.

20   E 1046 (for 1049) D 1052 (for 1051) C 1049 E 1048 (for 1051). E is out of
      synchronisation with other texts until 1052 when it omits entries under
      several years and begins again at 1052.

21   C, D and E 1052, plus Florence of Worcester and F under 1051. Then C, D
      and E 1053.

22   E 1052; Mason, pp.52-3; Stenton, p.561; Barlow, pp.164-5.

23   C.W. Previté, *Shorter Cambridge Medieval History*, vol. I; Orton, 1952, p.399.

24   *Vita*, p.37; E 1048 (10510 D 1052 (1051); Florence of Worcester 1051. For
      Emma, C 1043 E 1042 (1043) D 1043 and Florence of Worcester; Barlow,
      p.115; Mason, p.66; Walker, p.36; Oman, p.620; Stenton, p.565. He says 'to live
      in retirement'. John E.H.R. 94, 1979.

25   Osbert of Clare, *Vita Beati Edwardi*. Barlow, intro. to *Vita* lxxvi; Walker, p.35;
      Barlow, pp.80-83; William of Malmesbury, G.R. i. 239, for adultery charge:
      he is sceptical. *Vita* devotes little time to idea that chastity meant virginity.
      Osbert speaks only of 'purity of the flesh' and 'chastity', neither of which
      entails virginity. Canonisation was granted for evidence of miracles and
      incorruptibility of the body.

26   Barlow, p.82.

27   Barlow, p.83; *Vita*, p.23, 28 and 43; Barlow in E.H.R. 80 1965 and *Vita* intro.
      lxxvi; Osbert, p.14; Orderic Vitalis, *Eccles. Hist.* ii 47.

28   *Vita*, pp.59-60; C and D 1054, D. and E 1057.

29   D 1052 (1051) for the visit. Florence of Worcester repeats.

30   John, pp.179-80; Mason, p.110ff and 67; Walker, p.37; Oman, p.620; Stenton,
      pp.565-6; Douglas, p.169; Barlow, E.H.R. 80, 1965; Douglas, E.H.R. 68,
      1953; M.W. Campbell, 'A Pre-Conquest occupation of England?' *Speculum* 66,
      1971; *The Anglo-Saxons*, ed. J. Campbell, p.225; Eric John: 'the tensions and
      possibilities of a Norman alliance made the crisis of 1051'; Hill, p.109.

31   William of Poitiers, G.N.D. pp.121-23; Oleson, E.H.R. 72, 1957. For William's
      visit as a search by Edward for a Norman alliance, E. John, E.H.R. 94, 1979.

32   F. Barlow, *The Godwins*, p.44; C, D and E 1052 and Florence of Worcester;
      Oman, pp.620-21; Barlow, pp.120-25; Stenton pp.566-69.

33   C.D and E 1052; *The Godwins*, pp.450-7; Mason, Ch.5; John, pp.180-81;
      Walker, p.35 and 43-49.

34   C, D and E 1052.

35   C, D and E 1052.

36   C, D and E 1052; William of Jumiéges G.N.D., p.160 sec.31.

37   C, D and E 1052 and Florence of Worcester.

38   Walker, p.50; Mason, pp.78-9; Barlow, p.149; Stenton, p.465.

39   Death of Godwine: C, D and E 1053 plus Florence of Worcester; Oman, p.622,
      on choking story; from William of Malmesbury G.R. 197, Roger of Wendover,

Flores Historiarum I. 492 and Henry of Huntingdon, *Historia Anglorum* pp.378–9; Mason, pp.79–81.

4 The Earl in his Earldom

1   P. Hunter Blair, *An Introduction to Anglo-Saxon England*, p.106.

2   E.H.R. 94, 1979; Eric John, *Edward the Confessor and the English Succession*.

3   *English Historical Documents*, vol.II, nos 184 and 187.

4   *Abingdon Chron*. 'C' 1049 and 1050; A. Williams, 'Land and Power in the Eleventh Century; the Estates of Harold Godwinson', *A.N.S.* 2 1979.

5   Stenton, pp.547–49; Walker, p.54.

6   *Worcester Chron*. 'D' 1052; E.H.R.85 1970.

7   III Edgar 5; Walker, *op.cit* p.50.

8   *Vita*, pp.10–11; E.H.R. 80 1965; F. Barlow, *Edward the Confessor; Early Life, character and attitudes*.

9   Edgar's Code; *Wihtbordesstan*, IV Edgar 15.

10 S.Barber, 'The Earls of Mercia and their commended men in the Eleventh century' *A.N.S.* 23 2000; 'The New Wealth, the New Rich and the New Political Style in Late Anglo-Saxon England', *A.N.S*, 23 2000 p.20.

11 *Waltham Chronicle*; L. Watkins and M. Chibnall, *Oxford Medieval Texts*, 1994 xvi. R. Fleming, 'The Domesday estates of the King and the Godwines; a study in late Saxon politics', *Speculum* 58 1983; also E.John, E.H.R. 94 1979.

12 J.L. Grassi, 'The Lands and Revenues of Edward the Confessor', E.H.R. 117 2002.

13 E. John, E.H.R. 94 1979, p.70.

14 F. Barlow, *The Godwins; the Rise and Fall of a Noble Dynasty*, p.61.

15 E.H.R. 94 1979.

16 F.W. Maitland, *Domesday Book and Beyond*, p.183 and 282.

17 D. Roffe in Donaldson, *The Inquest and the Book*; Domesday.

18 Ann Williams, *Aethelrede the Unready: the Ill-Counselled King*, p.102.

19 F. Barlow, *Edward the Confessor*, p.174.

20 E.Fernie, *Saxons, Normans and their buildings*, *A.N.S.* 19 1996, p.8.

21 *A.N.S.* 19 as above; *Medieval Knighthood* ed. C. Harper-Bill and C. Harvey, Woodbridge 1992; Fleming, *A.N.S.* 21 2000, p.9.

22 C. Coulson, 'Peaceable Power in English Castles', *A.N.S.* 23 2000.

23 N.S.G. Pounds, *The Medieval Castle in England and Wales; a social and political history*, pp.223–4.

24 *Archaeological Journal* cxxxiv, 1997.

25 Vict. C.H. Kent vol.I 1908, p.435.

26 *Current Archaeology* xii, 1969.

27 D.Hinton, 'Archaeology, Economy and Society', *A.N.S.* 24 2001; *Waltham Chron*. intro. xvi.

28 K.Mack, *Journal of Medieval History*, 12 1986.

29 K. Mack, 'Kings and Thegns; aristocratic participation in the governance of Anglo-Saxon England', unpublished research paper, University of California at Santa Barbara, 1982.

30   *The Godwins;* F.Barlow, p.27.
31   G.R. Owen-Crocker, *Dress in Anglo-Saxon England*, p.150 and 153-6; Fleming *A.N.S.* 23 2000, p.9.
32   *Vita,* pp.54-7.
33   *Waltham Chron.,* cap. 16 and 22; Fleming, *A.N.S,*23 2000, p.9.
34   E. John, E.H.R. 91, 1976.
35   Bayeux Tapestry, plates 3-6, 27-31; *Vita,* p.21; *Worcester Chron.* 'D' 1063 and 1065.
36   *Waltham Chron.,* introduction *passim* and caps 6-13 and 22; Florence 1052.
37   William of Poitiers, G.G. 204-5; Hugh the Chanter; *History of the Church of York,* ed. C. Johnson, p.4-5.
38   William of Jumièges, G.N.D. ii 18; Northlaga I 458-61.
39   Florence of Worcester 1051.
40   Florence of Worcester 1040
41   *Vita,* pp.36-7; Florence 1051.
42   *Wulstan Cantor Narratis Metrica de Sancto Swithuno,* ed. A. Campbell.
43   *Anglo-Saxon Chronicles* C,D and E 1017.
44   William of Malmesbury, G.R. 1. 35-9, *A.N.S.* 23, 2000, 'Keeping up with the Godwinsons; in pursuit of aristocratic status in late Anglo-Saxon England', C.Senecal.
45   *Rectitudines Singularum Personarum,* 1. 76 and 1. 444-5; Alfred's Code 42.5.
46   H.E.J. Cowley, *Towards an Interpretation of the Bayeux Tapestry, A.N.S.* 19, 1986; Walker, *op.cit.* p.69.

5 Earl of Wessex

1   *Vita Edwardi Regis,* ed. F. Barlow, introduction *passim; Waltham Chronicle,* ed. L. Watkiss and M. Chibnall.
2   *Vita Edwardi,* intro; I.W. Walker, *Harold the Last Anglo-Saxon King,* p.120.
3   *Vita Edwardi* as above; Orderic Vitalis, *Ecclesiastical History;* William of Jumièges, p.172, sec.35.
4   *Anglo-Saxon Chron.* C, D and E 1046-47 and 1052; Florence of Worcester 1063; *Vita Edwardi,* p.48; Brit. Library Add. MS 33241 fol.4.
5   *Encomium Emmae Reginae,* ed. A. Campbell, London 1949.
6   Bayeux Tapestry, various plates; Walker *op.cit.* p.120; Mason, p.102.
7   *The Story of British Coinage,* P. Seaby, London 1985; H. Grueber and C. Keary, *English Coins in the British Museum;* Mason, p.141.
8   Adam of Bremen, *Chronicle of the Archbishops of Bremen; Chronique de Saint Maixent* 751-1140 p.136; Sayles *op.cit.* p.160.
9   Walker, *op.cit.* p.66
10   Walker, pp.67-68.
11   *Vita Edwardi,* intro.
12   *Vita* as above.
13   *Vita* as above.
14   *Waltham Chronicle.*
15   A. Williams, *Land and Power in the Eleventh century, A.N.S.* 2 1979; R. Fleming,

The estates of Harold Godwinson; 'The Domesday Estates of the King and the Godwines: A Study in Late Saxon Politics' *Speculum* 58 1983; R.H. Davies, 'The Lands of Harold Son of Godwine', unpub. PhD thesis, Cardiff 1967; J.L. Grassi, 'The Lands and revenues of Edward the Confessor', E.H.R. 117 2002; K. Mack, 'Kings and Thegns; aristocratic participation in the governance of Anglo-Saxon England', unpub. research paper, University of California at Santa Barbara, 1982.

16   As above.

17   As above.

18   As above.

19   William of Jumièges, G.N.D. p.360 sec. 31; William of Poitiers, G.G. p.54; Lucien Musset, *La Tapisserie de Bayeux*.

20   *Waltham Chron.* II p.227; *E.H.D.* II Doc. 187.DB. fol.59 Essex; Williams, *A.N.S.* 2 1979.

21   F.W. Maitland, *Domesday Book and Beyond* 1897, p.207, 1965 edition, DB fol.101 Devon and 75 Dorset.

22   Walker, *op.cit.*; Williams, *op.cit.*

23   Williams, *op.cit.*; Walker, *op.cit.*, p.127ff; Mason, *op.cit.*, pp.138-41.

24   See Stenton, p.570; Oman, pp.623-4; Barlow, pp.201-3.

25   *Anglo-Saxon Chron.* C,D and E 1055 and Florence 1055; Oman, p.625; Stenton, pp.572-3.

26   Gerald of Wales, *Description of Wales*, trans. L. Thorpe, Book 2 Ch.3; Barlow, p.206 n.4; *Anglo-Saxon Chron.* D and E and Florence 1063; Stenton, p.576; Oman, pp.628-9.

27   *Anglo-Saxon Chron.* C and D 1055 and Florence; Oman, p.625; Stenton, p.573.

28   *Anglo-Saxon Chron.* C and D; Florence, also 1055; Gerald of Wales, Bk.2 Ch.3.

29   Walker, *op.cit.* p.83; Oman, p.626; Stenton, p.574.

30   Walker, *op.cit.* p.77; *Anglo-Saxon Chron.* D 1058.

31   Florence 1058; *Annales Cambriae* R.S. 20 1860 p.25; Stenton, p.575; *Annals of Tigernach* in A.O. Anderson, *Early Sources of Scottish History* ii.1; *Revue Celtique* xvii 1896; *Brut y Twysogion Peniarthi*, T. Jones, Cardiff 1952, p.14; Walker, *op.cit.* p.85; Barlow, p.209; Mason, p.94.

32   Gerald of Wales, Book 2 Ch.3; *Vita*, p.57; *Anglo-Saxon Chron.* D and E 1063 and Florence; Oman, p.628; Stenton, p.576; Walker, pp.87-9; Mason, pp.100-101.

33   Gerald of Wales, Book 2 Ch.3; *Vita*, p.87; and as note 32.

34   As note 32. Gerald of Wales, Book 2 Ch.7.

35   As note 32. *Anglo-Saxon Chron.* C and D 1065.

6 Queens and Countesses

1   Stafford, *Queeen Emma and Queen Edith*, p.256; *Vita*, pp.10-11; Mason, pp.34-5; Walker, p.10; Barlow, *The Godwins*, p.23

2   Walker, pp.11-12; *E.H.D.*ll No.184; Whitelock, *Anglo-Saxon Wills*, pp.30-34; Oman, *op.cit.* p.602; Harmer, *Anglo-Saxon Writs*, p.563; Mason, p.35; Stafford, p.256.

3   Mason, p.35; Stafford, pp.255-7; *Vita*, p.15.
4   Mason, pp.34-5; Walker, p.12; Oman, p.602; Barlow, *Edward the Confessor* p.293 note 2; Barlow, *The Godwins* p.112 and 115; 'Anglo-Latin Satirical Poets and Epigrammatists of the Twelfth Century' vol. 1, *Epig. Hist.* 4.
5   Stafford, p.3 and 209ff.
6   M.K. Lawson, *Cnut: the Danes in England in the early Eleventh Century*, p.55; Duggan, *Queens and Queenship* p.29 n.13; Stafford, *Queens and Concubines* p.4.
7   Stafford, *Queens and Concubines* and *Queen Emma and Queen Edith*. Also Duggan, *Queens and Queenship, passim*.
8   Walker, p.61ff; Stafford, *Queen Emma and Queen Edith*, p.113.
9   F. Barlow, E.H.R 80 1965; *Edward the Confessor: his early life, character and attitudes*; *Vita*, p.14; Duggan, p.37; Mason, pp.51-2.
10 Henry of Huntingdon, *Historia Anglorum* Ch.6; E.A. Freeman, *Norman Conquest* vol.1. p.332; Orderic Vitalis, *Eccles. Hist.* Bk 6 pp.168-9.
11 R. Fletcher, *Bloodfeud*, p.38; Lawson, *Cnut*, p.132; Van Houts, *A.N.S.* 2 1979; *Gesta Normannorum Ducum* p.16; Freeman vol 1. pp.612-14.
12 *Vita* p.9 and 14-15; Walker, p.17; Mason, p.43; Oman, pp.609-10; Barlow, p.56; *Anglo-Saxon Chronicle* C,D and E and Florence 1042.
13 *Encomium Emmae*, pp.52-3; *Anglo-Saxon Chronicle* and Florence as above.
14 *Encomium*, B.L. Add. M.S. 33241 fol.4 and *Liber Vitae of New Minster*, B.L. Stowe M.S. 914 fol.6; P. Cavell, *Vikings: Fear and Faith in England*, p.34; Duggan, intro.; Mason, p.4-5; Barlow, *The Godwins*, p.8; Stafford *op.cit.* p.263; *Medieval Europe* ed. S. Mews and B. Yorke.
15 Barlow, ed. and trans, *Vita*, intro. *passim*.
16 Stafford *op.cit.* Pref. viii; J. Campbell, *The Anglo-Saxons*, p.208; Lawson, p.55; De Boüard, *Guillaume Le Conquerant*, p.235.
17 Osbert of Clare, *Vita Edwardi* p.14; E. John, 'Edward the Confessor and the Norman Succession' E.H.R. 94 1979; Barlow, *Vita*, intro. pp.22-24 from Richard of Cirencester and p.81; Stafford, *Queens and Concubines*, p.5 and *Queen Emma and Queen Edith*, p.45 and 50.
18 Duggan, p.30; *Vita*, pp.24-5.
19 Stafford, *Queens and Concubines*, p.5.
20 John and Barlow, E.H.R. as above; *The Godwins*, p.20 and 263; Stafford, *Queen Emma and Queen Edith*, p.260ff; Duggan, p.81ff.
21 Stafford, as above, p.88; Walker, p.118; *Anglo-Saxon Chron.* C and D and Florence 1065.
22 Barlow, *The Godwins*, p.8.
23 Barlow *op.cit.* pp.263-5; Stafford *op.cit.* p.268; *Anglo-Saxon Chron.* sub anno 1051; *Vita* p.23.
24 Stafford *op.cit.* p.264ff.
25 *Anglo-Saxon Chron.* and Florence 1052 and 1054; Barlow, E.H.R. 80 1965; *Vita* pp.34-5; *The Godwins*, p.25.
26 Barlow, intro. to *Vita* lxvi; John, E.H.R. 94 1979; *Waltham Chron.* Sec. 9 (Harold 'next to the King'); Oleson, *Witanagemot* p.3; *Anglo-Saxon Chron.* 1065; Walker, p.105; Jolliffe, *Const. Hist.* p.135; N.J. Higham, *The Kingdom of Northumbria A.D. 350-1100*, pp.235-6.
27 Higham *op.cit.* p.236; *Anglo-Saxon Chron.* sub anno 1065 for negotiations.

28   *The Godwins,* p.23. *Vita* p.81.

29   Stafford *op.cit.* p.14.

30   Stafford as above; *Anglo-Saxon Chron.* D and E 1075 and Florence.

31   Stafford *op.cit.* p.15.

32   *Vita,* p.6 and 48; *Waltham Chron.* p.27.

33   William of Malmesbury, *Gesta Regum,* p.197; Osbert of Clare, cap.4; *Vita,* intro.
     lxvi; Stafford *op.cit.* p.268; Barlow, *Edward the Confessor,* p.293 note 2; Oman,
     p.602; Williams, *A.N.S.* 19; Walker, p.12; Mason, p.35.

34   Walker, p.66 and 131; Freeman, II, pp.545-6; Williams, *A.N.S.* 19; William of
     Poitiers G.G. pp.204-5; Orderic LL pp.178-80; Malmesbury G.R. LL pp.304-7.

35   *Anglo-Saxon Chron.* C and D 1067; Walker, p.192; Stafford *op.cit.* p.276; J.
     Hudson, *A.N.S.* 19 1996; *Chron. Abingdon* LL p.283; Freeman, LL note 2 p.351;
     New Monasticon vol.6 p.435.

7 The Wives of Harold Godwinson

1   Walker, p.61ff, 127, 195, 138-9; Domesday Book l. fol. 4; Freeman lll p.763,
     note NN; *De Inventione Sanctae Crucis,* p.21. *Vita Haroldi,* p.34; *Waltham Chron.*
     xliv and xlviii also p.55; *The Godwins,* p.56 and 90; Freeman ll Append. RRiv
     Append.M.; Searle, *A.N.S.* 2 1979; *Anglo-Saxon Chron.* sub anno 1066 R.W.
     Chambers, *England before the Norman Conquest,* pp.306-7; *Heimskringla. Harald's
     Stave of Stein Herdisarson.*

2   *Anglo-Saxon Chron.* sub anno 1063; Walker, pp.130-31 and 199; *The Godwins*
     p.90; Mason, pp.138-9.

3   Walker, pp.138-9; Mason, pp.139-40.

4   *Waltham Chron.* Xxxxliv-xlvii and p.55; *Vita Haroldi,* p.210; *The Godwins,*
     pp.177-79; Walker, p.181.

5   As *Waltham Chron.* Above; Walker, p.128 and 130; *Anglo-Saxon Chron.* sub
     anno 1068; Duggan *op.cit.* pp.63-66; Freeman l pp.612-14.

6   Walker, p.127, 131 and 199; *Vita Haroldi,* p.34; Searle, *A.N.S.2* 1979; Fletcher,
     Bloodfeud, p.127; Lawson, *Cnut,* p.132; Duggan, p.33; Freeman l pp.612-14; C.
     Morris, *The Papal Monarchy; the Western Church from 1050 to 1250,* p.103 7 329;
     M.Clunes Ross, *Basic readings in Anglo-Saxon History* vol.6, pp.251-64; Mason,
     pp.139-40; Walker, p.144.

7   Fletcher, p.126ff; Van Houts, *A.N.S.* 2 1979; Duggan, p.p32-3; Freeman l
     pp.612-14; Foote and Wilson, p.112; Morris, pp.329-30; Stafford *op.cit.* p.68 and
     72-76; Walker, p.131; Stafford, *Queens, Concubines and Dowagers,* p.74ff and 258ff.

8   *Waltham Chron.* p.55; Walker, p.61ff and 126; Freeman ll p.631 and lll Note
     NNN p.763ff and IV Append.M; *E.H.D.*ll nos 187-188-189; Domesday l fol.2;
     The Godwins, p.27 and 55.

9   Walker, p.61ff; Searle, *A.N.S.* 2 1979; Williams, *A.N.S.* 2 1979.

10   *Anglo-Saxon Chron.* sub anno 1068; Foote and Wilson, p.112.

11   As relevant entries in Domesday Book, ed. A. Williams A and G.H. Martin,
     Penguin 1992.

12   Walker, p.61ff; Searle, *A.N.S.* 2 1979; *The Godwins,* pp.116-7; Van Houts, *A.N.S.*
     2 1979.

13   *The Godwins*, pp.116-7; Walker, p.126; S.J. Rüdyard, *The Royal Saints of Anglo-Saxon England*; Letters of St Anselm, nos 168 and 169.

14   Walker, p.127 ff; Eadmer, *Hist. Nov.* 121-2; Barlow, *William Rufus*, pp.313-4; *Vita Wulfstani*, p.34.

8 The English Succession

1   Walker *op.cit.* p.75.

2   *Abingdon Chron.* C 1055; Florence 1055; Walker, p.75; T. Reuter, *Germany in the Early Middle Ages 800-1056*; Z.J. Kozstodnyk, *Five Eleventh century Hungarian Kings*; V. King, 'Ealdred of York; the Worcester Years', *A.N.S.* XVIII 1995; Oman, p.627; Mason, p.88; Barlow, *Edward*, pp.215-6; Freeman II Note Y p.370.

3   Barlow, *Edward*, p.217; *The Godwins*, p.57; E. John, E.H.R. 94 1979 citing Oleson, *Witanagemot*; De Boüard *op.cit.* p.256; Mason, pp.91-2; Brown, *The Normans and the Norman Conquest*, p.109; Stenton, p.571.

4   *Worcester Chron.* D 1057; *Peterborough Chron.* E 1057 and Florence; Grierson, 'A Visit of Earl Harold to Flanders 1056' P E.H.R. LI, 1936; *Vita* pp.408-12 and 53; Previté-Orton, *Shorter Cam. Med. Hist* vol. I p.399; E. John in J. Campbell, *The Anglo-Saxons*, p.231.

5   Grierson, E.H.R. LI 1936; Walker, p.82; *Waltham Chronicle*, Watkins and Chibnall; Barlow, *Edward*, p.219; *The Godwins* p.77; N. Rogers, 'The Waltham Relic List' in C. Hicks, *England in the Eleventh century*.

6   Domesday Book I f.208 Hunts; Freeman II note Y p.370; *Vita*, pp.24-5; Walker, p.83; *Worcester Chron.* D 1066.

7   *Peterborough Chron.* E 1068 and 1066; *Worcester Chron.* D 1067 and 1068; Mason, p.93; Walker, p.83; Barlow, *Edward*, p.218.

8   Barlow *op.cit.* 219-21 and 297; Oman, p.630; Stenton, p.585.

9   *Shorter Cam. Med. Hist.* I 399 and 461ff; G.O. Sayles, *The Medieval Foundations of England,* p.154; Florence 1066; Asser, *Life of King Alfred*; J. Stevenson, 1854 under 871, pp.453-4; Barlow, *The Godwins*, p.125; Mason, pp.120-21; *Larousse Encyclopedia of Ancient and Medieval History*, p.287 and 296; *Petit Larousse Illustré*, pp.600-601.

10   Bayeux Tapestry, plate 2; Onslow *op.cit.* p.162; Lucien De Musset, *La Tapisserie de Bayeux*.

11   Oman, p.162; E. John, E.H.R. 94 1979; Wace L. 2044 and 5571; *Medieval Latin* ed. F.A.C. Mantello and A.G. Rigg, Washington 1996, p.209; *Petit Larousse Illustré* p.91; Freeman I p.634, II p.56; *Vita*, p.27; *Waltham Chron.* p.6ff.

12   T. Oleson, *The Witanagemot in the Reign of Edward the Confessor*, p.3 and 87; J.E.A. Joliffe, *The Constitutional History of Medieval England* p.135; M. Chibnall, 'Feudal Society in Orderic Vitalis' *A.N.S.* I.1978; William of Jumièges p.160 sec.31.

13   Brown, *The Normans and the Norman Conquest*; E. John E.H.R. 94 1979 and *Re-Assessing Anglo-Saxon England*, Manchester 1996; Barlow, *Edward the Confessor*, London 1970; Mason, p.110; *The House of Godwine*; Walker *op.cit.*

14   William of Jumièges G.N.D. pp.132-36; Marx Ed. 1914. *E.H.D.* II, Douglas and Greenaway, London 1953, p.215; Mason, p.110 and note 21; Barlow,

Edward, pp.221-2.

15   P. Hill, *The Road to Hastings,* Tempus 2005, pp.23-4 and p.80.

16   Hill *op.cit.* p.68; S. Keynes, 'The Aethelings in Normandy' *A.N.S.* 13 1991.

17   William of Jumièges G.N.D. 1. xxxii; E. Van Houts, Oxford 1992 p.95; E. Van Houts, *Inventio et miracula Sancti Vframni, A.N.S.* 12 1990; *Historiography and Hagiography at St Wandrille.*

18   Mason, *op.cit.,* p.110; William of Poitiers G.G. in *E.H.D.* II, pp.217-31. William of Poitiers strengthens his presentation of his case by using technical legal and feudal terms such as *dona, beneficia, honores* and *haeredem,* even *adoptio filio loco,* for rhetorical effect. They are not applicable to the transmission of the crown in England. It was not a benefice to be bestowed at will. A king could recommend his successor to the Witan, that is all, unless there was a ceremony carried out in England appointing the successor as joint-king.

19   As above and P. Rex, *Hereward the Last Englishman.*

20   William of Poitiers as above; F. McLynn, *1066 The Year of Three Battles,* p.138.

21   Douglas *op.cit.* p.15 and 171; D. Matthew, *The Norman Monasteries and their English Possessions,* Chapter 2.

22   Douglas *op.cit.* p.169; William of Poitiers as above.

23   William of Poitiers as above.

9 Harold in Normandy

1   Barlow, pp.221-9; *E.H.D.* II p.218 and 215 and p.217 note 1; Florence 1065; Walker, p.91; Poitiers 110-12; Douglas, p.175 note 2; Lawson, p.26 note 23.

2   *Anglo-Saxon Chronicles,* Garmonsway p.190 note 1; *E.H.D.* I p.109; Introduction to *Anglo-Saxon Chronicles,* ed. M. Swanton; Florence 1065; Walker, p.91.

3   E. John, *Re-assessing Anglo-Saxon England,* pp.186-7; E.H.R. 90 1975.

4   Barlow, p.228; *Heimskringla;* Lawson, pp.26-31 (reviews the tales); K. De Vries, *The Norwegian Invasion of England,* Woodbridge 1999 (summarises recent opinion, as does Lawson in his note 34 p.29). See also Walker, *Harold;* P. Hill, *The Road to the Battle of Hastings;* Douglas; Barlow, *The Godwins.*

5   Stenton, p.578; Lawson, pp.29-31. References in note 4 above.

6   Walker. Ch.6; Barlow. Ch.10.

7   Bayeux Tapestry, plate 1 *et seq; E.H.D.* II pp.239-41.

8   Douglas, pp.62-6; Fletcher, *Bloodfeud,* p.164; Brown, *The Normans and the Norman Conquest,* p.99ff; Huscroft, *Ruling England 1042–1217* p.302; De Boüard, *Guillaume le Conquerant,* p.238.

9   De Boüard, p.247; Jumièges, p.132; Poitiers, pp.77-159, *E.H.D.* II Items 3 and 4, p.215 and 217.

10   Poitiers, 77-159; Chronicles C, D and E 1051-52; Barlow, p.107ff; Walker, p.37.

11   Barlow, p.107ff; *The Godwins,* p.47ff; Brown, p.98ff; Walker, pp.37-38; Lawson, p.23.

12   Douglas, p.169; Barlow, pp.107-9, Ch.3; Lawson, p.19 and 24; Poitiers, p.77; Jumièges, p.132.

13   *Shorter C.M.H.* vol.I, p.461ff and 320ff; Walker, p.75; Barlow, pp.214-19.

14   Onslow, *The Dukes of Normandy and their origin*, p.162; Florence 1066; Wace Ll 2044 and 5571 (Harold holds the seneschalcy and has England *en sa baillie*; compare Godwine, '*bajulus*', and Baldwin V, *procurator et bajulus* as regent to Philip I); John, E.H.R. 94 1979; Freeman II p.56 and 631; *Heimskringla* p.543; Florence 1064, submission of the Welsh princes; Larousse, *Ancient and Medieval History*, p.287.

15   See introduction to *Anglo-Saxon Chronicles*, Garmonsway.

16   Bennett, pp.19-20; Van Houts, E.H.R. cx 1995 and *A.N.S.* 19 1996; E. Tetloe, *The Enigma of Hastings*, 1974, p.10; Garnett, T.R.H.S. 5th Ser. xxxvi, 1986.

17   Barlow, E.H.R. 80 1965; Orderic V., p.24; Malmesbury G.R. ii 306; Freeman II 518 and 302; III 227; *A.N.S.* 4 1081; P. Hyams Garnett, 'Conquered England 1066-1215' in Lawson, pp.22-3; Onslow, p.162; Eadmer H.N. p.8; Orderic II 207.

18   Poitiers, pp.220-22; Huscroft, p.298; Orderic II 207; Malmesbury G.R. 238; Pierre Chaplais, *English Medieval Diplomatic Practice*, p.30.

19   See usual published accounts e.g. Walker, Barlow, Brown, Mason *et al.* and *Vita* p.23 and 51.

20   Orderic, 401-18; Forester Translation, 1854 (Vol.III, 227-49); Letters of Gregory VII No.9. in *E.H.D.* II, p.644.

21   Jumièges, pp.132-36; Poitiers, pp.77-159 in *E.H.D.* II.

22   Poitiers in *E.H.D.* II p.218; Bayeux Tapestry, plates 29-35 in *E.H.D.* II.

23   See discussion in all major accounts as above. Bayeux Tapestry, plates 29-30 and note in *E.H.D.* II p.235; *Vita*, St Gundleii, cap.13; *Lives of the Cambro-British Saints* ed. W.J. Rees, 1853; *Worcester Chron.* 1065.

24   'Bayeux Tapestry' in *E.H.D.* II *Anglo-Saxon England* 31 2002; G.R Owen-Crocker, 'The Bayeux Tapestry: invisible seams and visible boundaries', *A.N.S.* 19, 1986; H.E.J. Cowley, *Towards an Interpretation of the Bayeux Tapestry*.

25   Bayeux Tapestry, plate 27; Walker, p.83, citing Orderic.

26   *Harald's Saga*, 95; Freeman III 697; Anonymous of St Andreas, Cambrai *circa* 1133, vii 537; Cartulary of St Bertin, p.97; Van Houts, E.H.R. c110, 1995.

27   Freeman III 217ff; Eadmer, H.N. p.8; Wace II 258; De Boüard, p.266; Douglas, p.133.

28   *Harald's Saga*, 76 and 95; Freeman III 697; Lawson, p.30; Walker, p.99ff; Freeman III 217ff; Henry of Huntingdon, 760; E. Jerrold, p.335.

29   *Vita*, p.51; Jerrold, pp.335-6; *Shorter C.M.H.* p.399ff; Malmesbury G.R. iii 238; Freeman III p.217ff ('His fetters were gilded but he was still in fetters'); Walker, p.83; Barlow, p.219.

30   Lawson, *Cnut*, p.132; Walker, pp.99-102; Barlow, p.238.

10 Discord and Downfall

1   *Anglo-Saxon Chron.*, Worcester D and Abingdon C 1055; Oman, p.625; Walker, p.77; Mason, p.89; John, *Reassessing Anglo-Saxon England*, p.82. Barlow observed that to dispute a king's decision was to dispute his right to rule and was therefore treason.

2   *Vita Edwardi*, p.11 and notes p.166; Walker, p.103; Kapelle, p.88; Higham,

pp.233-35.

3 Walker, p.103ff; Higham, p.234; McLynn, p.303.

4 Simeon of Durham, H.R.ii 174; Barlow, p.303; Gaimar ll 5087-98; *Annales Dunelmenses*, p.508, Pertz; Orderic IV 270; William of Malmesbury, H.N. 4.

5 *Vita*, pp.64-5.

6 *Vita*, pp.31-2; Barlow, p.203; Kapelle, pp.92-4; McLynn, p.169; Walker, pp.104-5.

7 Kapelle, pp.92-4; Barlow, p.235; Walker, pp.107-8; Mason, p.126.

8 Mason, pp.96-7; Walker, p.106.

9 Mason, p.126; Walker, pp.106-7; Higham, pp.235-6; Florence 1065.

10 Kapelle, p.88ff; Mason, p.126; Walker, p.107; *Vita*, p.77; Higham, p.234; Williams, *Land and Power*, A.N.S.2 1979.

11 *Vita*, p.77; Simeon of Durham for Tostig; *Hist. Eccles. Dunelm.* 243-45; *Liber Vitae Dunelm.* p.2, 1841 edn; *Hist. Trans. S.Cuth.* Cap.5; Barlow, *The Godwins*, p.85; Mason, p.124. Walker, pp.103-4.

12 *Vita*, pp.76-9; *Peterborough Chron.* 1087; *Harald's Saga* sec. 77; Wace II 258; Higham, p.233; Mason, pp.123-4; McLynn, p.167.

13 Higham, p.234; Mason, p.125.

14 Higham, p.234; Hadley and Richards, p.69.

15 Kapelle, p.88; Higham, pp.232-4.

16 Kapelle, pp.96-8; Higham, p.214 and 236; Mason, p.126; Walker, pp.107-8; Domesday Book Yorkshire; *Abingdon Chron.* 1065; *Vita*, p.79.

17 Higham, p.231; Barlow, p.238; Kapelle, pp.25-6; Mason, p.42; Walker, pp.103-5; *Anglo-Saxon Wills* no. 121.

18 Walker, p.110; Florence 1065; Mason, pp.125-6; McLynn, pp.170-1; Kapelle, pp.94-5; Freeman II 477-78; Stafford, *Queen Emma and Queen Edith*, p.271; C.J. Morris, *Marriage and Murder in Eleventh Century Northumbria*.

19 *Vita*, pp.76-7; *Abingdon* and *Worcester Chron.* 1065; Mason, pp.126-7; *The Anglo-Saxon State*, Essay I, ed. J. Campbell, p.77; Higham, p.236; Walker, p.110; McLynn, pp.171-3; Freeman II 479; Barlow, p.236.

20 *Vita*, pp.50-2; Florence 1065; *Worcester* and *Peterborough Chron.* 1065; Barlow, p.236; McLynn, pp.172-3; Mason, pp.126-9; Walker, pp.110-3; Hill, pp.137-8.

21 *Vita*, pp.78-9; *Abingdon* and *Worcester Chron.* 1065; McLynn, p.174; Walker, pp.111-12; Hill, p.139; Mason, pp.127-8.

22 *Vita*, p.81; Chronicle 1065. C, D, E; Mason, pp.130-1; Walker, p.114; McLynn, pp.174-5; Hill, p.139.

23 McLynn, p.175; *Abingdon* and *Worcester Chron.* 1065; Barlow, intro. to *Vita Edwardi*; Barlow, *Edward*, pp.237-9; Walker, pp.114-5; Mason, p.130.

24 Higham, pp.236-7; Mason, pp.128-9; Barlow, pp.236-8; Hill, p.139; McLynn, pp.174-5.

25 Healey and Richards, p.69; J. Campbell, *The Anglo-Saxons*, Oxford 1982, p.212 and 215; William of Poitiers in E.H. D. II. p.236; McLynn, p.174; Mason, p.129.

26 Kapelle, p.97; Barlow, intro. to *Vita*; Higham, p.236; Freeman II 301; John E.H.R. LXXI; Barlow, p.250 and 253; Bayeux Tapestry, plate 32.

27 Barlow, pp.247-8; *Vita*, pp.75-6 and 88-90.

28 Barlow, pp.244-45 for Sulcard and Osbert of Clare; *Vita*, pp.71-2; K.C.D 824 and 825 (Sawyer 1043 and 1041).

29 Walker, p.118.

30   Barlow, pp.249-50; Hermann, *Miracula Sancti Edmundi*; Bayeux Tapestry, plates
      30 to 34.

11 *The Reign of King Harold*

1   *Worcester* and *Peterborough Chron.* 1066; Bayeux Tapestry, plate 33; N.P Brookes
      and H.E. Walker, *The Authority and Interpretation of the Bayeux Tapestry A.N.S.*
      I 1978; Barlow, *The Godwins*, p.6; J. Nelson, *A.N.S.* 4 1981; *The Rites of the
      Conqueror and Politics and Ritual in early Medieval Europe*, p.388ff.

2   Bayeux Tapestry, plates 31 to 36.

3   *Vita*, pp.80-81; Chronicle for 1065 and Florence.

4   Freeman I Note DD p.421; C.D. 162 and 172; *Worcester Chron.* 1063; Florence
      1066.

5   A. Williams, 'Problems connected with the English Royal Succession 800-
      1066' *A.N.S.* 2 1979; Barlow, p.249 note 1; William of Poitiers in *E.H.D.* II
      p.223; Freeman I. Note DD 421.C.D.IV 172 and 162.

6   As for note 6.

7   A. Williams, 'Problems connected with the English Royal Succession 800-
      1066'; Barlow, p.249 note 1; Chaplais, *English Medieval Diplomatic Practice*, p.30.

8   *Vita*, pp.79-80; William of Poitiers 166-68.

9   *Vita Wulfstani*; Walker, p.144; McLynn, pp.185-6 and189; Mason, p.132.

10   'The Participation of Aquitanians in the Conquest of England' *A.N.S.*9, citing
      Chronique de St Maixent, ed. J. Verdon, pp.136-7; William of Poitiers, *E.H.D.*II
      p.220; Bayeux Tapestry, plates 36-41; *Abingdon* and *Worcester Chron.* 1066;
      McLynn, pp.186-7.

11   William of Poitiers *E.H.D.*II pp.218-9; P.A. Maccarini, 'William the
      Conqueror and the Church of Rome' *A.N.S.* 6 1983; William of Malmesbury
      G.R.iii 238; G. Garnett, 'Coronation and Propaganda', T.R.H.S. 5th Ser. xxxvi
      1986; Orderic ii 142; Onslow, p.168; Raine Patterson, p.9; Van Houts, 'The
      Norman Conquest through European Eyes', E.H.R. 110 1995; *Ramsey Chron.*
      cap.cxx.

12   De Boüard, p.260; *E.H.D.*II No. 82; Maccarini, 'Allocation of Peter's Pence,
      Kent', *A.N.S.* 6 1983; Letters of Pope Gregory VII, No.9, 24 April 1080,
      *E.H.D.*II no. 99; Wenric of Verdun in M.G.H. Libelli de Lite I, 280-99.

13   C. Norton, Latomus 34 1975; *E.H.D.*II No.81; Freeman IV p.34; C. Morris,
      The Papal Monarchy; the Western Church from 1050 to 1250; Erdmann, *The Origin
      of the Idea of Crusade*; J. Gilchrist, 'Crusade and Settlement', ed. P.W. Edbury,
      History No.58 1973; J. Robinson, *Gregory VII and the Soldiers of Christ*.

14   Bayeux Tapestry, plate 73; Bennett, p.22; Z.N. Brooke, *The English Church and
      the Papacy*; Freeman III p.585; Wace I. 12393 and 1453.

15   *Chronicle of St Riquier Hariulf*, W.C.23 *c*.1085; A. Williams, *Land and Power*,
      A.N.S. 2 1979; *Chron. Johann de Oxenedes*; Stenton, E.H.R. 37 1922; *Worcester
      Chron.* 1065; Malmesbury. G.R. 280.

16   Florence 1066; Walker, p.139; Hugh Candidus, *Chron. of Peterborough*, re. Writ
      of Abbot Brand, A.S. Wills no. 71.

17   Stenton, pp.581-2; M. Dudley, *The Norman Conquest and English Coinage,* p.11;

Spink, 1966; Gaimar 1. 222. DB.I Hants fol.38 Glos. Fol. 162v; K. Mack, 'The Staller; an administrative innovation of the reign of Edward the Confessor', J.M.H. 12 1986; William of Jumièges 132-36; Walker, pp.140-42.

18   Walker, pp.142-44; M. Biddle, 'Seasonal festivals' *A.N.S.* 8 1985; William of Jumièges, *E.H.D.*II p.215.

19   D.B.I Sussex Fol.16; William of Poitiers, *E.H.D.*II p.218 and 220; Hill, p.146; McLynn, pp.187-8; *Harald's Saga*, sec. 78; Gaimar, p.792.

20   *Harald's Saga*, sec. 78. to 82; Gaimar, p.792; Hill, p.146; *Abingdon* and *Worcester Chron.* 1066.

21   All major sources give an account of Harold's activities in summer 1066. For example, Walker, p.145 and 150; Stenton, p.588; Mason, pp.146-7; Hill, p.147; McLynn, pp.190-91.

22   *Abingdon Chron.* C 1066; William of Poitiers, *E.H.D.*II p.220; McLynn, p.162; Hill, pp.161-2; J. Laporte, *Les Opérations Navales en Manche et Mer du Nord pendant l'année 1066*; *Annales de Normandie* 17 1967; Walker, p.166; Freeman III p.53; Cartulary of Holy Trinity, Rouen, pp.453-4; Mason, p.156 and 146-7; Bates, p.103, D.B. Essex Fol. 14v.

23   *Annals of Neider-Altach* 1075 in Van Houts, 'The Norman Conquest through European Eyes', E.H.R. 110, 1095; Hill, p.68; *Gesta Herewardi*, sec. xx; William of Poitiers p.131 and 160; Carmen l. 1319; C. Grainge and G. Grainge, 'Brilliantly Executed Plan or Near Disaster?' in S. Morillo, ed., *The battle of Hastings: sources and interpretations*, Woodbridge 1996, pp.129-4.

12 All Roads Lead to Hastings

1   Walker, p.159 and 165; *Abingdon Chron.* C 1066; Stenton, p.582 and 587-8; Mason, p.63.

2   *Anglo-Saxon Chron.* C, D and E 1066 and Florence; William of Poitiers *E.H.D.* II pp.220-21; Stenton, p.582; De Boüard, pp.289-90 and 301ff; P. Marren, *1066 The battles of York, Stamford Bridge and Hastings*, p.63.

3   *A.S.C.* C, D and E 1066 and Florence; Domesday Book fol. 298 and 298v Yorks; *A.S.C.* D and E 1068 and 1069; Stenton, 587-89; De Boüard, pp.310-12; Marren, p.61 and 65; Mason, p.143 and 147; Walker, p.157.

4   M. Magnusson and H. Pálsson, *King Harald's Saga*; R.W. Chambers, *England before the Norman Conquest*, Ch.VIII, Stamford Bridge and Hastings sec. XIX from the *Worcester Chronicle* sec. XX from the *Heimskringla*; Marren, p.64ff; Mason, 148-49.

5   *Harald's Saga*, par.84; Hill, *The Road to Hastings*, pp.149-50; Marren, pp.65-72 and 147; De Boüard, p.289; M. Bennett, *Campaigns of the Norman Conquest*, p.35; Hill, p.151.

6   Marren, pp.65-72; Hill, p.150; *A.S.C.*, C, D and E 1066.

7   *Harald's Saga*, par. 85; Marren, pp.65-72.

8   *Harald's Saga*, par. 85.

9   *Harald's Saga*, par. 85; *Worcs. Chron.* D 1066.

10   *Harald's Saga*, par. 84 and 85; *A.S.C.*, C, D and E 1066.

11   Introduction to *King Harald's Saga* pp.24-26; William of Poitiers *E.H.D.* II

P.225.

12 Marren, pp.73-75.

13 *A.S.C.*, C, D and E and Florence 1066; Marren, p.73; Bennett, pp.35-36; Walker, p.158 and 160.

14 Walker, pp.161-64; Hill, pp.152-55; *Harald's Saga*, par.86; *A.S.C.*, C, D and E and Florence 1066.

15 *Worcester. Chron.* D 1066; *Harald's Saga*, par.87.

16 *Harald's Saga*, par. 87-91; Marren, pp.75-86; Mason, pp.149-53.

17 *Harald's Saga*, par. 90, 92 and 99; Marren, p.75.

18 *Harald's Saga*, par. 89 and 91.

19 *Harald's Saga*, par. 92; Bennett, p.36.

20 *Abingdon Chron.* C 1066; *Harald's Saga*, par. 92; Lawson, p.41 (points out that both Malmesbury and Henry of Huntingdon knew of the lone defender of the bridge); G.R. 1. 420-21 and *Hist. Ang.* pp.386-9.

21 *Harald's Saga*, par. 93; Marren, p.84; Mason, p.152; P.G. Foote and D.W. Wilson, *The Viking Achievement*, p.285.

22 Marren, pp.72-3 and 82-3; Lawson, p.40; Orderic H.E. ii 168-9.

23 Gaimar, *L'Estorie des Engles,* 242-43; Lawson, p.73 and 206; Freeman, *Norman Conquest* III p.720.

24 Douglas, *William the Conqueror*, p.194; William of Poitiers *E.H.D.* II p.222; Marren, p.81; *Vita Edwardi*, p.89; Stenton, pp.590-91; Hill, p.147 and 153; Mason, p.152; E. John, *Reassessing Anglo-Saxon England*, p.191.

25 Poitiers *E.H.D.* II 224; *Waltham Chron.* 47.

26 Ord. Vit. interpolating William of Jumièges G.N.D. ii 166-68.

27 Walker, p.158; Barlow, *Edward*, p.62; D.B. I Worcs. 26;16 and Essex 6;15.

28 *E.H.D.* II pp.222-3.

29 Poitiers *E.H.D.*II 224; Bayeux Tapestry, plate 53, D.B.I.18v Sussex; Walker, p.172.

30 Jumièges *E.H.D.* II p.216; Poitiers *E.H.D.* II p.225.

31 *Peterborough* E and *Worcester* D *Chron.* 1066 plus Florence.

32 *Worcester Chron.* D 1066.

33 *The Godwins*, Barlow, p.102; *Vita Edwardi* pp.48-9.

34 Bayeux Tapestry, plates 72 and 60.

35 *The Godwins*, p.104.

36 *Song of Maldon* I. 17ff; Poitiers *E.H.D.* II 225.

37 Poitiers as above and p.226; Florence 1066.

38 *Chron. of St Maixent*, pp.136-7.

39 Carmen. I.863; see Marren, *1066 The Battles of York, Stamford Bridge and Hastings*; McLynn, 216-7; Mason, p.167.

40 Bennett, p.42; *Brevis Relatio* 7; Poitiers *E.H.D.* II 225.

41 Jumièges *E.H.D.* p.216; Bayeux Tapestry, plate 71; Marren, pp.166-7; 'Oops, who said "Charge"?', Andrew Roberts, *Sunday Telegraph*, Jan. 30 2005.

42 Poitiers *E.H.D.*II p.224; *A.N.S.* 2 1979; I.N. Hare, *The Buildings of Battle Abbey*.

43 *Harald's Saga*, 89 and 92; Wace, p.27 n.3.

44 Bayeux Tapestry, plates 62 to 69; *A.N.S.* 2 1979; R. Allen Brown, *The Battle of Hastings*.

45   Bayeux Tapestry, plates 21 to 23.
46   See accounts of the battle in Poitiers and Jumièges *passim* and *Carmen de Hastinge Proelio.*
47   Poitiers *E.H.D.*II 226-7.
48   Lawson, p.118 and 169 citing John of Salisbury, *Polycraticus;* Marren, p.150; Wace l.7819-30.
49   Poitiers *E.H.D.* II 228; *Battle Chron.* 38; *A.N.S.* 2 1979, Brown; *Harald's Saga*, 96; Hill, p.138 and 185.

13 Aftermath: The Lost King

1   *Annals of Innisfallen*, ed. S. MacAirt, Dublin 1951; Mason, p.194; *E.H.D.* II; Poitiers, p.228 and Jumièges, p.216; Florence 1066.
2   E. Van Houts, 'Scandinavian Influences in Norman Literature', *A.N.S.* 6. 1983; Carmen I.36-8; Poitiers, *E.H.D.* II 229.
3   Poitiers as above.
4   *De Inventione Crucis*, 30; *Vita Edwardi*, 210; *Waltham Chron.* xliv and xlvii and section 21.
5   *Waltham Chron.*; Stubbs, *De Inventione;* Carmen l.579-83; *Ramsey Chron.* 35.
6   As note 5.
7   *E.H.D.* II, Poitiers, 228 and Jumièges, 218; Hill, p.216 n.5; Florence 1066.
8   Poitiers as above, 229.
9   Eadmer, *Hist. Novel. in Anglia* p.8-9; Bayeux Tapestry, plate 76.
10   N.P. Brookes and H.E. Walker, 'The Authority and Interpretation of the Bayeux Tapestry', *A.N.S.* I 1978; McLynn, p.237, quoting R. Allen Brown.
11   McLynn, p.237; Marren, p.141 and 138-40; Lawson, p.90 and n.9; Poitiers *E.H.D.* II 227.
12   *Benoît de St Maure Chron.* l. 39680-85 and l. 39876 in *A.N.S.* 21 1998, P. Damian-Grynt; *E.H.D.* II Jumièges 216 and Poitiers 229.
13   Walker p.233, n.31; Mason, p.172; D. Bernstein, *A.N.S.* 5 1982, *The Blinding of Harold and the meaning of the Bayeux Tapestry;* McLynn, p.240.
14   *Harald's Saga*, 92; McLynn, pp.239-40.
15   *Waltham. Chron.* 49-50; Carmen p.34; Barlow, 1997, Oxford Med. Texts.
16   Bayeux Tapestry, plates 1, 33 and 74-77; *Brevis Relatio* 32.
17   Bayeux Tapestry, plates 49 and 65; C. Gibbs-Smith in *The Times*, 8 Oct. 1966; Lawson, p.226 *et seq.*
18   André Maurois, *Le Mémorial des Siècles; XI Siècle, Les événements.* 'La Conquête de L'Angleterre par les Normands', p.230 and 313; Lawson, pp.256-60.
19   Wace l. 118851-6; Marren, p.136, 146 and 155.
20   Florence 1066; Lawson, p.121.
21   Florence 1066; Sayles, *The Medieval Foundations of England*, London 1948, p.154.
22   Oman, pp.649-50; Grassi E.H.R. 117, 2002.
23   *Shorter Camb. Med. Hist.* vol.I p.399.
24   Poitiers *E.H.D.* II 217; *Harald's Saga*, 76; Walker, p.97; McLynn, pp.186-7.

25   R.A. Brown, *English Castles*, p.44, 1976 edn; T. Rowley, *The Norman Heritage 1066-1200*, London 1983, p.63 and 72.

26   P.J. Huggins and K.N. Bascombe, 'The Archaeology of Waltham Abbey, Essex 1985-91', *Archaeol. Journ.* 149, 1992; Oman, pp.648-51; *English Romanesque Art 1066-1200*, gen. intro. by Prof. G. Zarnecki, p.17, 42 and 80 (Stothard's Copy of Bayeux Tapestry); Rowley, p.156.

27   R. Tilbrook and C.V. Roberts, *Norfolk's Churches*, p.vii; Rowley, p.100.

28   *Eng. Roman. Art*, pp.17-22; Rowley, p.159 and 184-5.

29   Oman, p.50.

30   Jolliffe, pp.183-5,' D.B. I 46v and 50 Hants' *Harald's Saga* 77.

31   *E.H.D.* II p.483; Stenton, p.644 and 646-7; Douglas, *Feudal Documents*, p.67; *Peterborough Chron.* E 1087.

32   Jolliffe, pp.186-88.

33   D. Pelteret, *Basic Readings in Anglo-Saxon History*, *A.N.S.* 4 1981; P. Hyams, *The Common Law and the Fench Connection*; H.R. Loyn, *The Governance of Anglo-Saxon England*.

34   E. John in J. Campbell, *The Anglo-Saxons*, 1982.

35   Ord. Vit. III 126-7; Poitiers *E.H.D.* II 230; Barlow, *The Godwins*, p.92.

36   J. Campbell, *The Anglo-Saxon State*, London and N.Y. 2000; Kapelle, p.106.

14 Epilogue

1   Fleming, p.48ff.

2   G.O. Sayles, *The Medieval Foundations of England*, p.145; E.A. Freeman, *History of the Norman Conquest*, vol. I p.166ff; D.J.V. Fisher, *The Anglo-Saxon Age c.400-1042*, p.320; S. Reynolds, *Kingdoms and Communities in Western Europe*, p.266; Chronicles C, D, E, F 1002 and 1015 (*Anglo-Saxon Chronicles*, ed. and trans. J. Stevenson, 1853 and M. Swanton, 2000).

3   J.E.A. Jolliffe, *The Constitutional History of Medieval England*, p.62, 70-1 and 104-5; D.M. Hadley and J.D. Richards (eds), *Studies in the Early Middle Ages, Cultures in Contact; the Scandinavian Settlement in England in the Ninth and Tenth centuries*, pp.72-77 and 85; *Chronicles*, Worcester D, 926 and 1018.

4   A. Williams, *Aethelrede the Unready*, pp.56-9, 119 and 123; D.M. Hadley, *A.N.S.* 19, 1996; Stenton, *The Scandinavian Settlement*, p.504, 514-6 and 533-34; James Campbell, ed., *The Anglo-Saxons*, pp.200-1; Fisher, p.335; W.E. Kapelle, *The Norman Conquest of the North: the region and its transformation 1000-1135*, pp.62-68; M.W. Barley, *Lincolnshire and the Fens*, p.37 and 109; P. Cavill, *Fear and Faith in Anglo-Saxon England*, pp.210-11 and 227; F.W. Maitland, *Domesday Book and Beyond*, p.254; N. Hooper, *The Housecarl in England in the Eleventh Century*, *A.N.S.* 7 1984; N.J. Higham, *The Kingdom of Northumbria AD 350-1100*, Stroud 1993, pp.490-93; P.G. Foote and D.M. Wilson, *The Viking Achievement*, p.102, 123-4 and 272; I. Peirce, 'Arms, Armour and Warfare in the Eleventh Century', *A.N.S.* 8 1985; R. Fletcher, *Blood Feud: Murder and Revenge in Anglo-Saxon England*, p.102.

5   Jolliffe, p.104; James Campbell, 'The Late Anglo-Saxon State: a maximum view', *Proc. of the Brit. Acad.* 87 1994, p.10, citing S. Reynolds, *Kingdoms and*

Communities in Western Europe, p.266; Williams *op.cit.* p.125 and 149; Hadley and Richards, pp.84-5; R. Fleming, *Kings and Lords in Conquest England*, p.21 and p.47; Ian W. Walker, *Harold, the Last Anglo-Saxon King*, p.1; K. Mack, 'Changing Thegns: Knut's Conquest of the English Aristocracy', *Albion* 16, 1984.

6   Campbell, pp.33-4 and 36; Eric John, 'Edward the Confessor and the Norman Succession', *Eng. Hist. Rev.* 94 1979; Fleming, pp.40-1.

7   Walker, p.1; Fleming *op.cit.* p.40; F. Barlow, *The Godwins*, p.1; Chronicles C, D, E, F, 1009, 1010, 1015-1017.

8   Oman, p.624; Stenton, p.570; Barlow, p.202; Chronicles C and D and Florence 1054, D.E.F. 1055.

Recommended Further Reading

The books and periodicals listed in the bibliography comprise those works consulted during the writing of this book. Readers who wish to know more about King Harold and his background may find the following recommendations useful.

Anglo-Saxon England. Sir Frank Merry Stenton. Oxford History of England, vol. II, O.U.P. 1971. This is still the best introduction to the early history of England.
Edward the Confessor. Frank Barlow. English Monarchs series, Eyre Methuen, London 1979. Still the best available biography of King Edward, with much to say concerning the career of Harold.
William the Conqueror. David C. Douglas. English Monarchs series, Eyre Methuen, London 1977. A most compelling and perceptive biography.
William the Conqueror. David Bates. Tempus 2004. A readable account of King William, including the results of more recent research.
The House of Godwin: the History of a Dynasty. Emma Mason. Hambledon and London 2004. The most recent account of the rise of Earl Godwin and his family.
Harold: the Last Anglo-Saxon King. Ian W. Walker. Wrens Park Publishing 2000. Provides an alternative view of King Harold and his career.
1066: The Year of the Three battles. Frank McLynn. Pimlico 1999. A lively and rewarding account of 1066.
The Battle of Hastings 1066. M.K. Lawson. Tempus 2003. A comprehensive account of current thinking on the battle.
The Viking Achievement. P.G. Foote and D.M. Wilson. Book Club Associates, London 1974. A balanced and accurate survey of the Vikings 800–1200.
Cnut: the Danes in England in the Early Eleventh Century. M.K. Lawson. Harlow 1993. Casts a great deal of light on Cnut's activities in England.
Queen Emma and Queen Edith; Queenship and Women's Power in the Eleventh Century. Pauline Stafford. Oxford 1997. Provides insight into the role of royal women.

Bibliography

'The Abbey of Abingdon, its Chronicle and the Norman Conquest'. J. Hudson. *Anglo-Norman Studies* (cited as *A.N.S.*) 19, 1996.

The Aethelings in Normandy. S. Keynes. *A.N.S.* 13. 1991.

Aethelrede the Unready: The Ill-Counselled King. Ann Williams. London 2003.

Alexander II and the Norman Conquest. C. Morton. *Latomus* 34, 1975.

Amatus of Montecassino; Storia de' Normanni. Ed. V. de Bartholomeis. Rome 1935.

Anglo-Latin Satirical Poets and Epigrammatists of the Twelfth Century. Vol. 1. T. Wright. R.S. 1872.

Anglo-Norman England 1066-1166. M. Chibnall. Oxford 1986.

'Anglo-Norman Feudalism and the problem of continuity'. J.O. Prestwich. *Past and Present* 26, 1963.

The Anglo-Saxon Age c.400–1042. D.J.V. Fisher. Longman 1973.

Anglo-Saxon Chronicles. Ed. and trans. J. Stevenson. London 1853.

Anglo-Saxon Chronicles. M. Swanton. London 2000.

Anglo-Saxon Chronicles. Everyman edition, G.N. Garmonsway. London 1955.

Anglo-Saxon Chronicle. Version F in Latin and Old English, B. Mus. Cott. M.S. Domit. A viii.

Anglo-Saxon England. Ed. Sir Frank Stenton. Oxford 1988.

Anglo-Saxon Military Institutions on the Eve of the Norman Conquest. C.W. Hollister. Oxford 1962.

The Anglo-Saxons. Ed. J. Campbell. Oxford 1982.

The Anglo-Saxon State. Ed. J. Campbell. London and N.Y. 2000.

Anglo-Saxon Wills. D. Whitelock. Cambridge 1930.

Annals of Innisfallen. Ed. S. MacAirt. Dublin 1951.

'A Pre-Conquest Occupation of England?' M.W. Campbell. *Speculum* 46 1971.

'Archaeology, Economy and Society'. D. Hinton. *A.N.S.* 24. 2001.

'Archaeology of Waltham Abbey, Essex 1985-91'. P.J. Huggins and K.N. Bascombe. *Archaeological Journal* 149. 1992.

Arms, Armour and Warfare in the Eleventh Century. I. Peirce. *A.N.S.* 9. 1986.

Authority and Interpretation of the Bayeux Tapestry. N.P. Brookes and H.E. Walker. *A.N.S.* I. 1978.

Basic Readings in Anglo-Saxon History, Vol.6. M. Clunes Ross. 2000.
The Battlefield of Hastings. F. Baring. E.H.R. 20, 1905.
The Battle of Hastings. J. Bradbury. Stroud 1998.
'Battle of Hastings'. C. Gibbs-Smith in *The Times,* 8 Oct. 1966.
The Battle of Hastings, England and Europe. S. Körner. Lund 1964.
The Battle of Hastings; sources and interpretations. Ed. S. Morillo. Woodbridge 1996.
'Battle of Hastings', *Weekend Telegraph.* Gen. H. Essame, 7 Jan. 1966.
'Battle of Hastings', *Sunday Times Magazine,* Gen. Sir Bernard Montgomery, 24
    April 1966.
Baudri de Bourgeuil: Adela Comitissa in *Baldricus Burgulianus Carmina.* Ed. K. Hilbert.
    Heidelberg 1979.
The Bayeux Tapestry and Schools of Illumination. C.R. Hart. *A.N.S.* 21 1998.
The Bayeux Tapestry and the French Secular Epic. C.R. Dodwell, *Burlington Magazine*
    civ, 1966.
'The Bayeux Tapestry: invisible seams and visible boundaries'. G.R. Owen-Crocker.
    Anglo-Saxon England 31, 2002.
'The Bayeux Tapestry: Why Eustace, Odo and William?' *A.N.S* 12, 1989.
The Blinding of Harold and the meaning of the Bayeux Tapestry. D. Bernstein. *A.N.S.* 5,
    1982.
Blood Feud: Murder and Revenge in Anglo-Saxon England. R. Fletcher. Penguin 2002.
'Bookland and Fyrd Service in Late Saxon England'. R. Abels. *A.N.S.* 7, 1984.
Brevis relatio de Guillelmo nobilissimo comite Normannorum. Ed. E. Van Houts. Camden
    Misc. XXXIV 5th series Vol. 10. Cambridge 1997.
Brut y Twysogion Peniarth. Ed. T. Jones. Cardiff 1952
Brut y Tywysogion: The Chronicle of the Princes. T. Jones. Cardiff 1955.
The Buildings of Battle Abbey. I.N. Hare. *A.N.S.* 2, 1979.
Burh-Geat-Settle. W.H. Stevenson. E.H.R. 12, 1897.
Campaigns of the Norman Conquest. M. Bennett. Osprey 2001.
Carmen de Hastinge Proelio. Ed. C. Morton and H. Muntz. Oxford Medieval Texts
    1971.
Carmen de Hastinge Proelio. F. Barlow. Oxford 1999.
Carmen de Hastinge Proelio. R.H.C. Davis. E.H.R. 92, 1978.
Cartularium Monasterii de Rameseia. Ed. W.H. Hart and P.A. Lyons. R.S. 3 vols,
    London 1884.
Change and Continuity in Eleventh Century Mercia. E. Mason. *A.N.S.* 8, 1985.
'Changing Thegns: Knut's Conquest of the English Aristocracy'. K. Mack. *Albion*
    16, 1984.
Chronicle of Battle Abbey. Ed. and trans. E. Searle. Oxford 1980.
Chronicle of Florence of Worcester. Ed. and trans. J. Stevenson. London 1853.
Chronicle of Johann de Oxenedes, with the history of the Abbey of St Benet Holme. Ed. H.
    Ellis. R.S. 1859.
The Chronicle of John of Worcester. Vol. II. Ed. R.R. Darlington and P.J. McGurk.
    Oxford 1995.
Chronique de Saint Maixent 751-1140. Ed. J. Verdon. Paris 1979.
'Chronique des Ducs de Normandie: Benoît de St. Maure'. P. Damian-Grynt.
    A.N.S. 21, 1998.
'Cnut's Law Code of 1018'. A. Kennedy. *A.N.S.* 11, 1988.

Cnut: the Danes in England in the Early Eleventh Century. M.K. Lawson. Harlow, 1993.

'Cockles among the Wheat: Danes and Englishmen in the Western Midlands in the first half of the Eleventh Century'. A. Williams. *Midland History* 11.

'The Common Law and the Fench Connection.' *A.N.S.* 4, 1981

Communications and Power in Medieval Europe. K.J. Leyser. London 1994.

Conquest, Co-Existence and Change: Wales 1063-1415. R. Davies. Oxford 1987.

The Constitutional History of Medieval England. J.E.A. Jolliffe. London 1937.

'Coronation and Propaganda. Some implications of the Norman claim to the throne of England in 1066.' G. Garnett. T.R.H.S. 5th Ser. xxxvi 1986.

Crusade and Settlement. Ed. P.W. Edbury. Cardiff 1985.

The Danelaw. C.R. Hart. London 1992.

De Inventione Sanctae Crucis nostrae apud Waltham. W. Stubbs. Oxford 1861.

Domesday: A search for the roots of England. M. Wood. London 1999.

Domesday Book. Ed. A. Williams and G.H. Martin. Penguin 1992.

Domesday Book and Beyond. F.W. Maitland. Cambridge 1887, 1965 ed.

'The Domesday Estates of the King and the Godwines. A Study in Late Saxon Politics'. R. Fleming. *Speculum* 58, 1983.

Dress in Anglo-Saxon England. G.R. Owen-Crocker. Manchester 1986.

The Dukes of Normandy and their Origin. Rt. Hon. the Earl of Onslow. London 1945.

Encomium Emmae Reginae. Ed. and trans. A. Campbell. Cambridge 1998.

'Ealdred of York: the Worcester Years'. V. King. *A.N.S.* 18, 1995.

'Earl Godwine of Wessex and his political loyalties'. D.G.J. Raraty. *History* 74, 1989.

'The Earls of Mercia and their commended men in the Eleventh century'. S. Barber. *A.N.S.* 23, 2000.

The Early Charters of Northern England and the North Midlands. C.R. Hart. Leicester 1979.

Ecclesiastical History, The. Orderic Vitalis. Ed. and trans. M. Chibnall. Oxford 1969-80.

Edward the Confessor. F. Barlow. London 1979.

'Edward the Confessor and the Norman Succession'. Eric John. E.H.R. 94, 1979.

'Edward the Confessor, Duke William of Normandy and the English Succession.' D.C. Douglas. E.H.R. 68, 1953.

'Edward the Confessor: Early Life, character and attitudes.' F. Barlow. E.H.R. 79, 1965.

'Edward the Confessor's Promise of the Throne to Duke William of Normandy.' T.J. Oleson. E.H.R. 72, 1957.

'Edward the Confessor's return to England in 1041.' J.R. Maddicott. E.H.R. 118, 2004.

England before the Norman Conquest. R.W. Chambers. London 1928.

England before the Norman Conquest. P. Clemoes and K. Hughes. Cambridge 1971.

England before The Norman Conquest. Sir Charles Oman. London 1921.

England in the Eleventh century (N. Rogers, 'The Waltham Relic List'). C. Hicks. Stamford 1992.

England under the Normans and Angevins. H.W.C. Davis. London 1949.

The English Abbey. F.H. Crossley. London 1935.

The English and the Norman Conquest. A. Williams. Woodbridge 1995.

The English Church and the Papacy. Z.N. Brooke. Cambs. 1952.

English Coins in the British Museum. H. Grueber and C. Keary. London 1970.
English Medieval Diplomatic Practice. Pierre Chaplais. Hambledon and London 2003.
English Historical Documents vol.2. Ed. D.C. Douglas and G.W. Greenaway. London
    1953 (cited as *E.H.D.*)
The English Nobility under Edward the Confessor. P.A. Clarke. Oxford 1994.
English Romanesque Art 1066-1200. Arts Council of G.B. 1984.
The Enigma of Hastings. E. Tetlow. New York 1974.
Essays in Anglo-Saxon History. J. Campbell. London 1986.
Fear and Faith in Anglo-Saxon England. P. Cavill. London 2001.
Feudalism. F.L. Ganshof. London 1966.
'Feudal Society in Orderic Vitalis'. M. Chibnall. *A.N.S.* I. 1978.
The First Century of English Feudalism. F.M. Stenton. Oxford 1932.
Five Eleventh century Hungarian Kings. Z.J. Kozstodnyk. New York 1981.
The Foundations of England. Sir James Ramsay. London 1898.
The Foundations of Medieval England. G.O. Sayles. London 1947.
'The French in England before the Norman Conquest.' C.P. Lewis. *A.N.S.* 17, 1995.
Geoffrey Gaimar, L'Estorie des Engles. Ed. and trans. J. Stevenson. London 1854.
Gerald of Wales; Journey Through Wales and Description of Wales. Trans. L. Thorpe.
    Penguin, London 1978.
Germany in the Early Middle Ages 800-1056. T. Reuter. Harlow 1991.
Gesta Hammaburgensis Ecclesiae Pontificium. Adam of Bremen. Ed. B. Schmeidler.
    Hannover 1917.
'*Gesta Normannorum Ducum*; a history without an end.' E. Van Houts. *A.N.S.* 2,
    1979.
Gesta Normannorum Ducum. William of Jumièges. Ed. E. van Houts. 2 vols, Oxford
    1995.
Gesta Regum Anglorum. William of Malmesbury. Ed. W. Stubbs. R.S. London 1897.
Giso of Wells. S. Keynes. *A.N.S.* 19, 1996.
The Godwins, The Rise and fall of a Noble Dynasty. F. Barlow. Harlow 2002.
Gregory VII. C. Norton. Latomus xxxiv 1975.
Gregory VII and the Soldiers of Christ. J. Robinson. History 58, 1973.
Guillaume Le Conquerant. Michel de Boüard. Librairie Arthème Fayard 1984.
Harold and William: the Battle for England 1064-1066. Benton Raine Patterson. Tempus
    2004.
Harold, the Last Anglo-Saxon King. Ian W. Walker. Stroud 1997.
Hereward the Last Englishman. P. Rex. Tempus 2005.
Historia Novorum in Anglia. Eadmer. M. Rule R.S. London 1884.
'Historiography and Hagiography at St Wandrille *(Inventio et Miracula Sancti
    Vfranni)*'. E. Van Houts. *A.N.S.* 12, 1990.
History of the Norman Conquest. 6 vols, E.A. Freeman. Oxford 1862.
'The Housecarl in England in the Eleventh Century'. N. Hooper. *A.N.S.* 7, 1984.
The House of Godwine: The History of a Dynasty. Emma Mason. London and New
    York 2004.
Hugh the Chanter: Hist. of the Church of York. Ed. C. Johnson. Oxford 1990.
'The Instituta Cnuti.' B. O'Brien. *A.N.S.* 25, 2001.
An Introduction to Anglo-Saxon England. P. Hunter Blair. Cambridge 1956.
The Introduction to the History of England. D. Jerrold. London 1949.

'Keeping up with the Godwinsons; in pursuit of aristocratic status in late Anglo-Saxon England.' C. Senecal. *A.N.S.* 23, 2000.

Kingdoms and Communities in Western Europe. S. Reynolds. Oxford 1984.

'King Harold's Books.' C.H. Haskins. E.H.R. 37, 1922.

Kings and Lords in Conquest England. R. Fleming. Cambridge 1991.

The Kings and Queens of England. Ed. W. Ormrod. Tempus 2004.

'Kings and Thegns: aristocratic participation in the governance of Anglo-Saxon England.' K. Mack. Unpublished research paper, University of California at Santa Barbara, 1982.

The Kingdom of Northumbria. A.D. 350–1100. N.J. Higham. Stroud 1993.

King Harald's Saga. M. Magnusson and H Pálsson. Penguin 1966.

Kings and Lords in Conquest England. R. Fleming. Cambridge 1991.

The Knight in Medieval England, 1000-1400. P. Coss. Stroud 1996.

'Land and Power in the Eleventh Century: the Estates of Harold Godwinson.' A. Williams. *A.N.S.* 3, 1980.

'The Lands and Revenues of Edward the Confessor.' J.L. Grassi. E.H.R. 117, 2002.

'The Lands of Harold Son of Godwine.' R.H. Davies. Unpub. PhD thesis, Cardiff 1967.

'The Language of the Bayeux Tapestry.' I. Short. *A.N.S.* 23, 2000.

Larousse Encyclopedia of Ancient and Medieval History. M. Dunan. Paris 1963.

La Tapisserie de Bayeux. Lucien Musset. 2nd edn. Zodiaque Paris 2002.

The Laws of the Kings of England. A.J. Robertson. Cambridge 1925.

The Leofric Missal. Ed. F. Warren. Oxford 1883.

Le Mémorial des Siècles: XI Siècle, les événements. La Conquête de L'Angleterre par les Normands. André Maurois. p. 230 and 313.

'Letters of Pope Gregory VII.' P. Maccarini. *A.N.S.* 6, 1983.

Liber Vitae of New Minster. B.L. Stowe. M.S. 914 fol.6.

Lincolnshire and the Fens. M.W. Barley. London 1952.

The *Lives of Three Englishmen.* M. Swanton. 1984.

Marriage and Murder in Eleventh Century Northumbria. C.J. Morris. York 1992.

The Medieval Foundations of England. G.O. Sayles. London 1948.

Medieval Knighthood. Ed. C. Harper-Bill and C. Harvey. Woodbridge 1992.

The Medieval Castle in England and Wales: A social and political history. N.S.G. Pounds. Cambridge 1990.

Medieval Latin. Ed. F.A.C. Mantello and A.G. Rigg. Washington 1996.

Medieval Europe. Ed. S. Mews and B. Yorke. York 1992.

'The Memory of 1066 in written and oral tradition.' E. Van Houts. *A.N.S.* 19. 1996.

'The Military Administration of the Norman Conquest.' B.S. Bacharach. *A.N.S.* 8, 1985.

'Military Tenure before the Norman Conquest.' J.H. Round. E.H.R. 12. 1897.

'Naval Logistics of the Cross Channel Operation 1066.' C.M. Gillmor. *A.N.S.* 7, 1984.

'The New Wealth, the New Rich and the new political style in late Anglo-Saxon England.' R. Fleming. *A.N.S.* 23, 2000.

Norfolk's Churches. R. Tilbrook and C.V. Roberts. Norwich 1997.

The Norman Conquest. D.J.A. Matthew. London 1966.

The Norman Conquest and beyond. F. Barlow. London 1983.

The Norman Conquest of the North: the region and its transformation 1000–1135. W.E.
     Kapelle. London 1979.
'The Norman Conquest through European Eyes.' E. Van Houts. H.R. 110, 1995.
The Norman Empire. J. Le Patourel. Oxford 1976.
The Norman Heritage, 1066-1200. T. Rowley. London 1983.
The Norman Monasteries and their English Possessions. D. Matthew. Oxford 1962.
The Normans and their Histories. Propaganda, Myth and Subversion. E. Albu.
     Woodbridge 2001.
The Normans and the Norman Conquest. R. Allen Brown. Woodbridge 1969. 2nd edn,
     paperback, 1994.
The Normans in England before Edward the Confessor. R.L.G. Ritchie. Exeter 1948.
The Norwegian Invasion of England. K. De Vries. Woodbridge 1999.
'The Officers of Edward the Confessor.' J.H. Round. E.H.R. 19, 1904.
'Opérations Navales en Manche et Mer du Nord pendant l'année 1066.' J. Laporte.
     Annales de Normandie 17, 1967.
The Origin of the Idea of Crusade. Erdmann. Princeton 1977.
Origins of English Feudalism. R. Allen Brown. London 1973.
Oxford Illustrated History of the Vikings. Ed. P.H. Sawyer. Oxford 1997.
The Papal Monarchy: The Western Church from 1050 to 1250. C. Morris. Oxford 1989.
'The Participation of Aquitanians in the Conquest of England. 1066-1100.' *A.N.S.*
     9, 1986.
'Peaceable Power in English Castles.' C. Coulson. *A.N.S.* 23, 2000.
Petit Larousse Illustré. Paris 1987.
Politics and Ritual in Early Medieval Europe. J. Nelson. London 1986.
'Problems connected with the English Royal Succession 800-1066.' A. Williams.
     A.N.S. 2, 1979.
Queens and Queenship in Europe. Ed. A.J. Duggan. Woodbridge 1997.
Queens, Concubines and Dowagers. P. Stafford. London 1983.
Queen Emma and Queen Edith: Queenship and Women's Power in the Eleventh century. P.
     Stafford. Oxford 1997.
Reassessing Anglo-Saxon England. Eric John. Manchester 1996.
The Reign of Cnut. Ed. A. Rumble. Leicester 1994.
'The Rites of the Conqueror.' J. Nelson. *A.N.S.* 4, 1981.
The Road to Hastings: The Politics of Power in Anglo-Saxon England. P. Hill. Tempus
     2005.
Roman de Rou. Robert Wace. Ed. A.J. Holden. Paris 1970-73.
The Royal Saints of Anglo-Saxon England. S.J. Rüdyard. Camb. 1988.
Ruling England. R. Huscroft. Harlow 2005.
Runestenen ved Oddernes Kirke. M. Olsen. 1908.
Saxo Grammaticus Gesta Danorum. Ed. A. Holder. Strassburg 1886.
'Saxons, Normans and their buildings.' E. Fernie. *A.N.S.* 19, 1996.
'Scandinavian Influences in Norman Literature.' E. van Houts. *A.N.S.* 6, 1983.
'The Scandinavian Settlement.' D.M. Hadley. *A.N.S.* 19, 1996.
Shorter Cambridge Medieval History, Vol. I. C.W. Previté-Orton. Cambridge 1952.
'Some Notes and Considerations on problems connected with the English Royal
     Succession 860-1066.' A. Williams. *A.N.S.* 1, 1978.
'The Stallers: an administrative innovation in the Reign of Edward the Confessor.'

K. Mack. J.M.H. 12, 1986.

'St Benet of Holme and the Norman Conquest.' F.M. Stenton. E.H.R. 37, 1922.

The Story of British Coinage. P. Seaby. London 1985.

Studies in the Early Middle Ages, Cultures in Contact: the Scandinavian Settlement in England in the Ninth and Tenth centuries. Ed. D.M. Hadley and J.D. Richards. 2000.

'Thegnly Piety and Ecclesiastical Patronage in the Late Old English Kingdom.' R. Fleming. *Speculum* 58, 1983.

'Towards an Interpretation of the Bayeux Tapestry.' H.E.J. Cowley. *A.N.S.* 9. 1986.

Unification and Conquest: A political and social history of England in the tenth and eleventh centuries. P. Stafford. London 1989.

Vict. C.H. Kent. Vol.I. 1908.

Viking Age Sculpture in Northern England. R.N. Bailey. London 1980.

The Viking Achievement. P.G. Foote and D.M. Wilson. London 1970.

Vikings: Fear and Faith in England. P. Cavell. London 2001.

'Visit of Earl Harold to Flanders 1056.' A. Grierson. P.E.H.R. 51, 1936.

Vita Edwardi Regis: The Life of King Edward who rests at Westminster. Ed. and trans. F. Barlow. Oxford 1992.

Vita Haroldi. W. de Gray Birch. R.S. London 1885.

Vita Wulfstani. William of Malmesbury. R.R. Darlington. Camden Soc. 3rd ser. 40, 1928.

'Wales and the coming of the Normans. 1039-93.' J.E. Lloyd. Trans. of Hon. Soc. of Cymmrodorion 1899-1900.

Wales in the Early Middle Ages. W. Davies. Leicester 1982.

The Waltham Chronicle. L. Watkins and M. Chibnall. Oxford Medieval Texts 1994.

The Welsh Alliances of Earl Aelfgar. K.L. Maund. *A.N.S.* 11, 1989.

'Where did all the Charters go? Anglo-Saxon Charters and the New Politics of the Eleventh Century.' C. Insley. *A.N.S.* 24, 2001.

William the Conqueror. D. Bates. Tempus 2004.

William the Conqueror. Ed. D.C. Douglas. London 1964.

'William the Conqueror and the Church of Rome.' P.A. Maccarini. *A.N.S.* 6, 1983.

The Witanagemot in the Reign of Edward the Confessor. T.J. Oleson. Oxford 1955.

Wulstan Cantor Narratis Metrica de Sancto Swithuno. Ed. A. Campbell. Zurich 1950.

The Year 1000. R. Lacey and D. Danziger. London 1999.

1066 The Battles of York, Stamford Bridge and Hastings. P. Marren. Lee Cooper 2004.

1066 The Year of Three Battles. F. McLynn. Pimlico 1998.

List of Illustrations

Genealogical Tables and Map

Index

TEMPUS – REVEALING HISTORY

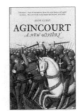

The Wars of the Roses
The Soldiers' Experience
ANTHONY GOODMAN
'Sheds light on the lot of the common soldier as never before' *Alison Weir*
£25
0 7524 1784 3

The Vikings
MAGNUS MAGUNSSON
'Serious, engaging history'
BBC History Magazine
£9.99
0 7524 2699 0

William the Conqueror
DAVID BATES
'As expertly woven as the Bayeux Tapestry'
BBC History Magazine
£12.99
0 7524 2960 4

Agincourt: A New History
ANNE CURRY
'Overturns a host of assumptions about this most famous of English victories... *the* book on the battle' *Richard Holmes*
£25
0 7524 2828 4

Hereward The Last Englishman
PETER REX
'An enthralling work of historical detection'
Robert Lacey
£17.99
0 7524 3318 0

The English Resistance
The Underground War Against the Normans
PETER REX
'An invaluable rehabilitation of an ignored resistance movement' *The Sunday Times*
£17.99
0 7524 2827 6

Richard III
MICHAEL HICKS
'A most important book by the greatest living expert on Richard' *Desmond Seward*
£9.99
0 7524 2589 7

The Peasants Revolt
England's Failed Revolution of 1381
ALASTAIR DUNN
'A stunningly good book... totally absorbing'
Melvyn Bragg
£9.99
0 7524 2965 5

If you are interested in purchasing other books published by Tempus, or in case you have difficulty finding any Tempus books in your local bookshop, you can also place orders directly through our website:
www.tempus-publishing.com